LAUGHING IN THE DARK

Horse Feathers *(Paramount, 1932)*

LAUGHING IN THE DARK

Movie Comedy from Groucho to Woody

Ted Sennett

Caught in the Draft *(Paramount, 1941)*

ST. MARTIN'S PRESS

NEW YORK

Design by Mary Moriarty

Library of Congress Cataloging-in-Publication Data
Sennett, Ted.
    Laughing in the dark/Ted Sennett.
        p. cm.
    ISBN 0-312-06280-X
        1. Comedy films—United States—History and criticism.   I. Title.
PN1995.9.C55S397   1992
791.43'617—dc20   91-25150
                                                                                    CIP

First Edition: January 1992
    10   9   8   7   6   5   4   3   2   1

*To all the gifted comic artists
who have made me laugh over
many years of moviegoing.*

Some Like It Hot *(United Artists, 1959)*

CONTENTS

Acknowledgments

I should like to thank the many good people who helped me carry out this project. Their support and cooperation have meant a great deal to me.

As before, I want to express my gratitude to Curtis Brown for his careful reading of my manuscript and his many valuable suggestions. I am also grateful to my astute editor, Michael Sagalyn, his helpful assistant, Ed Stackler, and to my zealous agent, Peter Miller. Thanks, as well, are due to John Springer, for generously allowing me to screen many comedy films from his astonishing collection, and to Jerome S. Ozer, for making his extremely valuable multivolume *Film Review Annual* available to me.

For once again providing me with so many stills from his collection, I would like to express my deep appreciation to Jerry Vermilye. I also thank Michael King for his beautiful posters, and Photofest for their color material.

I want to acknowledge the studio representatives who were cooperative in granting me feasible permissions to use their stills and who, in some cases, generously provided me with material: Ivy Orta, Terry Stull, and Helen La Varre of Columbia; Nancy Cushing-Jones, Bari Cohen, and Corinne DeLuca of MCA Publishing Rights; Joan Pierce of MGM/UA; Susan Nezami of Orion Pictures; Diane Isaacs of Paramount; Carol Bua of 20th Century–Fox, and Judith Singer, Jess Garcia, and Rob Lebow of Warner Bros. I am also grateful to the staff at the Billy Rose Collection at Lincoln Center and Charles Silver of the Film Study Center at the Museum of Modern Art for their help with my research.

Above all, I thank my wife, Roxane, whose love and support are blessings that carry me through every book I will ever write.

PROLOGUE
The Silent Years of Laughter

I n the cosmic scheme of things, we always have had greater reason to weep than to laugh. Faced with adversity, or cataclysm, or cruelty, we mourn our losses, nurse our wounds, and huddle together in the darkness. Then somebody slips on a banana peel and falls on his posterior. Or a witty remark punctures a mask of hypocrisy and pretension. Or a starving prospector, trapped in a Klondike cabin, consumes his shoe with exquisite delicacy, as if it were a gourmet meal.

And we laugh.

We laugh because, in the midst of trouble or chaos, laughter can be a healing balm that reminds us of how absurdly we behave, how ridiculous we sometimes appear in the eyes of others, and how gallantly we confront a universe that is usually hostile. More often than not, we mortals are not tragic figures howling at the wind, like Shakespeare's King Lear, but Fools with cap and bells, both mocking and mocked by the world. Laughter keeps us sane.

Laughter also has a long history in films that goes back to the very first movies, when filmmakers first projected flickering images on a screen. Years before movies began telling stories, pioneer filmmakers were striving for laughs. Even before the turn of the century, the Lumière brothers created the first movie farce, *L'Arroseur Arrosé* (*Watering the Gardener*), and inventor Thomas Edison made many brief comic films. Georges Méliès's pioneering fantasy films had a number of comic touches. Sometimes he himself was the prankster, having fun with the audience. When Charlie Chap-

Charlie, the Lone Prospector, looks like a tasty meal to starving Mack Swain in **The Gold Rush** *(1925). One of Chaplin's masterworks, the film is a sublime combination of slapstick and poignancy.*

lin was merely a new face at Keystone, a popular French comedian named Max Linder had already made a number of short comedy films over a period of ten years. The first star of American comic films was not Chaplin but a rabbity fat man appropriately named John Bunny.

Film comedy found its first great master in Mack Sennett (no relation to this author). Coming to films in 1908, he worked for years as an actor and director, then joined with two associates to form the landmark Keystone Company, turning out one- and two-reel slapstick comedies. Discarding any idea of plot, character, or motivation, Sennett made movies that had a brash, knockabout energy and a breathless pace that viewers found exhilarating. They responded gleefully to an endless round of chases, fights, and accidental falls. Soon Sennett's lunatic cops, mustachioed villains, and coy bathing beauties became staple attractions of early moviegoing. His Keystone company also served as a launching pad for many of the talented comedians of the silent years, including Roscoe ("Fatty") Arbuckle, Chester Conklin, Ford Sterling, and Mabel Normand.

One member of Sennett's stock company had comedy ideas of his own. Joining the Keystone players in December 1913 after years as an actor and entertainer in his native England, Charlie Chaplin had not been conspicuous in the roughhouse antics that the studio purveyed. One finds only rudimentary evidence of the immortal Tramp in over thirty films he appeared in at Keystone. However, his work at Essanay studios, starting in 1915, showed unmistakable signs that he was developing his own comic persona, and one film, *The Tramp* (1915), gave the first true indication of his vagabond character. As the bowler-hatted hero, he falls for a farmer's daughter (Edna Purviance), foils a robbery attempt, and then toddles down the road in the first of what would become a signature ending of his movies. In this and other Essanay films, Chaplin developed the plucky, resilient, put-upon character who always survived life's travails.

Joining the Mutual Film Corporation in 1916, Chaplin at last was given a free hand to make films in his own way, and after a few perfunctory efforts, the artist in him began to emerge. In such short films as *The Rink* (1916), *Easy Street* (1917), and *The Immigrant* (1917), Chaplin was now able to refine his comedy techniques and to bring together all the elements that went into the creation of the Tramp. All the ingredients were here: the physical mannerisms, such as lifting his hat straight up or turning corners on one foot; an air of courtly elegance contradicted by his shabby appearance; the physical grace with which he eluded pursuers; and the resourcefulness with which he solved the many problems that came his way. More significantly, the Mutual films, particularly *The Immigrant*, reveal that Chaplin was moving beyond burlesque and slapstick to a romantic sensibility, to a belief that compassion and empathy were possible even in sordid circumstances. These movies also contain traces of bitter irony and social commentary.

Chaplin finally achieved artistic maturity with his films for First National, starting in 1918 with *A Dog's Life*. His best films during the four-year period showed that, given a free rein, he could stitch together a seamless pattern of slapstick comedy, social awareness, and pathos. Occasionally the pathos would spill over into heavy-handed sentimentality, or his gags would retain the vulgarity of his earlier work, but the defects paled beside the mastery he revealed in such films as *Shoulder Arms* (1918), *The Kid* (1921), and *The Pilgrim* (1923). *The Kid*, in particular, has remained one of Chaplin's best-loved films. The story of the tramp and the waif (Jackie Coogan) he raises as his own contains many mawkish moments, but Chaplin's brilliance shines through in such sequences as the Tramp's first thwarted attempts to rid himself of the baby he has found.

Leaving First National in 1922, Chaplin began making films for United Artists, the releasing and distribution company he had cofounded in 1919. After directing a serious drama entitled *A Woman of Paris* (1923), he returned to comedy with *The Gold Rush* (1925), the film that is widely regarded as his greatest. A wondrous achievement that serves up renewed pleasure with every viewing, the film combines slapstick and poignancy with peerless artistry. As the Lone Prospector who struggles for survival in the Klondike, and who falls in love with a tempestuous dance-hall girl (Georgia Hale), Chaplin provokes laughter and tears, sometimes simultaneously. Nowhere is this more evident than in the scene in which the starving Prospector boils and eats one of his grimy shoes, savoring each shoelace or nail as if it were a delicacy. Six years would pass before the release of his next major film, and by then sound was firmly entrenched. In defiance of sound, but more as a way of demonstrating the continuing viability of silent film, Chaplin used only a few moments of gibberish speech in his 1931 masterwork, *City Lights*.

Chaplin's closest rival in the silent era worked in an entirely different mode. Both men were assaulted by people and even objects in a hostile universe, but where Chaplin revealed the pain, sympathy, or anger behind his humor, Buster Keaton was impassive. His famous poker face concealed feelings he was not about to share with a world that seemed bent on destroying him. Instead, he used his body, coiled and ready, to avoid life's hazards. In film after film, Chaplin expressed

irritation, dismay, pity, or smiling obsequiousness. Keaton, however, permitted his humor to come from what he did rather than what he was. Sometimes he could be most eloquent by doing nothing, a small, stoical figure standing alone against adversity.

Far more interested in the camera and camera techniques than Chaplin, Keaton was the supreme master of the ingeniously devised physical gag. The films from his peak period of 1923 to 1928 are filled with astonishing moments painstakingly set up by Keaton himself. One recalls any number of scenes in *The Navigator* (1924) that are marvels of comic construction, such as one in which Keaton and the none-too-bright heroine, adrift at sea in an ocean liner, try to signal a rescue ship. Nor is it easy to forget the awesome, almost surrealistic cyclone sequence in *Steamboat Bill Jr.* (1928), in which Keaton's bed becomes a vehicle moving through the streets, or the moment when a house frame collapses on him, just missing crushing him to death as he stands, unperturbed. Through every crisis, Keaton remains a model of composure, his face a grave, melancholy mask, his body as limber as his wits.

Most film historians regard *The General* (1927) as Keaton's finest film, and with good reason. An elaborate, richly detailed comedy-adventure, it works as both a straightforward Civil War melodrama and a treasury of ingeniously devised comic set pieces. (Often the two elements are intertwined.) As a Southern engineer who fights to retrieve his beloved train, known affectionately as "The General," from Union forces, Keaton overcomes any number of harrowing obstacles, while trying to cope with the "help" of his dim-witted fiancée, played by Marian Mack. Sequences of inspired slapstick—Keaton contending with a cannon that refuses to fire or fires in the wrong direction; Keaton and the girl meeting comic mishaps as they flee through enemy territory—alternate with moments of brilliantly staged spectacle, as when a bridge collapses just when a Union troop train is crossing it. Like a monster in its death throes, the bridge falls in ruins, creating a scene both unsettling and oddly beautiful. The subsequent decline in the quality of Keaton's films, due to mounting personal problems and a calamitous decision to sign a contract with MGM, seems doubly tragic in the light of his achievement in *The General*.

Like Keaton, Harold Lloyd had a distinct flair for brilliantly constructed gags, but there the resemblance between these actors ends. A cheerful, irrepressible sort rather than a stone-faced stoic, Lloyd either played a weak mama's boy longing to prove his worth or a pushy go-getter who triumphed against all odds, mostly through luck and dogged persistence. With his straw hat and oversized black horn-rimmed glasses, he represented the clean-cut American youth who craved success and an admiring girlfriend. Lacking Chaplin or Keaton's skill and intricate comedic timing, he turned to "thrill" comedy as his métier, placing himself in hair-raising situations that had audiences screaming, and not only with laughter. The most famous moment occurred in *Safety Last* (1923), in which he dangles from atop a skyscraper, holding on to nothing but the hands of a huge clock. (He did not use a double for such scenes.) The actor's best film was probably *The Freshman* (1925), in which he played an eager beaver mocked and humiliated by his fellow students—until he wins the big football game. This climactic contest, filled with inventive slapstick moments, is undeniably the movie's highlight.

Harry Langdon is less remembered than Chaplin, Keaton, or Lloyd, but he, too, won attention from critics and the public during his relatively brief period of popularity. Of all the leading comedians of the era, he seemed least well equipped to cope with trouble or adversity. His persona, depending on an odd and sometimes bewildering combination of childlike innocence and adult cunning, was emphasized by his white makeup and his tightly buttoned undersized jacket. (Critic James Agee described him aptly as "an elderly baby" and "a baby dope fiend.") His rather specialized talent reached fruition under the aegis of Frank Capra, who wrote *Tramp Tramp Tramp* (1926) and directed *The Strong Man* (1926) and *Long Pants* (1927), Langdon's three best films. Langdon's decision to leave Capra in order to write and direct his own material had disastrous results, and the actor's career never recovered.

Other notable silent comedians emerged from the bustling studio of producer Hal Roach. They included rotund Oliver Hardy, who teamed with long-faced Stan Laurel in 1927 to create one of the greatest and most durable of movie comedy teams; Charlie Chase, who played either the fussy, henpecked husband or the dapper man about town, and later had only a modest career in the sound years; James Finlayson, sour-faced and squinty-eyed; "Snub" Pollard of the drooping mustache; and Edgar Kennedy, master of the "slow burn," who later starred in a long-running series of short comedies. A number of Roach's films also starred homespun Will Rogers, though this comedian achieved popularity only after moviegoers could hear his amiable Oklahoma drawl.

With the advent of sound, many of the great silent comedians declined, starring in low-budget two-reelers or inappropriate feature vehicles. A few, like Chaplin and Lloyd, were wary of sound, or unsure of its relevance to their particular style. Yet no period of film history stands apart from any other, and the influence of these figures extended far into the sound years and even into the here and now. (Red Skelton admired and emulated Buster Keaton and had his help on several films; the shadow of Charlie Chaplin hovers over much of Woody Allen's work; and there are even traces of Harry Langdon in Pee-wee Herman.)

Acknowledging the impact of the silent comedians on those who followed them, this book begins with the early sound years and moves across six decades to the present day. Along the way, *Laughing in the Dark* pays homage to the performers who have given us the blessed gift of laughter. As long as we can sit in a darkened theater and dissolve our troubles in giggles and guffaws, these stars will be remembered and loved.

A famous scene from **Safety Last** *(1923): Harold Lloyd, master of the "thrill" comedy, hangs perilously in space over a busy street. Amazingly, Lloyd performed all of his own stunts.*

Part 1

GETTING AWAY FROM IT ALL

Movie Comedy in the Thirties

A decade of poverty and despair, followed by ominous rumblings of a world war . . .

Throughout the country, the Depression exacts a terrible toll in human misery, with millions of jobless and hungry people. Fear and unrest sweep the nation, until the presidency of Franklin D. Roosevelt, elected in 1932, promises relief and new hope. Progress is slow, but times are hard.

In the last years of the decade, concern over the Depression gives way to a new threat from overseas, as the Nazis in Germany launch their devastating *Anschluss* in Europe. Ironically, in April 1939, the same month in which the New York World's Fair opens "to all mankind," Hitler's troops invade and occupy Czechoslovakia. Later that year, war erupts in Europe, spurred by Germany's unprovoked attack on Poland.

Still there are advances and achievements, both large and small, throughout the decade. . . .The Empire State Building, the world's tallest building, is formally opened in New York City (1931), and the engineeering marvel called the Golden Gate Bridge opens in San Francisco (1937). . . . Amelia Earhart becomes the first woman to fly solo across the Atlantic Ocean (1932). . . . At Berlin's Olympic Games, a black American named Jesse Owens proudly becomes the world's fastest athlete (1936) . . . And the decade sees the first appearance of detective Dick Tracy (1931), *Newsweek* magazine (1933), Donald Duck (1934), the board game of Monopoly, and both the book (1936) and film (1939) versions of *Gone With the Wind.*

The thirties are the decade of Shirley Temple and contract bridge . . . of Astaire and Rogers and John Dillinger . . . of heavyweight Joe Louis and the Dionne quintuplets. . . . Among the best-attended movies of these years are *Frankenstein, King Kong, Top Hat, The Good Earth, The Adventures of Robin Hood,* and to crown the decade, *The Wizard of Oz.*

Animal Crackers *(Paramount, 1930). Groucho Marx, as African explorer Captain Spaulding, tells the party guests, including Louis Sorin and Margaret Dumont, about his African safari. ("One morning I shot an elephant in my pajamas. How he got in my pajamas, I don't know.")*

Chapter 1
The Early Sound Years
Slapstick and Sophistication

I n October 1927, with the arrival of *The Jazz Singer*—the first feature film with sound sequences—audiences were stunned and exhilarated by hearing Al Jolson sing. Overwhelmed by a demand for more of the same, the film industry went into a frantic state of upheaval. Producers who had scoffed at the potential of "talkies" suddenly scrambled to accommodate the new medium. Actors who had never spoken a line on screen took voice lessons, or contemplated early retirement. Writers who had grown comfortable producing on-screen titles now learned to compose spoken dialogue, and in the first sound years, many films sank under the weight of their words. It was, in all, a hectic, terrifying, exhilarating period for the industry.

In front of the camera, it was not a happy time for the icons of silent comedy, and for some, the sound era spelled the veritable end of their careers. After firing Frank Capra in 1927, Harry Langdon, claiming to follow his own creative bent, went on to make several films that blended Chaplinesque pathos with his own familiar slapstick antics, without success. Langdon apparently never recovered from the films' poor reception. Buster Keaton suffered an equally unhappy fate. Signed over to MGM by his longtime mentor Joseph Schenck, the great comic lost artistic control of his work. The films Keaton made for the studio bore little trace of the comic genius that had ranked him with Chaplin in the silent years. Racked by alcoholism and marital trouble, his life and his career became a shambles.

For other star comedians, the coming of sound marked an unmistakable but not necessarily devastating decline. After a number of sound films, including *Welcome Danger* (1929), *Feet First* (1930), and *Movie Crazy* (1932), Harold Lloyd found that his sort of "thrill" comedy was no longer popular, nor was his characterization of the breezy go-getter in step with the times. He retired from films a wealthy man, returning only for Preston Sturges's *Mad Wednesday (The Sin of Harold Diddlebock)* in 1947. On the other hand, Stan Laurel and Oliver Hardy moved with

Design for Living *(Paramount, 1933). Miriam Hopkins, Gary Cooper, and Fredric March make up an odd ménage à trois in Ben Hecht's adaptation of Noël Coward's comedy. The play was actually demolished rather than adapted— Hecht retained only one Coward line, a toast delivered by Cooper "to the good of our immortal souls."*

ease into sound, adding their distinctive voices while retaining their emphasis on beautifully executed physical gags.

At first, the greatest silent comedian stubbornly opposed the coming of sound. Like many others in the industry, Charlie Chaplin insisted that sound merely diluted or compromised the purity of silence; he felt that all emotions and ideas could be expressed on film without uttering a word. Only a month after completing *The Circus* in 1928, he had started to work on *City Lights*, then decided to halt production when sound films took over. Several years later, still in defiance of sound, he boldly completed the movie as a silent feature, adding only some sound effects. It would be five years before he made another film, and when he did, *Modern Times* (1936) turned out to be mostly silent again, his last great tribute to a bygone era. He ended the movie with a gibberish song, still mocking the screen's obsession with spoken words, *any* words. In the films that followed *Modern Times*, he did speak in his mellifluous British voice. These later sound films, for all of their weaknesses, would contain inspired Chaplinesque moments, though his greatest work by far had been achieved during the silent years.

In the beginning, the filmmakers, confronted with the new device of sound, found it much easier to continue the silent emphasis on raucous slapstick. For a while, a new kind of comic hero emerged, replacing the energetic but naïve eager beaver represented by Harold Lloyd with confident, urbane, and even smart-alecky young men played by such actors as Reginald Denny, William Haines, and Glenn Tryon. Sometimes the slapstick comedians arrived in pairs, as teams whose stock in trade was not subtlety ground out movie after movie. Bert Wheeler and Robert Woolsey, two recruits from vaudeville and Broadway, soon established themselves as busy low comedians in a series of frantic farces. Wheeler played the amiable boob and Woolsey was the wisecracking, cigar-chomping con man in ramshackle comedies—*The Cuckoos* (1930), *Half Shot at Sunrise* (1930), and others—that strained an audience's tolerance for hoary gags and outrageous situations. Bobby Clark and Paul McCullough, two other popular Broadway veterans, starred from 1928 to 1935 in a group of frenetic short comedy films—*False Roomers* and *Odor in the Court* were typical entries—that featured a barrage of quips and sight gags.

On the distaff side, Marie Dressler, a large and homely woman of sixty whose performance in *Min and Bill* (1930) had already made her an unexpected and most unlikely star, joined another well-seasoned actress, Polly Moran, in a series of hectic farces that took advantage of their bumptious personalities. In such movies as *Reducing* (1931), *Politics* (1931), and *Prosperity* (1932), the actresses threw subtlety to the winds as they cavorted in a variety of contrived situations. *Politics* was perhaps the funniest of the group, casting Dressler as an outspoken widow who runs for mayor of her corruption-ridden city. Moran played her rowdy friend.

Other actresses teamed up for the short comic films that were a staple of this early sound period. At the busy Hal Roach studios, vivacious blonde Thelma Todd, who had served as a foil for virtually every leading comedian, joined with fluttery ZaSu Pitts in a series of comedy shorts that ran from 1931 to 1933. As inseparable pals who get into lots of trouble, the two were subjected to knockabout gags that ranged from the raucously funny to the painfully humorless. When ZaSu Pitts left the studio, she was replaced by an entirely different type, the brassy, leather-lunged Patsy Kelly, who starred with Todd in a number of shorts, many with such punning titles as *Air Fright* (1933) and *Bum Voyage* (1934).

In the rush to fill the movie audience's seemingly insatiable demand for comedy talkies, headliners from two-a-day vaudeville and the Broadway theater were drafted by Hollywood, often with less than happy results. Performers who had delighted audiences in live stage performances fared poorly when their work was transferred to celluloid. It may be that they lacked the irreverence and insolence that Depression audiences seemed to prefer in their comedians. Or perhaps they were unable to muster the sort of material that would show them at their best. At any rate, such notable stage stars as Ed Wynn, Fanny Brice, and Charlotte Greenwood failed to make a major impact as starring film comedians. Wynn and Brice found more receptive audiences in radio, and Greenwood later became a likable supporting actress in Fox musicals and comedies.

Other comedians from vaudeville and the stage were much more succcessful in making their mark in sound films. As the thirties began, new figures (and a few who had started in the silent years) were getting ready to begin the first matchless flowering of sound comedy. Stepping into the spotlight were comic artists who would quip, connive, stumble, and insinuate their way into screen immortality.

While some filmmakers were dispensing the low comedy of Wheeler and Woolsey and their ilk, others were taking heed of the new propensity for talk and the novelty of spoken dialogue. And what better place to utter this dialogue than in the salons and drawing rooms (and occasionally, the bedrooms) of high society, where men and women of breeding and refinement could either discuss or act on their wicked inclinations? In the first sound years, the lines in many a sophisticated comedy were spoken by the chattering well-to-do, who either

amused the audience or sent it into a stupor. The vogue for these high-society comedies was brief, but for a time, it gave comedy seekers an alternative to rowdy slapstick.

Inevitably, a number of these comedies were adapted from the stage, where the talk was plentiful and drawing rooms were always available. In many cases, the films were so intent on serving up witty dialogue that they forgot to be cinematic. The camera remained stationary, frozen in its admiration of the well-appointed rooms and their well-dressed occupants. Norma Shearer, chic and elegant, appeared to be a favored resident, whether playing a jewel thief posing as a rich widow in Frederick Lonsdale's stage comedy *The Last of Mrs. Cheyney* (1929), or a dowdy duckling turned soignée swan in a static version of Rachel Crothers's play *Let Us Be Gay* (1930). Forever game despite her acting limitations, Shearer even took a stab at Noël Coward, joining Robert Montgomery in delivering Coward's brittle, stylized dialogue in an adaptation of *Private Lives* (1931). As a divorced couple who reunite at a chalet in Switzerland, they came across as smug and self-indulgent rather than wickedly witty, as intended.

If Shearer seemed ill at ease mouthing Noël Coward's sophisticated bons mots, other actresses with more developed comic skills fared little better. In *Tonight Is Ours* (1933), adapted from Coward's minor play *The Queen Was in the Parlour*, Claudette Colbert grappled helplessly with the role of the princess of a fictional Middle European country. She falls in love with a commoner enacted by Fredric March. And Miriam Hopkins tried gamely to bring some verve to Ernst Lubitsch's film version of Coward's *Design for Living* (1933), playing the apex of a curious romantic triangle that involved Gary Cooper and Fredric March. Onstage, the play had served Coward and the Lunts as a stylized vehicle, but the movie floundered when scenarist Ben Hecht and director

Trouble in Paradise *(Paramount, 1932). Kay Francis and Miriam Hopkins vie for Herbert Marshall's amorous attention. Pure sparkling champagne, Ernst Lubitsch's film marked a peak of achievement in sophisticated comedy of the thirties.*

Lubitsch were ordered to tone down the plot's sexual innuendos. Only one line of Coward's play survived, although Hecht managed to work in a few lines from the playwright's other works.

Adaptations of stage comedies about life and love among the rich, the royal, and the sophisticated proliferated in the early sound years. Philip Barry's play *Holiday* became a 1930 film with a miscast Ann Harding as the rebellious daughter of a rich and snobbish family, who falls for her sister's fiancé. Robert Montgomery starred as a golf champion with romantic problems in *Love in the Rough* (1930), derived from Vincent Lawrence's stage comedy *Spring Fever*. And John Barrymore and Diana Wynyard took over the Alfred Lunt and Lynn Fontanne roles in a film version of Robert E. Sherwood's play *Reunion in Vienna* (1933). Barrymore was in characteristically flamboyant form as Austria's Crown Prince Rudolph, who returns to Vienna on the hundreth anniversary of the Hapsburg Empire and tries to rekindle his romance with an old flame (Wynyard), now comfortably married. If many of these drawing-room comedies seemed rather bloodless and rarefied, too special for thirties audiences, the best of them had a bracing wit that compensated in large part for the ceaseless jabber. Occasionally, a film of these years dispensed with theater origins altogether and offered a original screenplay that could match any stage play in all particulars, and even exceed it in some. One of them, and much the best of the lot, was Ernst Lubitsch's delectable comedy *Trouble in Paradise* (1932).

By this time, Lubitsch had established himself as one of the masters of screen sophistication. His films were noted for their wry, mocking tone and their visual sheen. Arriving in Hollywood in the twenties after successes in Europe, the Berlin-born director had made *The Marriage Circle* (1924) and other comedies that managed to be lightly risqué and witty, even without spoken dialogue. His early sound films, especially *One Hour with You* (1929) and *Monte Carlo* (1930), added dialogue that was deft, sparkling, and rife with sexual innuendo, then stirred in some songs. The resulting mix, staged by Lubitsch with the mixture of mischievous wit, irony, and suggestiveness that became his trademark "touch," delighted knowing audiences.

Trouble in Paradise marked the peak of his achievement in these years. From an adroit screenplay by Samson Raphaelson, adapted by Grover Jones from a play by Laszlo Aladar, Lubitsch fashioned an enchanting tale of Lily (Miriam Hopkins) and Gaston (Herbert Marshall), two resourceful high-society thieves who become lovers. Joining forces, they decide to steal the jewels of Mariette Colet (Kay Francis), a rich and amorous widow, with Gaston becoming her trusted secretary and Lily his typist. Jealousy causes a rift in Lily and Gaston's relationship, but by film's end, they are reconciled, and make off with their stolen goods. Around this bauble of a story, Lubitsch weaves a mood that manages to be both romantic and sardonic.

As Lily and Gaston meet, instantly fall in love, and plot their maneuvers, the dialogue sparkles as brightly as the jewels of Mme. Colet. In their first scene together, in which they reveal their true identities (they have been posing as baron and countess), the quick-witted give-and-take they exhibit while stealing from each other is especially felicitous. After taking Gaston's watch, Lily tells him, "It was five minutes slow but I regulated it for you." His tender reply ("I hope you don't mind if I keep your garter") arouses her and she flings herself into his arms with a cry of "Darling!"

Best of all are the techniques by which Lubitsch and his collaborators score a point and a laugh at the very same time. To show that Mme. Colet is not only extremely wealthy but also a woman to be reckoned with, a series of quick cuts from one servant to another, each saying "Yes, Madame" or "No, Madame" establishes her character economically. At various moments throughout the film, Lubitsch suggests, subtly and characteristically, what *might* be happening off-screen between the players. As Lily and Gaston sink amorously onto a sofa, they suddenly vanish from the frame, and a hand reaches out to place a Do Not Disturb sign on the door. No further comment needed. The camera lingers on the door for a second or two.

Before the decade was over, this sort of sophisticated romance among the rich was becoming obsolete as audiences began to prefer the more plebeian romance of the screwball comedies. For a while, jewel thieves remained in style—Frank Borzage emulated Lubitsch with *Desire* (1936), in which glamorous thief Marlene Dietrich has an affair with automobile engineer Gary Cooper. As the worst days of the Depression passed into history, however, moviegoers were no longer as entranced with ostentatious wealth.

There was, of course, another reason why audiences were abandoning sophisticated romance. They were much too busy laughing at the icons of sound comedy who were soaring to popularity from the earliest years of sound. In place of elegant lovers embracing in drawing rooms or in the moonlight came the outrageous, anarchic, and deliriously funny clowns who would never be caught dead or alive in a drawing room, unless it was to steal the silverware or humiliate the host. A glorious new age of sound comedy was under way. Historically, it would last the decade. In every other way, it has never ended.

Chapter 2

The Comedy Icons of the Thirties

One of the most durable comedy icons of the thirties was heard before she was seen. In *Night After Night,* a routine Paramount film of 1932, we are in one of those fancy Depression clip joints where watered bootleg liquor is served and an orchestra plays tinkly dance tunes of the period for sleekly attired couples. At one table, the club's owner, an ex-boxer with patent-leather hair, is coming on to a haughty Park Avenue beauty. Suddenly, there is a commotion at the door, and a voice asks, "Who's dere?" Another voice answers, "The fairy princess, ya mug!" The nasal no-nonsense tone belongs unmistakably to the lady known as Mae. As soon as Mae West, playing Maudie Triplett, has walked, or rather sashayed, into the room, all eyes are riveted on this buxom blonde with the undulating hips and insinuating manner.

From the first, it was clear that Mae West was no dewy-eyed damsel, fair game for men on the make. "Goodness, what beautiful diamonds!" the hatcheck girl exclaims. "Goodness had nothing to do with it, dearie," Maudie retorts, and immediately we know that she did not acquire the gems by selling violets to passing strangers. In fact (surprise!), it turns out that Maudie is something of an entrepreneur—she runs a string of beauty parlors, the latest of which is called The Institute de Beaut. Like the heroine of *Working Girl* (1988), nearly six decades later, Maudie "has a mind for business and a bod for sin." She is also ready with a quip, many of which were added by West herself when the producers allowed her to tailor the role to her own ample measurements. Much of the fun in *Night After Night* comes from Maudie's banter with a bogus society swell named Mabel Jellyman, ripely played by veteran actress Alison Skipworth. "Do you believe in love at first sight?" Miss Jellyman asks Maudie. "I don't know," Maudie replies, "but it sure saves an awful lot of time."

Inevitably, Mae West's unabashed sexuality stirred up a storm of protest. (This was nothing new—her earlier stage appearances had caused shock and alarm.) The scandalized critics failed to notice, however, that she was not really

The Bank Dick *(Universal, 1940). New bank detective Egbert Sousé (W. C. Fields) wrestles a toy gun away from a boy. The boy's mother is not too pleased. Fields believed that "anyone who hates dogs and children can't be all bad."*

erotic. In fact, West's love scenes never generated any sexual heat. (Paramount saw to that, giving her such uncharismatic leading men as Paul Cavanagh, Edmund Lowe, and Victor McLaglen; even Cary Grant seemed wan in her overwhelming presence.) There had been nobody like her until then—the heroines of the twenties vamps were black widow spiders who devoured their mates, or nobly boring wives, or Mary Pickford clones who were as pure as the driven snow. (So was West, but she drifted.) West loved men, but she also loved besting them and then discarding them. She laughed at sex but she enjoyed it, too. In some quarters, to be both amused and delighted by sex was a sin punishable by censorship. While the bluenoses fumed, Paramount exulted, and cast her immediately in a film version of her 1928 stage hit, *Diamond Lil,* which they renamed *She Done Him Wrong* (1933).

The film gave West her first starring role, and in many ways it was one of her best. For one thing, she could never have asked for a grander entrance, riding in a coach through the streets of Gay Nineties New York in her wide Floradora-girl hat and diamond-spangled gown. She is Lady Lou, Queen of the Bowery, and, by her own admission, "one of the finest women who ever walked the streets." Occupying the film's center for all of its sixty-six minutes, she inspires the ardent admiration of every male in the cast, from leading men to extras. Although they prostrate themselves before her, Lou regards them all with scorn. What's more, she has very little regard for everyone else—she treats her black maid with mocking condescension, and she looks on the law as an encumbrance to be avoided.

The plot of *She Done Him Wrong* is arrant nonsense, as saloon singer Lou tangles with her dangerous admirers, frees an innocent waif from white slavery, and spars with an upright Salvation Army officer (Cary Grant) who is not what he seems. Against a flavorsome backdrop of the raffish Bowery streets and saloons, West and the cast move through their paces with enthusiasm. The screenplay is credited to Harvey Thew and John Bright, but the quips that punctuate the text are pure Mae, reflections on life and love by a lady who's been around the block: "When women go wrong, men go right after them." Lou is West's first bold woman, an unabashed sexual aggressor who can look the righteous Captain Cummings up and down and ask him, "Why don't you come up sometime and see me? I'm home every evening."

West's disdainful attitude extended to her next (and probably best) film, *I'm No Angel* (1933). As Tira, queen of the traveling circus, she is not only the mistress of her honky-tonk domain but also the smartest and toughest person in the vicini-

ty. By her own admission, she's also the most alluring: gazing in a mirror, she remarks, "When I was born with this face, it was the same as strikin' erl!" Buoyed by her ego, Tira has little use for anyone else: the suckers who come to her tent to be fleeced, the society swells who look down on her, and even the lions she tames in the circus ring. Like Lady Lou, she also gets what she wants, and once again it's Cary Grant who plays the object of her lustful attention.

As in *She Done Him Wrong*, West makes an eye-popping entrance in *I'm No Angel*. As eager men gather before the makeshift tent on the runway, a trumpet blares, a carpet is rolled out, and emerging in a spotlight is an undulating Tira, emitting little moans of pleasure as she works the crowd ("A penny for your thoughts!"). Like all other West characters, Tira has little use for the opposite sex—her credo is "Find 'em, fool 'em, and forget 'em"—and yet she constantly becomes involved with them in unsavory ways. When she finds herself in trouble over a chump she's been vamping, Tira tries to flee. Instead, to get the money she needs, she agrees to remain with the carnival in a daring new act that has her putting her head in a lion's mouth. Soon, Tira has become a sensational attraction in the big-time circus, with a swank Park Avenue apartment and a handsome socialite lover named Jack Clayton (Grant). Their first encounter is ripe with insinuations and double entendres. (Clayton: "Do you mind if I get personal?" Tira: "Go right ahead. I don't mind if you get familiar.")

The film's unquestionable high point is the trial scene, in which Tira, having been tricked into losing Jack Clayton, decides to sue him for breach of promise. Dressed to the nines, or possibly tens, in floor-length black gown, long strand of pearls, fur wrap, and feathered chapeau, West acts as her own lawyer in making her case. Tira's brash cross-examinations of the men summoned to attack her character are essences of West; while admitting freely that she has known many men, she exposes their double standards where women are concerned. At the press conference after her inevitable victory, she leaves her adoring audience with a classic quip: "It's not the men in your life that counts, it's the life in your men." Inevitably, she is back with Clayton in the end, purring in his arms and singing a few bars of the title song.

West's next movie, *Belle of the Nineties* (1934) returned her to the Gay Nineties to play Ruby Carter, a music-hall entertainer and courtesan who is "the most talked about woman in America." As before, she enters the film in spectacular fashion, appearing onstage in a series of fantastic guises and then topping them all with an incarnation of the Statue of Liberty, proudly holding her torch. With such an entrance, any plot would be anticlimactic, and the story of *Belle of the Nineties* is the usual melodramatic mix involving West with jealous and ardent lovers, all of whom are putty in her hands. Although the censors were breathing down her neck after all the sly innuendos of her first films, West still managed to implant her wisecracks and put-downs in the script. Arriving in New Orleans, she is asked, "Are you in the city for good?" "I expect to be here," she replies, "but not for good."

By this time, West was enjoying phenomenal popularity, if not with moralistic critics then with paying audiences who found her earthy approach to life and sex wholly refreshing. To her great annoyance, the Hays Office was demanding that she tone down her naughtier wisecracks and subdue her frankly libidinous attitude. West complied to a certain degree, taking some of the bite and tang out of her subsequent films, giving them the sort of blandness that might have wrecked her early career in films. The ingredients are all present: the hard-breathing plots, the parade of lovers stunned by her beauty, the barrage of one-liners designed to titillate and/or outrage. Yet some spark is lacking: a tamer Mae West is less funny, less of an impudent reproach to puritanical behavior. The pleasures of *Goin' to Town* (1935), *Klondike Annie* (1936), and *Go West, Young Man* (1936) are only incidental, and after the listless *Every Day's a Holiday* (1937), West was released from her Paramount contract.

Sometime later, approached by Universal Studios to make a film with W. C. Fields, West accepted, beginning a turbulent collaboration that ended with *My Little Chickadee* (1940). At first, the two stars appeared eager to work with each other, but as the movie got under way, the storm clouds broke. Although both stars are credited with the screenplay, Fields insisted on adding many of his own distinctive touches, some of which, West claimed, had nothing to do with the film. He also circumvented West's strict "no liquor" clause by bringing his whiskey onto the set in a Coke bottle. The tension between them was pervasive and inescapable.

For whatever reasons, the resulting movie is not all that it should have been: It has an oddly perfunctory air, the plot line is even sillier than most, and for long stretches, the two stars seem to be inhabiting separate films. Still, there are lines and sequences that continue to draw hearty laughter. West plays Flower Belle Lee, a lusty vixen who, at the film's start, is being ushered out of town by its irate citizens. This shady lady is *not* contrite: "Are you trying to show your contempt for the court?" the judge asks her. "No," she answers. "I'm trying my best to conceal it." Fields is Cuthbert J. Twillie, a confidence man with a penchant for card playing, hard liquor, and women like Flower Belle.

My Little Chickadee never surpasses their meeting on the train to Greasewood City. It is a memorable encounter, with Flower Belle sizing up his bankroll and Twillie ogling her measurements. "Flower Belle!" he exclaims. "What a euphonious appellation! Easy on the ears, and a banquet for the eyes!" Not even an Indian attack can slow up his courtship. "Ah, what symmetrical digits," he cries, fondling her fingers. "Soft as a fuzz on a baby's arm!" For her part, Flower Belle is receptive only because of his money, and even agrees to marry him. Never mind that she is harboring a secret passion for the masked bandit who kidnapped her earlier in the movie. Twillie is enraptured, even when Mrs. Gideon (Margaret Hamilton), a disapproving passenger, tells him that she "can't say anything good" about Flower Belle. "I can see what's good," Twillie remarks. "Tell me the rest."

For West, *My Little Chickadee* marked the end of her film career. It was not her last film—she appeared in a disastrous minor musical called *The Heat's On* in 1943, and staged a poorly received comeback as licentious literary agent Letitia Van Allen in the abominable film version of Gore Vidal's novel *Myra Breckinridge* (1970). Her final movie was the dreadful *Sextette* (1978). Thankfully, when she ambled off the screen at the close of *My Little Chickadee,* she was already strolling into the pages of film history.

She has remained there ever since: a phenomenon rather than an actress, a woman who boldly and impudently acknowledged on-screen that sexual aggressiveness was not confined to males. Mae West insisted that a woman could be master of her own fate and mistress to anyone who was willing to abide by her rules of the game. Her game, however, was not the game of love but lust—unbridled physical lust—in which West was the queen and her men were the pawns whose only goal was to possess her entirely. There were two players, but West was the only winner. Moviegoers who had been used to helpless ingenues in the thrall of villains, or flappers who considered an all-night party the very depth of depravity, had never seen the likes of Mae West. In her best movies, she was a woman and an entertainer who blithely exposed the hypocrisy and double standard in matters of sex that lay just below the surface of American gentility.

Durable film comedy, the comedy that delights us even decades after its first appearance, can take the unlikeliest form. Could we have expected that U.S. movie audiences would warm to an entertainer who was alcoholic, mean-spirited, and, above all, hostile toward children, women, dogs, automobiles, clergymen, and clean living? Imagine this basically lazy, larcenous-minded man deliberately confusing our attitude toward him by also being, on occasion, a devoted father to a demure young girl, or a henpecked husband burdened with a vicious family.

In the silent era, Chaplin and Keaton engaged our

Belle of the Nineties *(Paramount, 1934). As usual, Mae West's Ruby Carter is the center of attention. At her left: suitor John Miljan. Ruby's philosophy: "Don't let a man put anything over ya 'cept an umbrella."*

25

sympathies. Suddenly, here was a man who was both victim and victimizer, often in the same movie. What could we make of this odd creature with the braying voice and bulbous nose, this mountebank who despised respectability, abstinence, and virtue? Many were bewildered, and even today many viewers are unable to find him funny. However, most of us continue to laugh with glee at William Claude Dukinfield, alias Mahatma Kane Jeeves, alias Otis Criblecoblis . . . also known as W. C. Fields.

Tracing his life and theatrical career from his Dickensian childhood and youth, we can guess at the source of his hostility: the deprivations and betrayals that (he felt) extended even into his years of fame. Born in 1879 in Philadelphia, the son of an English father and an American mother, Fields learned to live by his wits in the streets after running away from home at age eleven. Acquiring skill as a juggler, he toured backwater America with a ramshackle road company, then moved from cheap to prestigious vaudeville with an act that combined juggling and pantomimic comedy. After years in vaudeville, he joined Florenz Ziegfeld's spectacular *Follies* in 1915, appearing in seven consecutive editions. By the twenties, he was a full-fledged stage star.

As a master of pantomime, he was an inevitable candidate for silent movies, and in 1915, he made his first film, a one-reeler called *Pool Sharks*, in which he repeated the trick pool routine he had worked up during his vaudeville years. It was nine years, however, before he made another film, taking a small role in a 1924 historical epic called *Janice Meredith* and then starring in D. W. Griffith's *Sally of the Sawdust* (1925), a film version of his stage success *Poppy*.

Over the next three years, Fields appeared in eight additional silent films, many shot in the studios on Long Island. By the late twenties, after starring in several Broadway musicals, he decided to pull up his Eastern stakes and move to the West Coast for a career in the burgeoning new area of the talkies. His first sound film, *The Golf Specialist* (1930) was a two-reeler in which he essentially repeated the golf routine he had performed many times on the stage. Interestingly, it contained the seeds of the character he would play in his later films: the hapless man who is assaulted or intimidated by objects (golf clubs) and people (a caddie, a local sheriff), but who gets in a few licks of his own.

Venturing into feature sound films, Fields appeared with blond Ziegfeld star Marilyn Miller in a heavy-handed Warners musical called *Her Majesty, Love* (1931), then moved to Paramount, where he first appeared in one of the oddest films he would ever make, the lunatic farce *Million Dollar Legs* (1932). Based on a story by

Joseph L. Mankiewicz and directed by Edward Cline, this film astonished moviegoers with an array of sight gags and non sequiturs. Fields is not meant to be the star, yet he dominates the proceedings as the crackpot president of Klopstokia, a fictional country overrun with nuts and goats, mostly the former. (One of its many oddities is that all the women in Klopstokia are named Angela.) To raise badly needed funds, President Fields enters the country in the Olympics, with himself as a champion weight lifter and his majordomo (Andy Clyde) as the world's fastest runner (the "legs" of the title). Contributing to the comic mayhem are Jack Oakie as a brush salesman named Tweeny and Lyda Roberti as slinky spy Mata Machree ("The woman no man can resist").

In a mere sixty-four minutes of running time, *Million Dollar Legs* deliriously satirizes a number of subjects: crazy bureaucratic governments in which major decisions are made on a whim; seductive Mata Hari–like spies who drive men to distraction on a regular schedule ("Madame is only resisted from two to four in the afternoon"), and Olympic contests where anything goes. As the foul-tempered President, Fields makes a memorable entrance, arriving for a meeting with his own trumpet and drum and asking his cabinet, "Any of you mugs been playing with my harmonica? It's busted."

Following a role opposite Alison Skipworth in a segment of the all-star omnibus film *If I Had a Million* (1932), Fields signed to appear in a series of shorts for Mack Sennett, the undisputed king of silent comedy, who had been down on his luck after the arrival of sound. Released by Paramount, these brief twenty-minute comedies offered Fields the chance to distill his special brand of comedy into a small, self-contained space, with no distractions of plot. (He wrote all the screenplays.) It was his first opportunity to present the sort of offbeat, mocking, and unmistakably original humor he would develop into a unique art. Two of these short films (*The Pharmacist* and *The Barber Shop*, both 1933) drew him closer to the sort of full-length comedy he was about to launch at Paramount.

After resuming his feature-film appearances with roles in two of the studio's helter-skelter all-star productions of the period (*International House* and *Alice in Wonderland*, both 1933), Fields finally won the chance to expand on his character of the rascally, disreputable vagabond with larceny—and perhaps a drop or two of sentiment—in his heart. In *Tillie and Gus* (1933), he played Augustus, a ruffian and card shark who is reunited with his former wife, Tillie (Alison Skipworth), and joins with her to save their niece and her husband from being swindled out of a ferryboat franchise. Working with obvious relish and ease under Francis Martin's direction, Fields and Skipworth make a likable pair, and Fields gets to mutter some ferociously funny lines, including one of his best-remembered. Asked whether he likes children, he replies, "I do, if they're properly cooked," a remark possibly inspired by his tiny costar, Baby LeRoy, whom he reputedly despised.

In 1934, he was kept exceptionally busy as one of Paramount's top-grossing players, appearing as either one member of a stellar cast (*Six of a Kind*), or as the star of films that allowed him to dominate the screen with his unique and outrageous persona. Not unexpectedly, he excelled in the latter, creating original characters in such movies as *You're Telling Me* and *The Old-Fashioned Way* (both 1934). In *You're Telling Me*, a sound version of his silent *So's Your Old Man*, he played Sam Bisbee, the town reprobate burdened with a shrewish wife. (Told that she's the luckiest woman in the world, she asks cold-bloodedly, "Why, is my husband dead?") *The Old-Fashioned Way*, derived from Fields's silent *Two Flaming Youths*, cast him as the flamboyant, essentially dishonest McGonigle, head of a group of thespians who perform *The Drunkard* across the country. (He would repeat the role later in *Poppy*, 1936.) In both films, Fields managed to direct some well-aimed barbs at familiar targets, including crooked politicians, foolish women, and obnoxious children.

Fields's best 1934 release, and one of his very best comedies, was *It's a Gift*. Drawing on elements from two of his silent movies, *The Potters* and *It's the Old Army Game*, the film synthesizes Fields's double-edged creation of a character that remains his unique contribution to comedy: a man who is badgered and intimidated by life but can triumph in the end nonetheless. To say this, however, is to make Fields sound like Chaplin and Keaton, and it must be remembered that he inhabited a different world from theirs. Fields's outlook is imbued with a deep-seated malice and hostility, rather than the basic kindness and generosity of his comedic peers from the silent era. In the world of *It's a Gift*, a blind person is not a sweet flower girl, as in *City Lights*, but an ornery codger who destroys things with his cane. A dog is not a devoted pal, as in any number of silent comedies, but a nuisance who reduces his master's pillow to shreds.

As usual in a Fields movie, the plot of *It's a Gift* hardly matters. He plays Harold Bissonette, a small-town grocery owner constantly under attack by his wife, his relatives, and his customers. Out of desperation, and to his family's distress, he buys an orange ranch in California, a plot of land that is subsequently chosen as the site of a proposed racetrack. The eternally cowed Harold is suddenly rich. Around this story of a worm finally turning, Fields spins a web of hilarity that many are pleased to be caught in, and others resist stubbornly.

Under Norman McLeod's direction, the movie earns many laughs. Its undisputed highlight is the porch scene, Fields's beautifully orchestrated study in mounting frustration. Unnerved by his wife's strident complaining, Harold retreats to the porch to spend a peaceful night outdoors. First, his hammock collapses noisily, the milkman wears squeaky shoes, and a coconut topples from the ledge above and clatters down several flights of stairs. Harold is even forced into a bizarre encounter with an insistent insurance salesman who is looking for one "Karl La Fong." After driving poor Harold to distraction, the man finally leaves, but the situation worsens, until Harold cracks and pursues a noisy vendor with a gun. The entire sequence has an edge of accelerating hysteria and irrationality that is both humorous and faintly disturbing.

After leaving Paramount temporarily for a role in MGM's *David Copperfield*, Fields returned to the studio to appear in a mildly pleasing musical called *Mississippi* (1935), in which he shared star billing with Bing Crosby, and *The Man on the Flying Trapeze* (1935), a distilled example of the comedian at his best. A heady mixture of physical and verbal gags, laced with more than a few dashes of malice and misanthropy, the latter film cast Fields as small-town office worker Ambrose Wolfinger. A poor soul even more victimized than usual, Ambrose is forced to endure the endless complaints of his family. His only consolation is a loving daughter, played by Mary Brian. Small wonder that when burglars invade his basement, he would rather drink applejack with them, and join in boisterous three-part harmony, than protect his beastly relations.

The movie's story line is even frailer than usual: more of an incident than a plot. Seeking to leave his job to attend a wrestling match, Ambrose tells his boss that his mother-in-law has died from drinking "bad liquor." ("It must be hard to lose your mother-in-law," the sympathetic boss tells him. "Yes, it is," Ambrose replies, "very hard. Almost impossible.") Complications ensue when his lie spirals out of control. The movie's highlight is an extended sequence involving one of Fields's favorite props, the automobile. Driving to the wrestling match, Ambrose's luck is all bad. Orchestrated mayhem occurs as his jalopy knocks over a policeman's motorcycle, suddenly refuses to start, and crashes into another car occupied by an irate chauffeur. When the car finally backs up into an ambulance, a patient in a stretcher slides out into the street.

Fields made two more films for Paramount before leaving the studio. *Poppy* (1936), adapted from his Broadway success and *Sally of the Sawdust*, its silent version, offered a classic image of Fields in his cutaway coat, white stovepipe hat, spats, and cane: high fashion concealing low intentions. He plays "Professor" Eustace McGargle, an itinerant medicine man and shell-game expert, who tries to pass off his doting adopted daughter, Poppy, enacted demurely by Rochelle Hudson, as the heiress to a fortune. Fields's last film for Paramount, *The Big Broadcast of 1938*, cast him in a dual role—a millionaire playboy and his twin brother—in yet another of Paramount's star-filled music and comedy revues of the thirties.

By this time, Fields's steady consumption of alcohol had taken its toll, and he was frequently—and sometimes seriously—ill for much of his last few years at Paramount. For a while, he continued the radio appearances he had started in 1937, most notably a recurring mock feud with ventriloquist Edgar Bergen's mischievous dummy Charlie McCarthy, on the popular "Chase and Sanborn Hour." By late 1938, Fields was feeling better and ready to return to films. He signed a lucrative contract with Universal Studios, where he hoped to have a freer hand in creating his special brand of anarchic humor.

Made between 1938 and 1941, his four Universal films proved to contain some of his best work. Less polished, less cohesive, and less expensive to produce than most of the films he completed at Paramount, they were also, on the whole, funnier and devoid of intrusive sentiment. Fields did not require polish, cohesion, or money to make his comic points, and in writing some of the films (*My Little Chickadee* was cowritten with Mae West), he simply allowed his ideas to wander at will.

His first Universal film, *You Can't Cheat an Honest Man* (1939), placed him in a circus atmosphere where, as circus owner Larson E. (read "Larceny") Whipsnade, he was able to bamboozle the public while trading insults with his radio nemesis, Edgar Bergen's dummy, Charlie McCarthy. Bergen himself was involved romantically with Whipsnade's daughter, Vicky, played by Constance Moore. The slender plot had Vicky agreeing to marry a rich suitor only to improve her father's financial lot, but as usual the story took a backseat to Fields's outrageous antics. He also mutters, sotto voce, a choice variety of Fieldsian remarks, such as "Some weasel took the cork out of my lunch." The entire film seems to have been made up by Fields as he went along, although veteran George Marshall is credited with the direction.

After teaming with Mae West in *My Little Chickadee* (1940), Fields appeared in his most highly regarded movie, *The Bank Dick* (1940). In many ways, it represents the apex of his career in films: an almost perfect juxtaposition of his contempt for

Poppy *(Paramount, 1936). W. C. Fields, known here as "Professor" Eustace McGargle, charms Rosalind Keith. Fields had played the role twice before, in a Broadway play and in a 1925 silent version called* Sally of the Sawdust.

middle-class morality and hypocrisy and his jaundiced, eccentric approach to making people laugh. In a sense, the movie harkens back to his Paramount years. As Egbert Sousé, the town drunk and best customer of the Black Pussy Cat Cafe, he is saddled with yet another of those nasty families that seems to exist only to humiliate him.

The story line (once again Fields contributed the plot under an alias) hurtles from one wildly improbable incident to another. Sousé, it appears, would be content to spend his life drinking at the bar, but during the course of the movie, he is called on to (1) substitute for a drunken director on a movie being filmed in his town; (2) work as a bank detective as a "reward" for accidentally thwarting a bank robbery; and (3) foil a *second* bank robbery, again by accident. These and other complications make up a more cluttered plot than usual for a Fields comedy, but somehow, under Edward Cline's direction, Fields manages to juggle them all.

Forced to leave his natural habitat of the bar when he is hired as the bank detective, Sousé is not exactly a runaway success. Shouting "Is that gun loaded?" he wrestles a toy gun from a small boy's hand, prompting the boy's irate mother to respond, "Certainly not. But I think you are!" Trouble looms when Sousé must deal with a conscientious examiner named J. Pinkerton Snoopington (Franklin Pangborn), who is auditing the bank's books. (Sousé just happens to have "borrowed" bank money to pay for some beefsteak bonds.) Sousé's efforts to keep Snoopington from the books results in some delightful shenanigans. In the end, fortune smiles on Sousé, proving that larceny and alcoholism have their rewards. Helter-skelter in its style, throwaway in its humor, and sardonic in its attitude, *The Bank Dick* is generally regarded as the bellwether by which W. C. Fields can be admired and judged.

Fields's final movie for Universal, *Never Give a Sucker an Even Break* (1941), is by far the most bizarre, the most incoherent of the four. Apparently given free rein to indulge his fancies, Fields came up with a screenplay that makes little sense. Somehow it has to do with a film within a film: As Fields himself peddles his screenplay to Esoteric Studios producer Franklin Pangborn, the movie cuts to the story he is relating— a demented tale concerning wealthy Mrs. Hemoglobin (Margaret Dumont), who lives in a remote mountain hideout with her daughter Ouliotta (Susan Miller). Fields drops into the hideout (literally, from an airplane), where he dallies for a while with Ouliotta and then her mother. Through this madness, Fields manages to carry off some funny remarks. (As he falls off a high cliff, he comments philosophically, "It's the last foot that's dangerous.") Alcohol is his character's only consolation, as it was in life, and when his secretary warns him, "Someday, you'll drown in a vat of whiskey," the idea is not displeasing: "Drown in a vat of whiskey? Oh, Death, where is thy sting?"

Fields's last years were sad indeed, racked by serious illness and spotted with only a few more perfunctory "guest star" appearances in lackluster films. Not long afterward, weakened by a number of maladies, he withdrew to a sanitarium, where he died on Christmas Day of 1946. It was said that just before he died, he opened his eyes and winked.

A unique figure in the annals of film comedy, W. C. Fields looked with bleary eyes on a world he found both absurd and antagonistic. Objects assaulted him, and people harassed him—not just vicious wives and nasty mothers-in-law but also babies and well-meaning fools. He opposed his oppressors with deceit and ridicule, mocking pomposity by pretending to be pompous ("Flower Belle! What a euphonious appellation!"), or giving an odd Fieldsian spin to ordinary conversation. In *You're Telling Me,* he remarks to his drinking buddies, "It's a funny old world. A man's lucky if he gets out of it alive."

Whether moviegoers admired or disliked Fields's acerbic style, he was the perfect comic gadfly for the thirties, a man who made many of us laugh even as he embodied our worst instincts. If he wasn't lucky enough to get out of the world alive, he continues to live on the screen.

If Mae West represented liberated sexuality, and W. C. Fields registered contempt for middle-class morality, the Marx Brothers signaled the sound era's entry into a heretofore unexplored realm of nihilism. It was cheerfully lunatic nihilism, but nihilism nevertheless: an attitude that said if we live in a crazy world that lurches from one disaster to another (war to poverty and back again), why respect its guiding principles and institutions? Instead, the Marx Brothers decreed that disorder was the order of the day; with a gleeful disregard for the norm, they aimed their biggest comedic guns at, among other targets, holier-than-thou moralizing, cultural pomposity, and legal chicanery.

Tumbling out of New York City's mean streets and the raucous world of two-a-day vaudeville, Groucho, Chico, and Harpo—sometimes also Zeppo—Marx burst onto the nation's screens in 1929 with *The Cocoanuts.* In a time of breadlines and despair, the brothers offered neither comfort and reassurance nor a lecture on the nation's ills. Instead, they thumbed their noses at such bedrock institutions as government, education, and art, while indulging in more than a little misanthropy

(Groucho), chicanery (Chico), and lechery (Harpo). Theirs was not the precisely aimed satire of Voltaire, but irreverent and scattershot humor aimed at deflating pretentiousness and inducing laughter. And weary Depression audiences laughed.

Not everyone was amused by the tomfoolery of the Marx Brothers. Nor, for that matter, were Mae West and W. C. Fields always immune from a similarly negative response. The antics of Groucho and company irritated a number of moviegoers. The Marx Brothers looked and behaved like no other comedians or, for that matter, like no other residents on planet Earth. Groucho's face, with its bushy eyebrows and intimidating mustache, could express either a sneer or a leer, and he scurried from scene to scene in that peculiar loping gait, firing off wisecracks and puns. Chico was the conniving, easily corruptible layabout, speaking in an improbable Italian accent and playing the piano in his own loose-fingered style. And the incomparable Harpo, that demented Pan, barely resembled *Homo sapiens*. A curly blond wig (it was red at first) framed the face of a cheerful moron who could register childlike glee as well as unbridled lust. Instead of speaking, he used a taxi horn for emphasis and punctuation. Once in every film, this enfant terrible would become an idiot savant when he played a lovely harp solo.

The rags-to-riches tale by which three hustling New York brothers named Leonard, Adolph (later Arthur), and Julius Marx were transformed into, respectively, Chico, Harpo, and Groucho is now part of show-business lore. (Herbert, nicknamed Zeppo, left the act in 1933.) Much has been written about their growing up poor on New York's Upper East Side, and about their mother, Minnie, a tenacious woman who was determined to turn her sons into a major stage attraction. Somehow, against all odds, she succeeded, transforming a ragtag band of run-of-the-mill vaudevillians into the Marx Brothers, with their familiar nicknames and props. As the act took shape, more by trial and error than by design, Groucho's mustache and cigar, Harpo's wig, horn, and copious coat, and Chico's broken—or shredded—Italian accent became permanent fixtures. After touring the vaudeville circuit for years, the brothers finally landed a booking at New York City's legendary Palace Theater. Within a few years, they were starring on Broadway.

In 1929, while the brothers were still cavorting on stage in *Animal Crackers*, the stock market collapsed, wiping out their assets. Needing new sources of income, the Marxes turned to the newly burgeoning film industry. Or rather, the film industry turned to them, in urgent need of new faces and new material for the sound movies being churned out by the studios. In fact, the Marxes were eminently suited for sound—their verbal dexterity (Groucho's put-downs and puns,

Chico's fractured English) were as essential to their routines as their fast-moving slapstick. For their first film, *The Cocoanuts*, produced at Paramount's studio in Astoria, Queens, the studio adapted their successful stage show of the same name, keeping the basic characters and Florida setting.

Although primitive and tacky, *The Cocoanuts* set the mode for the Marx films to come, and also established the basic characters of the brothers: Groucho as the sarcastic, opportunistic con man who becomes involved with the equally crooked activities of Chico, a self-styled "Italian" with taking ways, and Harpo, a mute and happy imbecile blissfully free of morals. Here, Groucho is the manager of a seedy Florida resort hotel. His single-minded goal is to get the wealthy Mrs. Potter (the indispensable Margaret Dumont) to invest her money in his worthless stretch of land. Curiously, his way of wooing this haughty matron—the first of many subsequent courtships—is to insult her repeatedly. Even at the start, Groucho is unable to keep a compliment from turning into a nasty remark. ("Your eyes! Your eyes! They shine like the pants of a blue serge suit!")

Chico and Harpo make their entrance into movies playing themselves: two men with dishonest intentions. When Groucho points out to Chico that his suitcase is empty, Chico replies, "I know. We fill it up before we leave." Unlike Groucho and Harpo, Chico's face never betrays a single emotion—he leaves all expressions of lust, disgust, and mistrust to his brothers. Harpo has already settled into his persona, pursuing every girl with lascivious delight and displaying his odd and insatiable appetite by consuming, among other things, the buttons from a bellboy's uniform and a sponge seasoned with glue. *The Cocoanuts* also introduces us to Groucho's outrageous puns ("On this site, we're going to build an eye-and-ear hospital. It's going to be a site for sore eyes.")

Inevitably, the second Marx movie turned out to be an adaptation of their second stage success, *Animal Crackers.* Filmed again at Paramount's Astoria Studio, *Animal Crackers* (1930) merely lifted the original musical play by Morrie Ryskind and George S. Kaufman and photographed the pandemonium that results when the brothers are set loose on a palatial Long Island estate. As with *The Cocoanuts*, there was no pretense that the movie was anything more than a transcription of the play, or that the director, this time a Paramount regular named Victor Heerman, was more than a traffic cop trying to prevent a nasty collision.

In this antique piece of Marxian mayhem, Groucho plays his most famous character, the not exactly reputable African explorer Captain Jeffrey Spaulding, who makes a imposing entrance into the home of society matron Mrs. Rittenhouse

(Margaret Dumont). Borne on a stretcher by four African natives, he announces in song, "Hello, I must be going," but the assembled guests, as usual impervious to his rudeness, launch a chorus of "Hooray for Captain Spaulding!" Soon afterward, the captain's two partners in crime arrive on the scene, Chico as a musician named Emanuel Ravelli and Harpo as a demented soul called the Professor (of what, nobody knows).

The stage, of course, is set for chaos. Groucho is in fine fettle throughout, bombarding highfalutin Mrs. Rittenhouse with insults and toying playfully with the English language. The movie contains his best-known monologue, in which he regales Mrs. Rittenhouse's guests with an account of his African exploits. ("One morning I shot an elephant in my pajamas. How he got in my pajamas, I don't know.") Amazingly, no guest appears to be the least bit baffled by his "lecture."

Never one to be upstaged, Chico takes part with Harpo in one of the movie's choicest sequences, a four-handed bridge game in which the brothers reduce Mrs. Rittenhouse and her friend Mrs. Whitehead to total confusion. Harpo insists on presenting his leg to Mrs. Rittenhouse, or falling into Mrs. Whitehead's lap, or, in a memorable moment, winning the hand by playing thirteen aces. ("He plays a good game," Chico says admiringly.) Harpo also gets to use his copious-coat routine for the first time. Questioned by the police, an innocent-seeming Harpo manages to shake an endless amount of cutlery—and even a coffeepot—from his sleeve.

With the success of *Animal Crackers,* the Marx Brothers moved to Hollywood and Paramount Studios, where they could take advantage of the more expansive resources. Luckily, the brothers were given another advantage: the writing services of the noted humorist S. J. Perelman. Bringing his iconoclastic wit to the screen for the first time, Perelman collaborated with Will B. Johnstone and Arthur Sheekman on the screenplay for the Marxes' next venture, *Monkey Business* (1931). Director Norman McLeod was assigned to guide the brothers through their first Hollywood production.

Among Marx aficionados, *Monkey Business* is known as their shipboard adventure, although the film ultimately moves to yet another of those swank parties on a Long Island estate and ends in a barn. Here, the brothers, under their own names, are merely stowaways who become mixed up with bootleggers aboard ship. Margaret Dumont was absent, but Groucho found a suitable foil in Thelma Todd, who played the voluptuous blond wife of one of the bootleggers. They share one of the funniest scenes in the Marx canon. Finding Groucho hiding in her stateroom closet, Todd asks him, understandably, "What are you doing in there?" Eyes rolling lasciviously, Groucho replies, "Nothing. Come on in." As with Margaret Dumont, Groucho is not a conventional lover. "I know you're a woman who's gotten nothing but dirty breaks," he tells her. "We can clean and tighten those brakes, but you'll have to stay in the garage overnight." Soon the amorous couple move into a tango that sends Groucho spinning into the arms of her irate husband.

Horse Feathers (1932), their next Paramount movie, marked an advance for the brothers. The co-writers (Perelman and Johnstone) and the director (Norman McLeod) were the same as for *Monkey Business*—Bert Kalmar and Harry Ruby also contributed to the screenplay—but the setting of a college campus allowed for a wider range of satirical thrusts, and the entire film was less claustrophobic. Also, Groucho's quips are somewhat fresher than they were in *Monkey Business*, and the irrepressible shenanigans of Chico and Harpo play a more evenly spaced role in the proceedings.

Best of all, Groucho gets to puncture some holes in academia, spoofing the pomposity and long-windedness often associated with higher education. He plays Professor Quincy Adams Wagstaff, newly elected president of Huxley College, who wastes no time in revealing the backbone of his educational approach: nihilism. To the assembled faculty and student body, he announces in song, "Whatever it is—I'm against it!" His opening speech is so riddled with insults, one half-expects him to be driven out of the room by enraged educators; instead, everyone reacts with decorous silence to such remarks as "As I look over your eager faces, I can readily understand why this college is flat on its back." The scene ends with one of Groucho's best-remembered ripostes. His secretary informs him that "the dean is furious. He's waxing wroth." To this Groucho responds, "Tell Roth to wax the dean for a while."

In a tumultuous classroom scene, Groucho, abetted by Chico and Harpo as two unlikely, overage students, disrupts and takes over a session in biology. Boring lectures and professorial dignity go up in smoke as the brothers dispense with their teacher ("My students will bear me out," he says, and they do), and Groucho proceeds to instruct the class in the workings of the heart. ("Now, in studying your basic metabolism, we first listen to your heartbeat. And if your hearts beat anything but diamonds and clubs, it's because your partner is cheating—or your wife.") At the same time, those dubious intellectuals Chico and Harpo are doing their best to provoke chaos. When a tearfully contrite Harpo is told by Groucho

that "you'll find as you grow older, you can't burn the candle at both ends," his face is suddenly wreathed in smiles as he produces flaming evidence to the contrary from under his coat.

In their next film, *Duck Soup* (1933), the Marxes reached the apogee of their movies at Paramount, and, for many fans, the summit of their screen work. It is the purest form of Marxian madness, unsullied by a vapid romantic subplot or conventional musical numbers. Although the brothers would balk at being called serious satirists, *Duck Soup* is studded with barbs aimed at government leaders and officials who would plunge their countries into war over trifling matters. The Marxes and their primary writers, Bert Kalmar and Harry Ruby, really have one overall intention—to make everyone laugh—but along the way, the laughter is at the expense of asinine politicians, inept spies, and knee-jerk patriots.

Steered by Leo McCarey, already a veteran director of comedy, *Duck Soup* benefits from his well-developed sense of comic pacing. It is set in Freedonia, a country beset with financial woes and plagued with dim-witted officials who apparently believe that the only way to solve the nation's problems is to start a war with their neighbor Sylvania. Groucho plays Rufus T. Firefly, who has just been named Freedonia's president at the insistence of its richest citizen, Mrs. Teasdale (Margaret Dumont, happily returned to the fold). When the film opens, he is being welcomed at a reception that wickedly spoofs all such gala events for dignitaries, complete with a song of greeting, a trumpet fanfare, and girls strewing petals. Firefly, of course, is unimpressed and even hostile, tossing one insult after another at Mrs. Teasdale. (She recalls her late husband: "I was with him to the end." Firefly retorts, "No wonder he passed away." She adds, "I held him in my arms and kissed him." Firefly: "So it was murder, eh?")

One scene is a pure example of Marxian lunacy. For obscure reasons, Chico and Harpo, as spies Chicolini and Pinkie, are required to disguise themselves as Groucho, with all three attired in nightshirts and caps. At one point, Harpo must pretend that he is Groucho's mirror image. In exquisitely timed pantomime, Harpo manages to match every one of Groucho's movements until the illusion begins to break down. When a third "Groucho" enters the scene in the person of Chico, the jig is up, and the three scatter.

Not surprisingly, President Firefly's diplomatic blunders plunge Freedonia into war with Sylvania, a wild and woolly affair in which outrageous jokes, puns, and sight gags are deadlier—and much funnier—than weapons. Since the brothers constitute virtually the entire armed forces, Freedonia seems to have little chance

Horse Feathers *(Paramount, 1932). Dog catcher Harpo shows off his collection of police badges to a suspicious cop. In all of his movies, larcenous Harpo's capacious coat could hold everything from cutlery to a coffee pot.*

Duck Soup *(Paramount, 1933). Zeppo, Groucho, and Chico wage war against Sylvania, with the support of Mrs. Teasdale (Margaret Dumont).*

of winning. A messenger rushes into Firefly's besieged headquarters to announce that a general is undergoing a gas attack. Firefly's advice: "Tell him to take a teaspoon of soda and half a glass of water." Pinkie's main contribution to the war effort is to put up a HELP WANTED sign when Chicolini telephones for help. Soon the screen is inundated with fire engines, marathon runners, long-distance swimmers, packs of baboons, herds of elephants, and schools of porpoises. Mrs. Teasdale shows up to offer moral support, but Firefly is not about to soften: "Remember: you're fighting for this woman's honor, which is probably more than *she* ever did!" When the war is won simply by catching Sylvania's ambassador (showing that wars end as foolishly as they begin), Mrs. Teasdale breaks into an enthusiastic rendition of Freedonia's anthem. The brothers pelt her with oranges.

Today's fans may cherish *Duck Soup*, but at the time, its indifferent critical reception and poor audience response threatened the career of the Marx Brothers. Some felt that the brothers were washed up, and when Zeppo left the act to become a theatrical agent, the outlook seemed bleak. Unexpectedly, however, Hollywood's most prestigious studio, Metro-Goldwyn-Mayer, came to the rescue. One of Chico's poker-playing friends was Irving Thalberg, MGM's head of production, who was establishing a reputation as the studio's fair-haired young genius. Although Thalberg liked the Marxes' films, he felt that there was no relief from the onslaught of jokes, and that the brothers would fare better as sympathetic characters in a genuine story than as freewheeling clowns. He proposed to steer their floundering careers in a new direction, and signed them to a generous contract. Their first MGM film would be *A Night at the Opera* (1935).

True to his word, Thalberg assembled top-grade components. For the screenplay, he brought back the Marxes' original writers, George S. Kaufman and Morrie Ryskind, who had a special rapport with the brothers' unique style. (A Hollywood gagman named Al Boasberg provided some additional dialogue.) Thalberg also chose Allan Jones and Kitty Carlisle to play the young lovers who punctuate the comedy with music, and whose plight arouses the sympathy of the Marxes. He assigned the studio's reliable Sam Wood to direct, and he bathed the entire film in MGM's expensive production values. Best of all, to sharpen the material, he had the brothers tour the vaudeville circuit in advance of filming in order to polish key scenes from the movie. The result was a hugely popular comedy that restored the brothers to public and critical favor.

Although *A Night at the Opera* may fall short of the sustained surrealist humor and satirical flourishes of *Duck Soup*, it does fire some well-aimed shots at

the pomposity of "culture vultures." Groucho appears as Otis P. Driftwood, business manager to millionairess Mrs. Claypool (Margaret Dumont). He is courting her with one eye, or maybe both eyes, on her bank account. Eager to carve a niche in cultural circles, Mrs. Claypool is talked into donating to the New York opera company managed by bombastic Herman Gottlieb (Sig Rumann). To thwart Gottlieb and his nasty star tenor Lassparri (Walter Woolf King), Driftwood joins forces with Fiorello (Chico) and Tomasso (Harpo). His aim is to boost the fortunes of young tenor Ricardo Baroni (Allan Jones), whose beloved is the opera company's leading soprano, Rosa (Kitty Carlisle).

Clearly, *A Night at the Opera* has a more fully developed plot line than any previous Marx movie, but the brothers take it all in their stride, never allowing the story to interfere too much with their crazy antics. As usual, Groucho and Chico are given one verbal exchange of quips, puns, and non sequiturs—here, it is the contract scene, in which Groucho assaults Chico with the mumbo jumbo of legalese ("The first part of the party of the first part shall be known in this contract . . ."), and Chico, in turn, rejects every clause until the contract is the size of a postage stamp. Groucho tries to pass over the sanity clause lightly but Chico is ready for him. "You can't fool me," he says, laughing. "There *is* no Sanity Clause!"

The movie contains a sequence that represents a peak of inspired Marxian slapstick. It is, of course, the celebrated stateroom scene, in which the brothers and Ricardo are crowded into a minuscule room aboard an ocean liner, along with the ship's personnel, plus a woman looking for her Aunt Minnie. The laughter builds as each entangled person calmly tries to find his or her own niche or corner. (Naturally, Harpo, propped up by two chambermaids, sleeps through it all, except to honk for hard-boiled eggs when food is being ordered.) When Mrs. Claypool arrives and opens the door, a torrent of bodies spills out into the corridor.

The climax of the movie is "a night at the opera," a sequence of sustained brilliance. Groucho and company are out to wreck this festive evening and especially to replace the despicable Lassparri with their friend Ricardo. Groucho succeeds in replacing Gottlieb in Mrs. Claypool's box and delivers an audacious opening-night speech to the audience: "I am sure the familiar strains of Verdi's music will come back to you tonight. And Mrs. Claypool's checks will probably come back to you in the morning." Harpo and Chico insert "Take Me Out to the Ball Game" into the overture, and when the music starts, the brothers are playing baseball in the orchestra pit. (Chico pitches, Harpo bats, and Groucho sells peanuts.) Harpo alone causes the most disruption, releasing backdrops so that the gypsy in "Il Trovatore" is singing before a railroad depot, a battleship, and a fruit stand. The brothers crown their mayhem by disposing of Lassparri and getting a triumphant Ricardo to take his place.

A Night at the Opera restored the popularity of the Marx Brothers, despite the criticism of many purists that Thalberg's formula of adding romance and music to the Marxes' comedic mix diluted and compromised their work. However, since the formula appeared to have succeeded, similar ingredients were assembled for their next movie, *A Day at the Races* (1937). Once again, the story had the Marxes creating a comic uproar as they assist young lovers in a time of trouble, or pause for several splashy production numbers. Despite major impediments, most notably the sudden death of Irving Thalberg in 1936 at age thirty-seven, the movie was completed. Surprisingly, it came reasonably close to the high level of the previous film.

For this outing, there were two settings that made an odd combination: the worlds of medicine and horse racing. Groucho played Dr. Hugo Z. Hackenbush, veterinarian and charlatan, who is called on to save the insolvent sanitarium owned by Judy Standish (Maureen O'Sullivan). (Just why anyone would trust this shiftless rascal is never made clear.) Naturally, there are complications: Morgan (Douglass Dumbrille), owner of the nearby racetrack, is scheming to turn the sanitarium into a casino. The sanitarium's richest (and only) patient, Mrs. Upjohn (who else but Margaret Dumont?), is threatening to leave because the doctors refuse to find anything wrong with her. And Judy's boyfriend, Gil, played by Allan Jones, has invested all his money in a racehorse named High Hat. Chico and Harpo are on hand as, respectively, a jockey and a racetrack tout who help Hackenbush save the day for Judy and Gil.

The funniest barbs in *A Day at the Races* are aimed at the medical profession. Not only does Dr. Hackenbush make a mockery of medical ethics and competence but all other doctors in the film, however "distinguished" they may seem, are also inept, self-important fools. Since Groucho is the least trustworthy of all, his examinations erupt inevitably into comic chaos. He prepares for his all-important examination of Mrs. Upjohn by using Harpo as a trial patient. Taking Harpo's pulse, he comments, "Either you're dead or my watch has stopped." A gleeful Harpo chews a thermometer and finds it delicious (Groucho: "Your temperature certainly went down fast!"), and he guzzles a drink from a bottle in the medicine cabinet (Groucho: "Don't drink that poison! It costs four dollars an ounce!"). With all this practice, Groucho is ready to take on Mrs. Upjohn and convince her that she is seriously ill. Chico and Harpo join him in an examination that remains one of the funniest sequences in the Marx films. Medical procedure and decorum go down the drain as they lather Mrs. Upjohn's face with shaving cream, shine her shoes (Groucho puts a MEN AT WORK sign on her feet), and proclaim that X rays are necessary, whereupon Harpo begins shouting a silent "Ex-ray! Ex-ray!" as he peddles invisible newspapers.

Inevitably, *A Day at the Races* ends with the big race, which High Hat must win to keep the sanitarium solvent. With High Hat and jockey Harpo kidnapped by the villains, things look bleak, but Groucho and Chico do their part, disrupting the race until High Hat can show up. They use a wind machine to blow the spectators' hats onto the course, and they reroute the track into the countryside. In a last-minute reversal of fortune, Harpo loses the race, until it is discovered that he was riding the wrong horse. Apparently, Morgan's jockey rode High Hat to victory!

Although *A Day at the Races* is now regarded as one of the better Marx films, the reviews at the time of its release were decidedly mixed. Some critics were sounding a warning note that MGM and the Marxes might well have heeded: The Thalberg mixture of comedy, romance, and music was already in danger of wearing thin, and the routines were beginning to suffer from overexposure. More telling, the creative atmosphere at MGM did not encourage experimentation or the Marxes' penchant for rude satire that might have produced another *Duck Soup.*

Much has been written about the Marxes' decline, which began with *Room Service* in 1938, and indeed their movies did take something of a precipitous slide in quality. The Marxes' sole venture away from MGM during that period, *Room Service* was based on the successful Broadway farce by John Murray and Allen Boretz, and as such it was the first Marx film to draw on material not written expressly for them. Moving to RKO for the occasion, the brothers were shoehorned into a plot that centered on a group of down-on-their-luck actors, headed by Groucho's theatrical producer, who are trying to avoid being thrown out of a hotel while scrounging for money to put on a show. Sadly, the movie failed to deliver sustained laughter. Despite a few choice bits and a cast that included Lucille Ball, Ann Miller, and such capable farceurs as Donald MacBride and Philip Loeb, the restricting plot was a deadweight that the Marxes could not support.

After *Room Service*, the Marxes returned to MGM, but their films never approached their earlier work. By now, the Thalberg formula was becoming visibly frayed: The plots were more of a nuisance than ever; the requisite lovers were increasingly insipid; and, worst of all, the Marx routines were seldom as funny as intended. *At the Circus* (1939) has little to recommend it, and although *Go West* (1940) is substantially better, it still falls short of the mark. However, there are moments to treasure: Groucho gets to fire off a few choice insults (coming upon a drunken cowboy, he asks, "Didn't we meet in Monte Carlo the night you blew your brains out?"), and Harpo has one diverting encounter—a parody of the Western showdown—with the villain in a saloon. Yet these moments are few and far between. The film's best sequence is a climactic train chase that rivals a similar pursuit in Buster Keaton's *The General*. (In fact, it was modeled after that classic chase, and Keaton himself acted as adviser.)

By this time, the Marxes realized that they were beginning to overstay their welcome, and they were also growing tired of the arduous work. After one final movie for MGM, an essentially stale comedy called *The Big Store* (1941), they were off the screen for the next few years. And even when they returned, their work had lost much of its luster. Neither *A Night in Casablanca* (1946) nor *Love Happy* (1949) contained many laughs, even for their most loyal fans. The rest of the Marxes' careers was hardly notable, marked by perfunctory appearances in films and television, and a long stint for Groucho as a radio and television quizmaster on "You Bet Your Life."

The images have faded, the brothers are gone, but the high regard in which their best work is held has remained secure. Over the years, they have influenced comedians from Ernie Kovacs to Mel Brooks. The universality of their humor rests in large part on their all-out assault on revered tenets and institutions—audiences in every decade (in some more than others) have enjoyed watching them merrily tweak pomposity in all its hues. The Marxes were never true anarchists or rebels, but they appealed strongly to those who believed that many figures of authority spoke pure humbug. Even now, when the national and international scene seems crowded with fools and madmen playing destructive games, we expect to see the shadow figures of Groucho, Chico, and Harpo suddenly appear out of the void. Like other great film comedians, they force us to take a clear-eyed look at our own pretensions, foibles, and failings.

They were also uproariously funny. As they romped through Freedonia, or an ocean liner, or an opera house, stopping only to insult an imperious Margaret Dumont, they succeeded in creating a comic universe unlike any that has existed then or since.

While the Marxes' provoked laughter in most moviegoers, some responded adversely to the brothers' grotesque appearance and rampant slapstick, and to their assault on "civilized" behavior. Other moviegoers were offended by W. C. Fields's sardonic put-down of conventional values, or Mae West's flaunted earthiness. Yet it is interesting to speculate on why these icons enjoyed such favor with the great majority. Depression audiences appeared to enjoy most the movies that would take them out of themselves: kaleidoscopic Busby Berkeley musicals, elegant Astaire-Rogers musicals, comedies that made fun of the rich, and gangster films that turned hoodlums into capitalist entrepreneurs with bad attitudes. Occasionally, moviegoers were reminded of the nation's plight by such serious social dramas as *I Am a Fugitive from a Chain Gang* (1932) or *Our Daily Bread* (1934). On the whole, however, they wanted to leave their troubles at the box office window.

Still, not even the comedians could avoid the fact that all the old traditions and values were crumbling in the harsh light of the Depression. The comic figures of the silent era had told them that adversity was everywhere but happiness was possible: A tramp could adopt a homeless waif, and a brash young go-getter could achieve success in business or on the football field. The early sound comedians were giving entirely different messages, however: Pesky infants needed a boot in the rear more than a good home (Fields); a woman's success depended on her being shrewder than a man (West); and all our institutions were overrun with lunatics and charlatans (the Marx Brothers). These comic icons were telling us that we were a nation of fools, chumps, victims, and hypocrites.

Yet most of us laughed, and we have been laughing ever since. In part, the laughter came from the grotesque appearance of these figures, their exaggeration of the flamboyant con man (Fields), the alluring vamp (West), and wicked children who never grew up (the Marxes). Another (and greater) part of the laughter derived from what they said and how they said it, in their own inimitable voices: the great boon of sound. Now, instead of titles, we could have gags, wisecracks, and philosophical asides spoken in the nasal, sardonic tones of Fields, West, and Groucho. (Blessedly, we also had the sublime silence of Harpo, who combined the sweetness of the twenties with the larceny and lechery of the thirties.)

So we laughed while being mocked, cheerfully accepting (or perhaps, in some cases, not noticing) the poisoned darts being hurled at our heads. We laughed mainly because, sarcasm and iconoclasm aside, these were uniquely funny people who created persona that were unlike any others: true creations born out of their artistry, and out of their private hungers and drives.

Not all of the major comic figures of the thirties had streaks of malevolence or bawdiness in their nature. Two men, in particular, managed to straddle the silent and sound eras, keeping intact a gentle innocence that was harshly buffeted by the winds of life. Stan Laurel and Oliver Hardy found that the comedy formula they had created in the twenties—two ingratiating, ever-hopeful fools, sweetly stumbling through a nightmarish world—wore well in the thirties. Laurel's lightly British-accented voice and Hardy's touch of a Georgia drawl seemed to match their comedy. Starting in 1929 with *Unaccustomed As We Are*, they made a series of short and feature-length comedies whose popularity didn't wane until the early forties.

The early sound movies of Laurel and Hardy were made at the bustling studio of Hal Roach, Mack Sennett's closest rival in inventive slapstick and a prolific filmmaker who, like Sennett, discovered and nurtured some of the leading comedians of the period. Laurel and Hardy's films offered variations on a theme: fat, fussy, genteel Ollie, his wide baby face registering peevishness and exasperation (but seldom genuine anger), is the perennial victim of easygoing, dim-witted Stan, forever scratching his head in utter bewilderment or wailing noisily at all the calamities he has perpetrated inadvertently. Whatever roles they played, the result was the same as in their silent films: beautifully orchestrated slapstick in which the gags were worked out with loving care.

Certainly the funniest of their short sound comedies was the Oscar-winning *The Music Box* (1932), which has the simple premise of Stan and Ollie as deliverymen trying to get a crated player piano up a long flight of steps and into a house. Their labors fail miserably and hilariously, until they are forced to pull the box through an open balcony window. (One sublime moment: When things are at their worst, Ollie turns on the piano, which starts to play a medley of patriotic songs. The boys do a fast-stepping little dance to the music.) Of course, they end up with a wrecked piano, an irate house owner, and many well-earned laughs.

Inevitably, Laurel and Hardy moved into feature-length films, appearing first as comical convicts in *Pardon Us* (1931), a fairly amusing parody of MGM's prison drama *The Big House* (1930), and then as bumbling World War I soldiers who befriend a little girl in *Pack Up Your Troubles* (1932). Often the studio cast them as comic relief in typical operettas of the early sound years, including *The Rogue Song* (1930), *The Devil's Brother* (also known as *Fra Diavolo*, 1933), and *The Bohemian Girl* (1936). The most successful of these films was *Babes in Toyland* (also known

Innocents in a hostile world, Stan Laurel and Oliver Hardy brightened movies for several decades with their inimitable form of tomfoolery, Laurel (left) with his sweet stupidity and Hardy (right) with his perennial exasperation.

as *March of the Wooden Soldiers*, 1934), a charming, elaborate fantasy adapted from Victor Herbert's operetta.

The team's other feature films in the thirties were a variable lot, ranging from the inspired slapstick in parts of *Sons of the Desert* (1933) and *Way Out West* (1937) to the middling fun of *Block-Heads* (1938) and *The Flying Deuces* (1939). Some critics regard *Sons of the Desert* as their best feature, and indeed it has more than a few funny moments. The plot is simple enough to have served for one of their short films: Stan and Ollie, determined to attend the Chicago convention of their lodge, the Sons of the Desert, lie to their wives and become entangled in a series of complications. Highlights occur at the convention, where the boys encounter a repulsively hearty lodge member (Charlie Chase), and later, when they are forced to hide from their wives on the roof of Ollie's house. Stan's bulb was seldom dimmer: He consumes a wax apple with gusto and, at one point, uses multisyllable words in the manner of an idiot savant, causing Ollie to stare into the camera with his familiar expression of exasperation.

Way Out West, directed by James W. Horne, is actually a better film, less of an extended sketch than *Sons of the Desert* and replete with some of the team's most endearing moments. Stan and Ollie play genial misfits who arrive in the wild western town of Brushwood Gulch and immediately tangle with a greedy couple named Finn (Jimmy Finlayson and Sharon Lynne) over the deed to a gold mine, which rightly belongs to the demure heroine (Rosina Lawrence).

The team's appeal was never more evident than in the dance they perform early in the film to a hit song of 1905 called "At the Ball, That's All." Beginning tentatively, they are soon transported by the music, dancing with charm and elegance to the sprightly tune. While Stan and Ollie are both in top form throughout the movie, Stan provides the most delightful moments. At one point, after an idle boast that he would eat Ollie's hat if they failed to recover the deed, Stan must consume the derby. Like Harpo, another sweetly dim-witted soul with a bizarre appetite, he finds the hat delicious, even salting it for added pleasure!

The movie's major set piece involves the boys' attempts to break into the Finns' safe in the saloon. In a series of deftly executed gags, Ollie, as usual, bears the brunt of Stan's divinely inspired stupidity. Using a block and tackle, Stan hoists a trussed-up Ollie to the Finns' second-story window, then pauses to spit on his hands, sending Ollie plummeting to earth. Another break-in attempt using Dinah the mule somehow ends with the mule carried into the air instead of Ollie, and Ollie crashing through the saloon's storm-cellar door.

While other feature films had their moments, they were relatively few and far between. *Bonnie Scotland* (1935), which had them enlisting in the Scottish army to fight in India, worked best in isolated moments of easy, eccentric charm: for example, Ollie trying to figure out yet another of Stan's "white magic" tricks—when he blows on his finger like a pipe, his helmet levitates. In *Our Relations* (1936), Stan and Ollie played two sets of twins who turn up together at the same beer garden, creating utter confusion. *A Chump at Oxford* and *Saps at Sea* (both 1940) offered the by-now familiar mixture of lame and funny sight gags. Their last films, poorly made by Twentieth Century–Fox, were merely tired rehashes of their old routines and marked a sad end to their careers.

Yet there is no doubt that they deserve to be remembered among the great comedians of the screen. Starting in the silent years as an integral part of the Chaplin-Keaton-Langdon tradition of innocent fools at large in a dangerous world, they had extended their careers into the sound years, all the while enriching their separate characters. Audiences around the world came to expect—and to cherish—their quirks and eccentricities: Ollie's tie-twiddling, his exasperated, bemused look into the camera, and his inventive use of the derby as an extension of his personality, along with Stan's eye-blinking, head-scratching expressions of befuddlement, and his high-pitched cry of lamentation.

In a sense, Laurel and Hardy were already anachronisms when they made their films in the thirties. Many moviegoers seemed to prefer the ruder, more sardonic humor of W. C. Fields and the Marx Brothers. Stan and Ollie had no axes to grind against any social or political institutions, no contempt for middle-class respectability. Purely and simply, they were nice people. There was no malice in either of them, either off-screen or on. What they had was a humorous concern for life's travails and a tender regard for the gentle, hapless souls they had created. In Stan and Ollie, they gave us two men who are the very soul of comedy.

While comic figures such as Mae West and W. C. Fields dominated the decade, there were other comedians who made their mark on the screen. They may have lacked the distinctive style or inventive humor of the masters, but they attracted large numbers of fans who enjoyed their antics. One popular team, George Burns and wife Gracie Allen, brightened the era in films and on radio. In both short films and features, he played the cigar-smoking, quietly forebearing straight man to her role as the cheerfully light-headed woman whose non sequiturs had a sort of crazy logic. Either starring in their own films (*Many Happy Returns*, 1934; *Love in Bloom*, 1935) or sharing footage with other stars in musical comedies (*We're Not Dressing*, 1934; *A Damsel in Distress*, 1937) they projected a likable quality. Perhaps because her comments seemed more zany than dim-witted, Gracie Allen never for a moment appeared to be mentally retarded, the way later comedians did. She was lovable rather than off-putting, attractive rather than grotesque.

Another recurring figure was Joe E. Brown, a genial comedian with an elastic face whose low-budget slapstick comedies, mostly for Warners, enjoyed some popularity in the thirties. With his trademarked wide mouth often emitting a yowl of dismay or indignation, Brown generally played the country bumpkin, naïve and eager to please, who became the target for larceny-minded city slickers. In the end, with more luck than brains, he would triumph over his adversaries. Among his better features were two derived from baseball stories by Ring Lardner: *Elmer the Great* (1933), in which he played a baseball home-run king who becomes involved with gamblers, and *Alibi Ike* (1935), where he was a pitcher with the exasperating habit of making an excuse for everything he does.

Another comedian who found audience favor in the thirties was Eddie Cantor. A veteran of vaudeville and burlesque, Cantor had achieved stardom in the *Ziegfeld Follies* and other elaborate musicals through his brash comedy and energetic way with a song. Under the auspices of producer Samuel Goldwyn, his hand-clapping, hopping, eye-rolling style found its way to the screen in a series of elaborate musical films. The formula seemed to work: Place the comedian in an environment (modern-day Spain, ancient Rome, an amusement park), add some music and a bevy of beautiful chorines, stir in some expensive production numbers, and wait for the lines to form. Indeed, given Cantor's popularity and Goldwyn's shrewd marketing tactics, the films were successful.

Unfortunately, they were not very good. In *The Kid from Spain* (1932), *Roman Scandals* (1933), and *Kid Millions* (1934), the jokes fall incessantly but heavily, and the situations in which Cantor becomes frenetically involved lack the inventiveness and polish of the best slapstick. Above all, Cantor, for all of his strenuous efforts, fails to adopt a consistent identity on screen. Sometimes the character he projects—the jittery, hyperactive babe in the woods—is at odds with the flippant, leering vaudeville patter he is given to speak. He never seems quite as ingratiating as he would obviously like to be. On the whole, Cantor's screen roles failed to duplicate the special appeal of his radio personality.

Cantor, at least, achieved star status under Samuel Goldwyn's aegis. Other talented comedians who had traveled the path from vaudeville and burlesque to theatrical stardom fared less well on-screen. A show-business veteran, Jimmy Durante had delighted audiences with his formidable nose, raspy voice, and air of befuddlement or mortification. Yet he was seldom able to find screen roles worthy of his special gifts, often functioning merely as an avuncular support to the stars. Bert Lahr, another splendid comedian with origins in vaudeville, burlesque, and the legitimate stage, also found it difficult to transpose his talent to film. By the sound era, his inimitable clown's face and matchless buffoonery, coupled with a bellow that could shatter glass, had established him as a peerless comic artist. Yet he made only a handful of films in the thirties, capped by his memorable performance as the Cowardly Lion in *The Wizard of Oz* (1939).

Still other comedians found comfortable niches in films without achieving legendary status. The inordinately funny Australian-born Leon Errol used his slack-jawed, hawk-nosed face and rubber legs to good advantage in a series of two-reelers and low-budget features. "Second banana" Edgar Kennedy came into his own with a long-running group of short films in which he perfected his "slow burn"—quiet irritation that grew into towering rage. For a while, Al, Jimmy, and Harry Ritz, a team of madcap brothers who traded in freewheeling zaniness, enjoyed popularity with moviegoers, if not with critics, Occasionally, women would enter the crazy knockabout world of comedy: Martha Raye enlivened many thirties comedies with her raucous antics and her lively songs, while Joan Davis used her gawky, loose-limbed style to project an amiable goofiness that kept her active into the early fifties.

And then there were those purveyors of violent slapstick, the Three Stooges. Coming out of vaudeville and Broadway revues onto the nation's screens in 1930, the three, consisting originally of brothers Moe and Shemp Howard and Larry Fine, began appearing in comedy shorts that remained popular for nearly a quarter of a century. Whatever the story line, the slapstick never changed—Curley, Moe, and Larry (and their later replacements) would subject each other to a nonstop orgy of head bangings, eye gougings, shin kickings, and nose tweakings that would probably have delighted the Marquis de Sade. Although no comedy team ever traded so heavily on abusive behavior, their champions have always insisted that the violence has no more reality for viewers than that of an animated cartoon.

Small wonder that people of the Depression years turned so often to the great and lesser comic figures of the screen. At a time when few had reason to laugh, these figures eased the pain and the hardship, if only for a few hours, by revealing the eternally foolish and endlessly funny side of being human.

Chapter 3

Love in Hard Times

Romantic and Marital Comedy in the Thirties

I n *The Purple Rose of Cairo*, Woody Allen's amusing, poignant 1985 comedy-fantasy, Cecilia (Mia Farrow), a Depression housewife, sits in a darkened movie theater, staring enraptured at the screen. Watching the dashing hero, who is about to descend from the screen into her life, she is totally transfixed in a dream of romance. Her daily life is drab and petty, but in these cherished moments in the theater, she has been transported to a world where love waits, rather than dirty dishes or a brutish, insensitive husband.

Unlike the scores of women who struggled to survive the bleak Depression years, Cecilia will, for a brief time, have the chance to live out her fantasy with the shadow figure she adores. Yet like the others, she finally will be back in her theater seat, submerging her thwarted feelings in flickering images. For most of the women (and the men) of the thirties, love was a distinct hope and possibility—even in a gray world, the world will sometimes shine, and someone could be waiting to share a cup of coffee, a sandwich, and his or her life. But romance was another matter. Romance was a luxury, not to be found in the mean streets or meager apartments but up on the silver screen. It could have its tragic aspects: suffering heroes and heroines forced, by death or disaster, to lose an undying love. But in hard times, how nice, how entertaining romance could be when it was spiked with healing, warming laughter.

In the silent years, although romantic comedies were being made and enjoyed, audiences preferred the rapid-fire slapstick that required no titles to be understood. After all, moving pictures required movement, rather than words, and car chases and pratfalls were much more fun than sweethearts who squabbled with or embraced each other. When sound appeared, however, it was possible for bright, witty, or just pleasantly amusing talk to supplement the physical action. Comic banter could express a love affair going full throttle or veering off the track and heading for collision.

It Happened One Night (Columbia, 1934). Reporter Peter Warne (Clark Gable) and heiress Ellie Andrews (Claudette Colbert) pause in their cross-country trek. Gable's rugged charm meshed well with Colbert's womanly warmth.

But what to talk about? Given the nature of the times, it is not surprising that romantic comedy in the thirties concentrated more on war between the classes than war between the sexes. In a period when the have-nots vastly out-numbered the haves, it was clear that the catalyst from which romantic comedy could spring would have to come largely from the deep, wide abyss that separated the poor from the rich. If Cupid aimed his arrows indiscriminately, the comedy would be precipitated by having them simultaneously pierce the hearts of heir-esses and reporters, princesses and commoners, working girls and their bosses.

At first, in the earliest years of sound, many filmmakers surmised that audi-ences wanted to swallow their fantasies whole; they often doused their comedies and musicals in images of affluence and splendor: high society salons and bed-rooms inhabited by haughty men and naughty women; Graustarkian kingdoms where royalty romped in three-quarter time. It soon became apparent, however, that the wistful Cecilias who had little but their dreams to go on (and women made up the larger part of the audience) were looking to the movies, particularly the romantic comedies, for more than just a trip to Never Never Land, or more accurately, Never-to-Be Land. They wanted these movies to deliver any one or combination of the following reassuring messages: (1) it was possible, in this gloomy world, to find a true prince who would carry you off to his castle; (2) you might be better off with a poor but loving commoner, and (3) it might not be so wonderful to be rich, after all. In the worst of all possible times, romantic comedy was becoming class-conscious, and it was evident which class had the upper hand in common sense, intelligence, and even sex appeal.

If one film could be said to have set the tone for romantic comedy in the thir-ties, it was Frank Capra's *It Happened One Night* (1934). To the surprise of virtually everyone, including its director and leading players, this modest movie with low expectations turned into an enormous hit that came to represent prevailing atti-tudes of the day. Its story of a spoiled runaway heiress who learns about life and love on a cross-country bus tour with a reporter was not, in itself, startlingly origi-nal. (Several movies about bus trips had already failed at the box office.) Nor was the Robert Riskin screenplay exceptionally witty, although it was undeniably clever and charming. Yet, due to a combination of factors, the movie struck a responsive chord in audiences everywhere. It appeared to crystallize the collective notion that high-handed rich folk (the only kind, according to movie tradition) could learn to share a common humanity with poor folk. And better yet, the haves and the have-nots eventually could fall in love.

The film's success, which included five Academy Awards, certainly could not have been predicted from its humble beginnings. The original story, "Night Bus," by Samuel Hopkins Adams, had appeared in *Cosmopolitan* magazine, where it was noticed by Frank Capra. Despite being rejected by Columbia head Harry Cohn and his executives, the property somehow found its way into the studio's schedule, largely through Capra's persistence. His problems continued, however, when the leading roles proved difficult to fill. A reluctant Claudette Colbert finally accepted the role of heiress Ellie Andrews after a number of other actresses had rejected it. And as punishment for rebellious behavior, Louis B. Mayer, lord and master at MGM, ordered his up-and-coming star Clark Gable to report to Columbia for the role of reporter Peter Warne.

By now, the cross-country trek of Ellie Andrews and Peter Warne has been so imbedded in movie lore that it comes as something of a surprise to note that the film remains a diverting romantic comedy. As Ellie and Peter travel by bus through a Depression America—she hoping to escape an irate father and marry the gigolo of her dreams; he to safeguard his exclusive story of her flight—the two come to share a mutual concern and understanding that ripens into love. For Ellie, the journey becomes an introduction to the small felicities and survival tricks in the real world of "little" people: how to dunk a doughnut, for example, and how to hitch a ride. Even more important, the bus and foot journey gives Ellie an eye-opening look at life outside of her gold-plated cocoon. Above all, she learns to have humility, the quality that can soften her hard edges for Peter, and convince him that he loves her. No film to date had managed to convey the feelings and the attitudes of Depression-weary Americans with such effortless charm.

Still, *It Happened One Night* was not a social tract, but a romantic comedy, and even after the years have made it slightly frayed around the edges, it retains a romantic aura. From the moment Ellie comes on the bus and falls into Peter's lap ("Next time you drop in, bring the folks," Peter tells her, with the wry Gable grin), the movie makes their ultimate affair not only inevitable but totally engaging. One still marvels at their first intimate scene at the auto camp when Peter divides the room by stringing a blanket along a clothesline. "Behold the walls of Jericho!" he tells her. "Maybe not as thick as the ones that Joshua blew down with his trumpet, but a lot safer. You see, I have no trumpet." He undresses, simultaneously revealing a bare chest and striking a blow at the manufacturers of men's undershirts. Ellie follows suit by flinging her undergarments on the blanket. Soon, on opposite sides of the blanket, the air has an amorous charge as Robert Riskin's blithe dialogue begins to spin an unmistakably sexual web. Colbert and Gable play this scene, and indeed all the film's scenes, with a skill and assurance that earned them both Oscars.

Inevitably, the surprising success of *It Happened One Night* led to a number of other "rich girl finds true love" comedies, such as *Love Is News* (1937) and *There Goes My Heart* (1938). One of the brightest of these films, entitled *Libeled Lady* (1936), employed a clever twist: Heiress Connie Allenbury (Myrna Loy), accused of being a "husband-stealer" by the *Evening Star,* furiously sues the paper for libel. To thwart Connie by proving she truly *is* a husband-stealer, the paper's beleaguered editor, Warren Haggerty (Spencer Tracy), enlists the aid of Bill Chandler (William Powell), a past master at breaking libel cases, and Haggerty's own long-suffering fiancée, Gladys, played by Jean Harlow. Complications ensue when Bill falls for Connie, but all is resolved amicably.

Under Jack Conway's direction, the screenplay for *Libeled Lady* (credited to Maurine Watkins, Howard Emmett Rogers, and George Oppenheimer) succeeds in stirring up considerable merriment. One of the funniest scenes occurs when Bill and Gladys, in order to carry out Warren's scheme of foiling Connie, agree to a temporary marriage. At the ceremony, a startled justice of the peace watches as best-man Warren bestows a passionate kiss on the new bride. "An old friend of the family," Bill explains. "A *very* old friend." William Powell, always the superb farceur, has one exceptionally amusing sequence in which, to impress Connie, he is obliged to display his nonexistent skills at trout-fishing. Once again, as in *The Thin Man,* Powell's debonair elegance meshes with Loy's piquant charm, but it is Harlow who virtually steals the film as Tracy's brassy girlfriend. She creates a delightful character in Gladys, incensed at her boyfriend's cold-hearted manipulations ("You'd make your crippled grandmother do a fan dance!").

If romantic comedies in the Depression years seemed duty-bound to teach its spoiled rich girls the virtues of humility and common sense in hard times, they also professed to show them that the lives they led were frivolous and empty. In film after film, as a sop to the poor folk who, after all, constituted the larger part of the audience, the well-to-do were depicted as snobbish, insensitive, and light-headed. Of course, since these were comedies and not social diatribes, they were also, on some occasions, inordinately funny.

Witness Gregory La Cava's *My Man Godfrey* (1936). A film deeply rooted in its time (a disastrous fifties remake proved the point), this nimble social comedy had the audacity to juxtapose the glittering, fashionable environment of the Park Avenue swells with the harsh Depression world of the hobo colonies. The Morrie Ryskind–Eric Hatch screenplay (from Hatch's novel) focused on the wealthy Bullocks: grumpy father Eugene Pallette, whose business is on the verge of ruin; featherbrained mother Alice Brady, and their two daughters, Irene and Cordelia (Carole Lombard and Gail Patrick). Living with the Bullocks as a permanent guest and Mrs. Bullock's "protégé" is Mischa Auer's Carlo, a scrounger with two talents: eating and imitating a gorilla.

My Man Godfrey *(Universal, 1936). Irene Bullock (Carole Lombard) eavesdrops on her sister, Cordelia (Gail Patrick) and their butler, Godfrey (William Powell). Gregory La Cava's social comedy twitted the Depression's rich folk.*

Into this ménage of crackpots steps a hobo named Godfrey, played by William Powell, whom Irene discovers during a scavenger hunt. Discreet and all-wise, he becomes not only the Bullocks' latest butler but also the catalyst for events that stir up the Bullocks' privileged lives. Before the film is over, he has thawed out the frosty Cordelia, restored Mr. Bullock's shaky finances, and won the heart of the rather overwrought Irene. It also turns out that he is not a "forgotten man" after all, but an affluent scion who deliberately withdrew from a family that was "never educated to face life." In an ending of pure Depression fantasy, Godfrey, the perfect benign capitalist, builds a lavish nightclub on the site of the city dump, where he employs his old hobo friends.

Like other films directed by Gregory La Cava, *My Man Godfrey* enjoyed twitting the rich and their selfish ways. With their headline-making pranks and their waste of time and money, the Bullocks signify the well-to-do as they were seen in thirties films. To Godfrey, the Bullocks are "empty-headed nitwits" who need to be shown the terrible disparities between their swanky existence and those of the "men who starve for want of a job." Few comedies of the period addressed the gap between the haves and have-nots with such a biting edge.

A rich girl who could match Carole Lombard's Irene Bullock as a bona fide flake turned up two years later in Howard Hawks's definitive screwball comedy *Bringing Up Baby* (1938). As played by Katharine Hepburn in the first role to reveal fully her comedy skills, Susan Vance is a tribulation. Like Irene Bullock, Susan is convinced that she is entitled to pursue freely whatever whim takes her fancy. Her goal in *Bringing Up Baby* is single-minded: to win the heart of David, the absentminded archaeologist played by Cary Grant. She has no concern with the facts, not even the obvious one that David finds her a total nuisance. On the way to falling in love, Susan and David have to deal with, among other things, a missing rare dinosaur bone, a frisky terrier who enjoys burying bones, and especially a pet leopard named Baby, sent to Susan as a gift from her explorer brother.

Bringing Up Baby is less concerned with mocking the rich than with finding new ways in which Susan can disrupt David's life before convincing him that he loves her. The key sequence in which they meet on a golf course consists of a series of mounting disasters that trigger dismay for David and hilarity for the audience. In a short time, yammering without letup in that inimitable Hepburn voice, she wrecks his car, disrupts his golf game with an influential man, and threatens not only his patience but his sanity as well. Before long, every shred of

David's dignity has vanished. In one of the film's funniest scenes, he and Susan wander through the Connecticut countryside, searching for the missing Baby as they sing the leopard's favorite song, "I Can't Give You Anything but Love."

After *Bringing Up Baby*, Katharine Hepburn left RKO to costar again with Grant at Columbia as an entirely different sort of rich girl in a second film version of Philip Barry's play *Holiday* (1938). Another comedy that belabored the rich for accumulating wealth at the expense of happiness, *Holiday* cast Hepburn as Linda Seton, a serious-minded and discontented debutante who falls in love with her haughty sister's fiancé, Johnny Case (Grant). When Johnny proves to be a free spirit who insists on taking an extended "holiday" to find his identity before settling down to earning money, he loses his status with the Setons. In the end, Johnny and Linda discover that they are perfect soul mates, with a deep-seated mistrust of wealth and a desire to live their lives untrammeled by convention.

Adapted by Sidney Buchman and Donald Ogden Stewart, *Holiday* contains the requisite thirties attitude toward the wealthy. (Linda tells Johnny that the Seton house is "haunted by ghosts wearing stuffed shirts and mink-lined ties.") Yet in spite of the incidental flavor of wormwood, *Holiday* remains a diverting comedy given a stylish turn by the leading players. Under George Cukor's direction, Hepburn and Grant reveal the same adroit give-and-take that had served them so well in *Bringing Up Baby*. Hepburn, in particular, gives Linda's rebelliousness the affecting vulnerability of a young woman whose only home is the secret playroom of her childhood.

Several years after making *Holiday*, Hepburn appeared as yet another sort of rich girl in George Cukor's *The Philadelphia Story* (1940), adapted from the Philip Barry play in which she had scored a personal triumph on Broadway in the spring of 1939. No warm and vulnerable Linda Seton, her Tracy Lord is cool and haughty, a "goddess" with exceptionally high standards for everyone, herself included. On the eve of her second marriage to a rather stuffy sort, her pedestal collapses: She clashes with her jovial ex-husband, C. K. Dexter Haven (Cary Grant), and has a brief romantic fling with Mike Connor (James Stewart), a magazine reporter who has come to her Main Line Philadelphia home to write about her wedding. The experience turns her into a humanized woman with "an understanding heart," and she returns to Dexter, who still loves her.

Although released in 1940, *The Philadelphia Story* belongs securely in the thirties, in its lightly satirical tone toward the well-to-do, its witty banter, and its

Holiday *(Columbia, 1938). Rich girl Linda Seton (Katharine Hepburn) has a yen for her sister's fiancé, Johnny Case (Cary Grant). Linda disdains her wealth—she urges Johnny not to get caught up in "a reverence for riches."*

wealthy young heroine who needs her "comeuppance." In the role that was tailored to her specifications and mannerisms, Hepburn gives one of her very best comedy performances; she moves with ease from the high society snob to the starry-eyed young woman who can say, "Put me in your pocket, Mike" in a romantic poolside scene. As the man who continues to love her despite her faults, Cary Grant acts with his usual aplomb, and James Stewart, in a performance that surprisingly won that year's Best Actor Oscar, is enormously likable as Mike.

Although a silken and adroit comedy, *The Philadelphia Story* was essentially looking backward to a time that was vanishing by 1940. Like comedy itself, romance would take a different shape in the years ahead. But for a while it was exceedingly pleasant to inhabit the film's privileged world.

While many thirties films were busily mocking the foolish extravagances and selfish ways of rich folk, many others were indulging in a favorite Depression fantasy: the poor working girl, trapped in her dingy life, suddenly gets the chance to spend the rest of her days with a rich and handsome prince. This was a choice fantasy, to be sure, one that allowed the viewer to dream and escape in the darkness for a few hours. The movies had yet another goal in mind, however, and that was to reassure the female viewer that her own true life was not a dreary ritual, and that happiness could be found in her own backyard. Since the women in the audience, the housewives, the clerks, and the secretaries, were not likely to find a prince waiting at the doorstep, furs and jewels at the ready, they were told that it was all right to be content with one's lot. And so in film after film, Cinderella was made to reject the prince and return to the working stiff who had always loved her. Sometimes she won the prince, but it almost invariably turned out that she never knew that the fellow was a prince, or, in true democratic fashion, she simply didn't care. Most frequently, however, the Depression Cinderella chose the stability and no-nonsense attitude of the Guy Next Door. On more than one occasion, he looked like unbuttered white bread, or Fred MacMurray.

Virtually every leading actress of the thirties was given a turn to portray a heroine who settled for a poor but loving husband. Claudette Colbert switched from spoiled heiress to independent-minded working girl in *The Gilded Lily* (1935) and *I Met Him in Paris* (1937), two comedies directed by Wesley Ruggles, in which she respectively dropped nobleman Ray Milland for reporter Fred MacMurray, and playboy Robert Young for insolvent playwright Melvyn Douglas. In William Wyler's *The Good Fairy* (1935), innocent young Margaret Sullavan preferred struggling lawyer Herbert Marshall over millionaire Frank Morgan, while Mitchell Leisen's *Hands Across the Table* (1935) had Carole Lombard choosing poor but loyal Fred MacMurray over wealthy Ralph Bellamy. At the film's end, she got to speak the motto of many a Depression heroine: "Hard-boiled Hannah was going to fall in love with a bankroll!"

Jean Arthur, an actress whose piquant personality and crackling voice provided one of the ongoing pleasures of the thirties, starred in one of the most amusing entries in the Cinderella cycle. Mitchell Leisen's *Easy Living* (1937) cast her as

Easy Living *(Paramount, 1937). A publicity pose for Mitchell Leisen's romantic comedy. Left to right: Ray Milland, Edward Arnold, Jean Arthur, Esther Dale, and Mary Nash.*

a working girl who suddenly (and literally) has luxury dropped into her lap. Written by Preston Sturges three years before he made his auspicious debut as a writer-director with *The Great McGinty,* the movie spins a diverting if improbable tale of the misunderstandings that occur over a sable coat. Enraged by his wife's extravagance, financier J. B. Ball (Edward Arnold) flings her sable coat out of the window, whereupon it lands in the lap of Mary Smith (Arthur), a passenger on an open double-decker bus. From this point, the complications mount swiftly: A bewildered Mary, mistaken for J. B. Ball's mistress, finds herself suddenly quartered in a luxury hotel. In the fashion of movies of the period, she also meets Ray Milland, an apparently unemployed young man, who turns out be J. B. Ball's son John, anxious to prove his worth to his father. Not surprisingly, they fall in love.

By far the funniest and best-remembered sequence in *Easy Living* stems from Sturges's fondness for slapstick, so evident in the pratfalls and frantic chases that occur in his later, more famous films. It takes place in an Automat, where John Ball has taken a job, and where a hungry and penniless Mary has come in search of leftovers. When he is fired for trying to help her, a fight ensues, and all the food slots suddenly open to the patrons. An expertly timed melee takes place as everyone scrambles for free food: A man carefully balances a tray heaped high, until someone crashes into him; another man sprinkles pepper in the air and absconds with the meals of the hearty sneezers, until someone knocks him over. Through all the confusion, Mary sits calmly enjoying her repast. Sturges and director Leisen whipped the scene into a memorable comic frenzy.

An actress who perhaps best represented the plucky, tenacious working-class heroine of the thirties (in this case, late thirties) was Ginger Rogers. Having spent the larger part of the decade dancing memorably in the arms of Fred Astaire, Rogers made a career change that called for her to bring her crisp, down-to-earth personality to romantic comedy. Even before she left Astaire, she began appearing in films without benefit of song or dance, notably as an aspiring actress in *Stage Door* (1937). She also acted with considerable charm in George Stevens's engaging *Vivacious Lady* (1938), playing a nightclub dancer who marries a shy, fumbling college professor (James Stewart) and finds herself with more problems than she bargained for. In one of her best nondancing performances of the thirties, Rogers made something real and credible of this outspoken girl's collision with academia.

By the decade's end, the actress was getting to play a succession of sensible but romantic-minded white-collar girls, culminating in her Oscar-winning performance as *Kitty Foyle* (1940). In *Bachelor Mother* (1939), directed by Garson Kanin, she gave a comic turn to the usually serious subject of unwed motherhood, playing a department store salesgirl who finds an abandoned baby and is mistaken by everyone for its unwed mother. In a few years, Rogers's performances would take on an icy, grande dame manner, but here she is pert and sympathetic as a girl bewildered by the brouhaha surrounding her and her foundling. Norman Krasna's screenplay may skirt the edge of propriety by thirties standards, but its good humor disarms any disapproval. Later in the year, Rogers retained her working-class credentials by appearing in Gregory La Cava's *Fifth Avenue Girl* (1939) as a jobless girl who helps an unhappy tycoon recover the love and attention of his selfish family, while she finds romance with his playboy son.

If there were few aspiring Cinderellas left by 1939, there was one who closed out the decade in full glory, turning up in what may well be the best Cinderella comedy of the period. In Mitchell Leisen's sparkling *Midnight* (1939), Claudette Colbert was, in fact, following closely in the footsteps of her fairy-tale predecessor as a penniless girl who finds unexpected romance and adventure on a rainy night in Paris. Yet Eve Peabody is no wide-eyed maiden, but a cheerful gold digger who

enjoys a life of affluence. Through the events of a single evening, she finds herself posing as a baroness and playing the central figure in a marital intrigue.

The premise of the Billy Wilder–Charles Brackett screenplay is refreshingly original: wealthy Georges Flammarion (John Barrymore), determined to get rid of his wife's newest lover, playboy Jacques Picot (Francis Lederer), hires Eve to seduce Jacques away from his wife, Mary Astor. In exchange, Eve will lead a plush existence as the imaginary Baroness Czerny. She agrees to the deception, at the same time that Tibor (Don Ameche), a taxi driver whom she met earlier and who has fallen in love with her, is trying frantically to locate her. Confusion reigns when Tibor turns up at the Flammarion château, claiming to be Eve's husband,

Midnight *(Paramount, 1939). Claudette Colbert (second from right) looks uneasy introducing her husband the baron (Don Ameche) to Mary Astor. In fact, he is neither her husband nor a baron. Also present (left to right): Francis Lederer, John Barrymore, and Rex O'Malley.*

Baron Czerny. This being Hollywood in the thirties, Eve ultimately forgets her dreams of wealth and ends up with Tibor.

One of the decade's peerless romantic comedies, *Midnight* fairly brims with sly and clever lines from the Brackett-Wilder pen. As Eve is driven about Paris in Tibor's taxi, he asks her about the kind of work she is seeking. "At this time of night," she replies, "I'm not looking for needlepoint." Marcel (Rex O'Malley), the eternal party guest, considers himself a telephone worshiper. "Whenever a day comes without an invitation," he tells his bridge partners, "I pray to my telephone as though it were a little black god. I beg of it to speak to me . . . to ask me out whenever there is champagne or caviar." And when Jacques sends flowers to Eve with a card reading, "Hosannas to the high gods for throwing us together," Georges comments wryly, "I should resent that. To my wife he only wrote, 'So glad we met.'"

As a new decade was about to get under way, comedies that focused on a young girl's dream of romance, her longing for a Prince Charming to fit her with a golden slipper, were receding into the past. By the start of World War II, Cinderella was dismissing money and adventure along with the romance—it was enough for her merely to be there for GI Joe. The war would demand democratic heroines who boosted the morale of any man in uniform, rich or poor. And many a Cinderella enlisted herself, putting dreams behind her for the duration.

At the same time that romance between the unmarried blossomed on-screen in the hard times of the thirties, marriage found its own inevitable niche as a popular subject for comedy or drama. Some films depicted, with unflinching reality, the harsh, meager lives of young married couples who had chosen to share what little they had. Movies such as King Vidor's late-silent classic *The Crowd* (1928) captured the sadness and the frail hopes of husbands and wives in the Depression. Other movies, however, dealt solemnly with troubled marriages among the well-to-do, giving such refined actresses as Norma Shearer and Ann Harding the opportunity to show their capacity for suffering while dressed in the height of fashion.

Turned on its ear, the dramatic muse could turn comic, and many movies in the thirties focused on the farcical or amusingly sophisticated consequences of marital infidelity. In the early years, as filmmakers struggled with the problems of sound, marital comedies either stressed the slapstick aspects of cheating wives and husbands or they overwhelmed the sound track with high-toned society chitchat. Couples seemed to spend much of their time in Art Deco rooms, planning, carrying out, and often regretting their indiscretions.

Then, in 1934, a very modest movie, a comedy-mystery of no pretensions whatever, changed the way the screen perceived marriage. With little fanfare, MGM released a film adaptation of Dashiell Hammett's popular mystery novel *The Thin Man*. On the surface, it appeared to be a routine story concerning the mysterious disappearance of an eccentric inventor (tabbed "the Thin Man" by the tabloid press), followed by several murders, a roundup of suspects, and a solution to the crimes. It was all fairly cut-and-dried material, directed competently by W. S. Van Dyke.

Yet there was one element that made all the difference and turned a small movie into a landmark. This element was the film's stars and the roles they played. As Nick and Nora Charles, a couple who happened to be wealthy, hard-drinking, and urbane sophisticates, William Powell and Myrna Loy brought a refreshingly candid new note to the movie-eye view of marriage. Powell, a frequent villain in the silent years, had graduated to leading roles in the early thirties by dint of his dry, sophisticated manner and a mellifluous speaking voice that fairly crackled with irony and skepticism. Loy had been busy in the silent and early sound years as an exotic vamp, and with a few exceptions, most notably her role as a man-crazy countess in *Love Me Tonight* (1932), she gave little indication of a flair for sophisticated comedy. Brought together for *The Thin Man*, the two struck a responsive chord that not only gave a new direction to their careers but also took the depiction of marital relationships in the movies to a new plateau.

Today, when films plunge fearlessly into the heights—and unmistakable depths—of modern marriage, the impact of Nick and Nora Charles may seem laughably simplistic. In 1934, however, it was virtually a novelty: Here was a married couple who not only liked being together, but who, from all indications, clearly enjoyed sleeping together as well. In actuality, there was not all that much banter between Nick and Nora in the Albert Hackett–Frances Goodrich screenplay, but what there was showed their mutual sense of fun and their warm regard for each other, tempered by an amused awareness of each other's weaknesses, mostly for martinis.

This husband and wife clearly share a marriage made in heaven. Always the perfect helpmate in movie terms, Nora never complains; she tolerates and is even amused by Nick's foibles (watch her expression as he shoots out balloons with his air gun), and frets about his safety when he is busy stalking murderers. Here was a wife who was not lofty, condescending, and holier-than-thou. She was smart, sassy, and sexy—and Nick appreciated and loved her. It is not surprising, then, that movie audiences liked what they saw, and wanted more of the same. Although the subsequent *Thin Man* sequels diminished in quality, Nick and Nora remained popular well into the forties. Encouraged by the unexpected success of *The Thin Man,* many other studios proceeded to turn out mystery-comedies in which an urbane couple bustled about, dispensing witty banter and crime solutions in equal proportions.

In those mystery-comedies, marriages were solid and secure. Although the couples enjoyed being flippant and sarcastic with each other, there was a clear sense that all was serene in the marital nest, and that their only real problem was finding the murderer. Other movie marriages, however, were not so lucky; in these marital nests, feathers were ruffled, beaks were sharp and biting, and much squawking could be heard. To extend the metaphor, some birds even flew off to their very own nests.

In thirties comedies of marital discord, there was an unmistakable pattern that extended well into the forties: Most often it was the husband who was required to play the fool, the one who was expected to endure comic humiliations and embarrassments in the marital conflict. While the wife was permitted to remain reasonably calm, the husband was called on to dither, plead, and take extreme measures to win the marital war or negotiate a truce. It was he who played the jabbering fool as he tried frantically to win back his ex-wife, or to romance his "kiss-less" bride.

Most likely, the principal reason for this doltish husband–wise wife syndrome in marital comedies of the thirties (and early forties) rests with the star actresses who played the wives. These women projected an attitude that made them seem more levelheaded and probably more intelligent than the men. In the womanly warmth of Claudette Colbert, or the slightly tongue-in-cheek superiority of Irene Dunne, or the cool (but not chilly) disdain of Myrna Loy, there was a confidence that carried them through every comic dilemma. They may have been the ultimate Hollywood fantasy of womanhood, but women admired them, and men wanted to be married to them.

If many movie wives ruled the roost, ex-wives had even more power. A number of thirties marital comedies involved a divorcing couple in which the husband, still in love with his wife, pursues her doggedly, enduring any kind of humiliation in the hope of winning her back. Often the wife, although sharing her husband's feelings, finds pleasure in letting him twist in the wind, until she relents and agrees to reconcile. Certainly, the classic example of this situation occurs in Leo McCarey's 1937 comedy, *The Awful Truth,* in which husband Cary Grant, divorced by wife Irene Dunne after being caught in a lie, spends most of the film trying to get back in her good graces.

The Awful Truth is one of the brightest, most durable comedies of the thirties, and yet by the time it appeared, it was hardly freshly minted. The original play by Arthur Richman had been filmed twice before in the twenties, and would be again in the fifties. In addition, the screenplay, credited to Viña Delmar but actually stitched together during less than six weeks of production by director Leo McCarey and others, has the simplest of premises: Lucy and Jerry Warriner divorce, although they really love each other. They each find somebody else, but, through a series of comic events, they are finally reconciled. There is nothing startlingly original here to warrant the movie's special cachet.

Yet it all works beautifully. Although the screenplay may not be especially witty, it abounds in funny moments, a number of which were improvised on the set by McCarey and the cast. One scene among many—a model of inspired slapstick—has Lucy trying desperately to keep her new beau and his formidable mother from discovering that her ex-husband and overly attentive music teacher are battling it out noisily in her bedroom. Sequences that virtually define the marital comedy of the period are happily present: the early courtroom encounter, with Lucy and Jerry contending for possession of their dog, Mr. Smith (the dog is asked to decide); the chance meeting at a nightclub where an embarrassed Jerry must explain his "date," a club stripper named Dixie Lee; and the climactic sequence in which the couple, stranded together in a remote cabin, are forced to deal with their still-simmering desire for each other. Perhaps funniest of all is the scene in which Lucy, determined to break up Jerry's engagement, impersonates his flamboyant "sister," storming the home of his fiancée and disconcerting everyone with her antics. Leo McCarey's deft improvisational touch with this material won him the year's Oscar as Best Director.

When marital comedies of the thirties were not concerned with divorced or estranged couples, they found other ways to discomfit or confound the hapless husband. In the game of marriage, the wife always seemed to hold all the cards, even when she was merely a wife of convenience. A 1935 comedy entitled *She Married Her Boss* centered on career woman Claudette Colbert, in love with her boss (Melvyn Douglas), who agrees to marry him for purely business reasons, then diligently steers him into a permanent and romantic relationship. In true thirties fashion, the boss, finally realizing that he loves his bride of convenience, must play the fool in order to effect a happy ending. Sometimes, the husband was depicted as a man whose marriage is in jeopardy not through any fault of his but through his own singular obtuseness. In *Wife vs. Secretary* (1936), magazine publisher Clark

Gable is so unaware of his attraction to women that he is mortified when jealous wife Myrna Loy accuses him unfairly of an adulterous relationship with his secretary, Jean Harlow. (The poor man is innocent—he resisted temptation when Harlow joined him at a Havana convention.)

No movie husband ever suffered as ignominiously, however, as Gary Cooper in Ernst Lubitsch's *Bluebeard's Eighth Wife* (1938). Here, Cooper played a much-married millionaire who meets and marries Claudette Colbert, the daughter of impoverished French aristocrat Edward Everett Horton. When she learns of his many previous wives (she is number eight), she consents to the marriage only if he agrees to pay her $100,000 a year for the rest of her life if they should divorce. Although she ostensibly loves him, she proceeds to drive him into a divorce by firmly insisting on remaining—in the euphimism of the day—"kiss-less." Her tactics in keeping him from consummating their marriage cause him to have a nervous breakdown. Eventually, of course, they are reconciled.

Lubitsch tries hard to extract humor from this essentially humorless concept, but here his usually airy and sardonic "touch" deserts him. Many thirties films contained a streak of cruelty that curdled the comedy and turned it sour. In this instance, we are inclined to cringe at the ploys Colbert uses to keep her groom at arm's length. Their constant bickering, as his frustration mounts, lacks any semblance of wit or reason. (Why is she doing this, if she loves him?)

Drawing on themes that extended into the war years, the marital comedies of the thirties were delivering an unmistakable message: In most marriages, it was the husband's obligation to keep the relationship on a straight path, without side excursions or distractions, whatever the cost to his pride or dignity. Marital comedy depended on a battle between the sexes, and in those years, it usually took the form of a beleaguered husband and an all-knowing, all-seeing wife. Only much later, with the impact of changing times and changing relationships, would the marital comedy take a different turn.

The Awful Truth (*Columbia, 1937*). *Jerry Warriner (Cary Grant, left) disconcerts soon to be ex-wife Lucy (Irene Dunne) before her new beau (Ralph Bellamy) and his mother (Esther Dale). Leo McCarey's comedy has wit and charm to spare.*

Chapter 4
Pure Brass
Spoofs, Satires, and Farces

n the thirties, when life seemed singularly bleak and the solid-rock institutions of family and government seemed unable to cope with even daily needs, there were many responses: numb resignation and hopelessness; anger and the call for reform; and a brash, nose-thumbing irreverence, a tweaking of the tails of all our sacred cows of the past. Irreverence, in fact, was the keynote of many thirties comedies: a mocking put-down of pompous cultural institutions, falsely pious attitudes, and hollow icons. With scarcely a wasted moment, these comedies tore through their simple plot lines, throwing logic and reason to the winds.

Certain topics seemed to prevail among the many brassy farces and satires that filled the theaters in the early thirties. One was inevitable: How could filmmakers resist poking fun at their own industry and its flamboyant lunacy? It was a time when moviegoers reveled in juicy gossip about the stars, and fan magazines cluttered the newsstands. The subject had everything: glamour, sex, scandal, and a giddiness that could be both mocked and glorified on the screen. Soon, Hollywood comedies were turning up regularly. George S. Kaufman and Moss Hart's Broadway play *Once in a Lifetime,* a delirious spoof of the sound revolution and Hollywood's nitwit inhabitants, became a breezy 1932 movie with Jack Oakie as a numbskull whose very ineptness turns him into a success story. Harold Lloyd played a similar character—dumbness incarnate—in *Movie Crazy* (1932), one of his several attempts to establish himself as a sound comedian. As an accident-prone Hollywood hopeful who becomes a star, Lloyd managed a few funny slapstick sequences, but his traditional character of an innocent who triumphs against all odds somehow seemed out of synchronization with the times.

By far the giddiest spoof of Hollywood's rampant lunacy appeared the following year. Fashioned for Jean Harlow, MGM's rising sex queen, Victor Fleming's *Bombshell* (1933) offered in its central character of Lola Burns the very personification of every movie fan's idea of a screen goddess. A volatile blonde with an

Twentieth Century *(Columbia, 1934). Producer Oscar Jaffe (John Barrymore) comforts his newest star, Lily Garland (Carole Lombard), née Mildred Plotka. Lombard was on the verge of becoming a consummate comic actress.*

extensive wardrobe and a limited IQ, Lola is not only a studio creation but also a pawn in the hands of her crafty press agent Space Hanlon (Lee Tracy). Lola's determination to adopt a baby and Space's ingenious efforts to thwart her make up the film's plot.

The screenplay by John Lee Mahin and Jules Furthman bubbles and crackles with the sort of brash, wise-cracking comedy typical of the period. Much of the humor stems from Lola's failed attempts to pass herself off as an ordinary girl ("I'm just my natural, simple self," she tells the adoption-agency people.) Her illiterate past keeps betraying her grandiose present: Interviewed by a magazine writer about her scandalous publicity, she remarks, "I ask you, as one lady to another, isn't that a load of clams?" Lola believes in movie myth and illusion: Impressed by the ardent lovemaking of a (fake) British suitor (Franchot Tone), she murmurs, "Not even Norma Shearer or Helen Hayes in their nicest pictures were ever spoken to like this!" Harlow plays Lola with a conviction that may be either instinct or acting skill, and Lee Tracy's Space Hanlon, his voice a clarion call to action, matches her every step of the way.

While the film community often laughed at its own follies, the theater also came in for some satirical drubbing. Although most films failed to have even an inkling of how the Broadway stage actually operates, an occasional movie succeeded in capturing some of the quicksilver quality, the self-indulgent behavior, and even the shining talent of many theater people. One was *Twentieth Century* (1934), Howard Hawks's funny, fast-paced adaptation of the Ben Hecht–Charles MacArthur play. Much of its story concerning flamboyant stage producer Oscar Jaffe (John Barrymore) and his tumultuous on-and-off relationship with his star protégé, Lily Garland, née Mildred Plotka (Carole Lombard), took place aboard the Twentieth Century Limited, but *Twentieth Century* was unmistakably a piece about the theater. Indifferent to the sycophants and eccentrics surrounding them, and unable to sustain any emotion for any longer than the two hours of a performance, Oscar and Lily inhabit their own private theatrical world, no matter where they may find themselves. Self-created monsters, they alternate between adoring and wanting to destroy each other.

Hawks's first sound comedy after several years of overseeing such hard-hitting dramas as *Scarface* (1932), *Twentieth Century* demonstrates the sense of pace and the ability to extract bravura performances from his leading players that would later inform his classic comedies, *Bringing Up Baby* (1938) and *His Girl Friday* (1940). Moving with the speed of its title, the film seldom pauses to catch its breath, from the time Oscar Jaffe bullies budding actress Lily Garland into a star-making performance ("You're not demonstrating underwear, you hear?") until they meet again on a Hollywood-bound train, ex-lovers and theatrical partners, now adversaries.

Other forms of occupation, legal or otherwise, were deemed suitable subjects for irreverent comedy and impudent farce. Many filmmakers were fascinated by the inner workings of newspapers, or at least the popular conception of newspapers as energetic, exciting places where headlined scandals and startling exposés were everyday occurrences. After a while, the ingredients for newspaper comedies were fixed: take one cheeky reporter or columnist (possibly with a press card tucked into his hatband), add a female colleague for romance and/or rivalry, plus an apoplectic editor, toss in some comic or melodramatic mayhem, a sprinkling of wisecracks uttered in rat-tat-tat fashion, and another brisk little film was ready for release.

Of the many newspaper comedies, none could match Ben Hecht and Charles MacArthur's 1928 play *The Front Page* for its scathing, acidulously funny view of the Fourth Estate. Filmed twice at either end of the thirties, and then remade again in the seventies and eighties, this rowdy tale focused on the efforts of Walter Burns, the unscrupulous editor of a Chicago newspaper, to keep his star reporter Hildy Johnson from marrying and leaving the paper. The plot also concerned both men's involvement with a convicted but pitiable killer who escapes from prison shortly before his scheduled hanging. The setting was the pressroom where the reporters, a cynical and insensitive bunch, await the execution.

First brought to the screen in 1931, *The Front Page* lost little of its impact in Lewis Milestone's adaptation. Filming in a near-expressionistic style, with odd camera angles and harsh close-ups, Milestone, only a year after directing his classic war film, *All Quiet on the Western Front*, emphasized the melodrama over the comedy. Adolphe Menjou as Walter Burns, and Pat O'Brien as Hildy Johnson, led the cast in a relentless pace, tossing invective at each other's head like lightning bolts.

Remade by Howard Hawks in 1940 as *His Girl Friday*, *The Front Page* took on a new coloration when it was decided to turn Hildy Johnson into a woman and make her not only Walter Burns's top reporter but also his ex-wife. The play's unromantic view of newsmen was retained, and its stinging indictment of a corrupt society still hovered around the edges. This time, *The Front Page* became a hybrid: a giddy and fast-paced mixture of romantic comedy, slapstick, and melodrama, with a pinch of social commentary. Luckily, it also costarred Cary Grant and Rosalind Russell, two players whose deft touch with comedy no longer needed proving.

There are those who claim that *His Girl Friday* has the fastest-spoken dialogue of any film to date, and this supposition is not difficult to believe. From first minute to last, the lines snap, crackle, and pop like so many Rice Krispies, only twice as delicious and ten times funnier. Grant and Russell bounce merrily off each other, Grant with his characteristic aplomb concealing a larcenous mind, and Russell, with her pinstriped suit and absurd hat, railing at him furiously. ("The stork that brought you must have been a vulture!")

Hildy and Walter spend much of the movie battling, yet it is clear from the start that these two really belong together. They move to the same rhythm, have the same lack of tolerance for fools, and derive the same deep pleasure from getting a scoop. When the two join Hildy's new fiancé Bruce Baldwin (Ralph Bellamy) for lunch, the scene is one of the film's funniest. His voice drenched with irony, Walter comments on the life Hildy will now lead ("A home with mother—in Albany, too!"), and the looks and foot-tappings he exchanges with an increasingly exasperated Hildy speak volumes for their past association. (Between fights, they had fun together.) Hildy and Walter speak to each other with what might be called married shorthand, no matter how long they have been divorced. By seducing Hildy back onto the *Morning Post*, Walter also seduces her back into his bed. Passion and profession have never been linked so closely.

Played at a dizzying speed, these newspaper comedies never allowed the audience to catch its breath, nor to wonder how a daily paper could be produced in the midst of such bedlam. At Warners, where pace was all, such films as *Back in Circulation* (1937) and *Off the Record* (1939) kept the presses jumping as they moved swiftly from comedy to melodrama. Warners, in fact, seemed to own the franchise on trim comedies in which people on the lower rungs of society's ladder fought to make a place for themselves. There was no art or artifice in these films, only a desire to divert viewers with an hour or so of staccato chatter, uncluttered plot lines, and acting that punched the material home.

The studio's kingpin for these films was indisputably James Cagney. A pugnacious bantam with Irish charm and a much-imitated quicksilver style, Cagney excelled at playing crafty con men, with a smile for his victims and a blow or a bullet for his enemies. His early thirties films had pace—at Warners, that was a given—but they also had a zest and vigor that made even the least of them watchable. Cagney represented the tough Depression survivor—like other members of

the Warners "stock company" of players, he was a surrogate for moviegoers who were struggling to eke out a meager living in the worst of times. In such brisk, raucous little comedies as *Blonde Crazy* (1931), *Hard to Handle* (1933), and *Jimmy the Gent* (1934), he seemed to be sharper, smarter, and more confident than anyone else. His only competition came from the unabashed, enterprising gold diggers played by Joan Blondell and Glenda Farrell in assembly-line comedies with such blunt titles as *Havana Widows* (1933), *Kansas City Princess* (1934), and *We're in the Money* (1935).

His Girl Friday *(Columbia, 1940). Reporter Rosalind Russell has reason to be wary about the affability of her ex-boss and ex-husband (Cary Grant, center) toward her new fiancé (Ralph Bellamy, left).*

On rare occasions, the frenetic comedies of the thirties turned to political satire, a topic generally regarded as anathema at the box office. The bombast and chicanery that often attends a political campaign inspired an artful 1932 Warners comedy called *The Dark Horse*, in which Guy Kibbee plays a gubernatorial candidate "so dumb that every time he opens his mouth he subtracts from the total sum of human knowledge." Only a shrewd political consultant (Warren William) can manipulate him into becoming a serious contender. Several other films hedged their bets by diluting the political satire with musical numbers. The weakness of the electorate for glitter and flash over substance was spoofed in Roy Del Ruth's *Thanks a Million* (1935), in which singer Dick Powell wins the governorship of Pennsylvania through a campaign of quips and songs. George Marshall's *Hold that Co-Ed* (1938) also mocked the political process with its tale of a flamboyant, ambitious governor (John Barrymore) whose suddenly acquired interest in higher education takes him to one of those Hollywood colleges where the principal subjects seem to be football, romance, singing, and dancing, in that order.

Every once in a while, a subject that usually received a solemn or melodramatic treatment would take a comic turn. The early sound years had seen a proliferation of stories reflecting the national concern with crime. Movies about gangsters and their mobs, including such harsh, violent films as *Little Caesar* (1930) and *Scarface* (1932), had struck the public fancy, and when pious warnings about the national scourge of crime were tacked on at the end, audiences were able to enjoy the bloodletting without feeling too guilty. However, if crime was hardly a laughing matter, it could occasionally inspire a comedy that poked fun at its methods and mores.

At the start of the sound era, only a few films, such as John Ford's *Up the River* (1930), dared to find humor in the criminal activities that were plaguing America's cities. Gradually, however, comedy intruded, so that even Edward G. Robinson, who has made his reputation as a vicious gangster in *Little Caesar*, could poke fun at his underworld figures. His best chance to portray the lighter side of gangsterdom came with *A Slight Case of Murder* (1938) adapted from Damon Runyon and Howard Lindsay's play. As Remy Marko, a prominent racketeer and beer baron who finds himself jobless after the repeal of Prohibition, Robinson used his familiar blustering style to comic effect. Trying to go "legit," Remy runs into a serious snag when the bullet-riddled bodies of his former colleagues in crime keep turning up in his Saratoga home. Adding to his mortification is a daughter (Jane Bryan), who becomes engaged to a state trooper (Willard

Parker). Everything is resolved in a frantic climax. Although it runs out of steam at the three-quarters point, *A Slight Case of Murder* is mostly boisterous fun, directed at a fast clip by Lloyd Bacon and brightly scripted by Earl Baldwin and Joseph Schrank.

While the crime film lent itself to humorous interpretation, other genres remained safely within their established guidelines. Most Western films, for example, offered the staple mixture of hard-riding action and adventure, with perhaps small doses of comedy and romance. One Western film, however, strongly emphasized comedy over action. Although it had its requisite share of gunfire (and indeed its heroine is shot dead at the end), George Marshall's *Destry Rides Again* (1939) was essentially concerned with spoofing the familiar conventions of the Western movie. A new version of the Max Brand story that had been filmed previously in 1932 as Tom Mix's first venture into sound, *Destry Rides Again* had as its hero not a hard-bitten, gun-totin' sharpshooter but a mild-mannered, reflective young man (James Stewart) who never carries firearms. Yet despite his pacifistic ways, he succeeds in routing the corrupt forces in the town of Bottleneck.

Destry Rides Again gives a satirical spin to other familiar characters in the Western. Until Tom Destry arrives to restore law and order, the sheriff of Bottleneck is no stalwart symbol of justice but, rather, the town drunkard, Wash Dimsdale (Charles Winninger), appointed as a joke. The town's mayor (Samuel S. Hinds) is not a man of rectitude but, rather, a self-serving crook. And Frenchy, the saloon's star attraction (Marlene Dietrich) seems to have wandered in by mistake from a Berlin music hall. In the role that revitalized her career, Dietrich is, in fact, the principal reason for the film's lasting fame. Her Frenchy is *The Blue Angel*'s Lola-Lola with a heart: a hot-tempered trollop who can hold her own in a fight—her wild brawl with Lily Belle Callahan (Una Merkel) is a well-remembered highlight.

The year 1939 was apparently a good one for female fisticuffs, since another hair-pulling match turned up in a sequence from that year's popular satirical comedy *The Women*. A film version of Clare Boothe's vitriolic stage play, the movie took a jaundiced look at the female sex in its nastiest form. Under George Cukor's direction, a cast of MGM actresses was assembled to portray, at full tilt, women of unadulterated viciousness. The glittering production took the viewer into the fitting rooms, powder rooms, and living rooms where the ladies gossiped, quarreled, and agonized over their main concern: men. To counteract this poisonous view of womanhood, the studio assigned the leading role of the noble, long-suffering heroine to Norma Shearer, its most popular actress in such roles. Other top actresses

Destry Rides Again
(Universal, 1939). Saloon queen Frenchy (Marlene Dietrich) is amused by mild-mannered sheriff Tom Destry (James Stewart). When a lusty new Dietrich sang about "the boys in the back room," audiences and critics sat up and took notice.

took up the slack in nastiness: Joan Crawford as a predatory man-stealer and Rosalind Russell as a strident, outrageous gossip.

Although some of the play's teeth were extracted in the Anita Loos–Jane Murfin screenplay, the movie retained a substantial dose of venom. As the marriage of Mary Haines (Shearer) unravels, the women who either precipitate or revel in her misfortune exhibit a thorough lack of sympathy toward their "friend." As Crystal Allen, the money-minded minx who steals Mary's husband, Joan Crawford gives a convincing portrait of hard-edged ambition wrapped in a shiny package. Her confrontation with Mary in a salon dressing room generates sparks of hostility that may be due, in part, to the actresses' mutual dislike. It is Rosalind Russell, however, playing two-faced Sylvia Fowler, who sets the film's prevailing tone. Her almost over-the-top performance established her as a comic actress after years of playing lofty types. Garishly dressed, her voice an ear-shattering trumpet, Russell's Sylvia is a mean-spirited virago who can betray a friend without blinking an eye.

If *The Women* seems less like authentic satire and more like a broadside aimed at the less attractive characteristics of some women, it may be because Hollywood has always shied away from satire in its purest state. Sharp-edged satire requires a sense of irony, a cutting wit, and a willingness to speak the truth fearlessly, attributes that are usually not in large supply in the film industry. On rare occasions, a writer will possess the satirist's skill, a skill that author Ben Hecht demonstrated with his lacerating screenplay for William Wellman's 1937 comedy, *Nothing Sacred.*

A caustic reflection on mankind's gullibility and celebrity worship, *Nothing Sacred* focuses on Hazel Flagg (Carole Lombard), a Vermont girl who is falsely diagnosed as dying of radium poisoning. Although she knows she is perfectly well, Hazel accepts the offer of a trip to New York City made by the New York *Star* and its top reporter, Wally Cook, played by Fredric March. Caught up in the hoopla, Hazel becomes a nationwide celebrity, the center of an orgy of sentiment and pity. On the verge of being exposed, Hazel realizes that everyone has been merely using her, and she flees into peaceful anonymity with her new husband, Wally.

Hecht concentrates his mockery on the hysterical idolization Americans love to bestow on even flash-in-the-pan celebrities. When Hazel arrives in New York with her alcoholic doctor (Charles Winninger), she is given a reception that Lindbergh might have envied. Wherever she goes, she is greeted with enthusiasm and tears—at a wrestling match, ten seconds of silence are observed in her honor, and at a nightclub, revelers watch a pageant featuring Great Women of History, including Hazel. Filmed in bright Technicolor hues that seem incompatible with the story's biting humor, *Nothing Sacred* takes a malicious look at the sentimentality and "humanity" with which most people conceal their greed and mendacity.

Satirical wit also informed many of the films of director Ernst Lubitsch, whose collaborative efforts with his writers resulted in movies that somehow managed to combine pointed satire with an aura of romance. When Lubitsch collaborated with Billy Wilder, Charles Brackett, and Walter Reisch, they succeeded in blending the two elements in the incomparable comedy *Ninotchka* (1939). Coming at a time when the Soviet Union's experiment with communism was regarded with interest rather than apprehension, Lubitsch and his writers chose to poke fun at the system's cheerlessness and lack of humor, as well as its pinched economic status. They also chose to submerge the satirical view of communism in a charming fable of a severe Russian woman who discovers love and laughter in Paris. This was not the Paris that, in 1939, faced the prospect of war, but the legendary city extolled in song and story.

To play the Russian wren turned swan, Ernst Lubitsch was fortunate to obtain another beautiful legend, Greta Garbo. Renowned by this time for her luminous face and her gifts as a dramatic actress, Garbo longed to play comedy after all the years as doomed heroines, and *Ninotchka* seemed an ideal choice. When she threatened to return to Sweden unless she was allowed to star in it, the studio agreed, and after a few games of musical chairs, Lubitsch was assigned to direct the film.

The result was magical. *Ninotchka* boasted the trademarks and the "touches" that Lubitsch had honed since the silent era: the visual elegance; the mischievous use of pantomime or the camera alone to score a point; and the astute mixing of sardonic, rueful, and romantic elements. Working with a witty screenplay, he traces the transformation of the dour Nina Ivanovna Yakushova into the bewitching Ninotchka after her arrival in Paris on a government mission. Checking on three buffoonish Soviet emissaries (Sig Rumann, Felix Bressart, and Alexander Granach) who had been sent earlier to Paris to sell the imperial jewels, she comes upon the exiled Grand Duchess Swana (the incomparable stage actress Ina Claire), who claims ownership of the jewels, and Swana's representative (and lover), Count Leon d'Algout, played suavely by Melvyn Douglas. Before long, Ninotchka's love for Leon changes her from a grim communist into a joyous capitalist, and after some setbacks, she and Leon are reunited.

By now, the satire in *Ninotchka* has taken on an antique charm, and yet it still amuses. The delight with which the Russian emissaries come upon their lavish Paris hotel suggests the deprivation they have known in Moscow ("Comrades, why should we lie to each other? It's wonderful!") Their willingness to surrender to Parisian pleasures is dramatized in a quintessentially Lubitschian scene in which the camera stays fixed on the doors to their hotel room as inside the three welcome the arrival of food-bearing waiters and fun-loving cigarette girls. By the time Ninotchka appears on the scene, her every word a reproach, they have been totally Westernized. Ready to take over negotiations for the jewels, Ninotchka assumes center stage, and the film immediately becomes Garbo's. She seems fully liberated in the role, transforming Ninotchka from the serious-minded woman who balks at staying at an expensive hotel into someone who responds to complex new emotions, especially love.

Released in the fall of 1939, *Ninotchka* capped a decade that had started deep in the heart of the Depression and was ending with the sound of gunfire as war began in Europe. In the first years of the thirties, with the movies as the principal escape hatch for a weary people, many films had mocked the status quo, brashly suggesting that the country was populated with con artists, power-seekers, and girls on the make. By the end of the decade, these films had become dusty anachronisms, and the times were turning in a different direction. In the same sense as *Midnight*, another Brackett–Wilder comedy released in 1939, *Ninotchka* marked the end of a Paris—and a world—that would not return again for many years.

Chapter 5
The Common Folk

While much of the comedy of the thirties revolved around the sardonic, even mean-spirited behavior of eccentrics, one large portion of comedy was reserved for the kinder, gentler common folk. These were the people who resembled, or at least approximated, the members of the audience: ordinary people whose tranquil, often small-town lives were disrupted by one crisis or another. Forever seeking the main chance, the Marx Brothers, W. C. Fields, and Mae West ploughed their comic way through circuses, carnivals, and saloons, or invaded the inner sanctum of society, strewing victims and suckers in their path. There were other comedians and comic actors whose characters inhabited quieter, less colorful places, however; cozy living rooms, inviting tree-lined main streets, quaint shops and stores became the settings in which they could resolve their dilemmas. For many filmmakers, these ordinary folk were the people who could summon hidden qualities of strength and endurance to thwart the forces of corruption. One director, Frank Capra, peopled his own cinematic dominion with such folk.

Until Capra's beleaguered heroes turned up in the second half of the decade, the home-and-hearth comedies were represented mainly by a gangly figure named Will Rogers. A genial entertainer, the Oklahoma-born Rogers had started in Wild West shows and had then moved to the stage, where his homespun comments and expert lariat-twirling brightened the *Ziegfeld Follies*. Beginning in 1918, he made many silent features and shorts, but his popularity soared with the coming of sound. His country drawl and easygoing personality slipped effortlessly into a series of appealing comedy-dramas in which he could play the wry, deceptively simple down-home man who approaches life's problems with a cracker-barrel philosophy. Such films as *State Fair* (1933), *Doctor Bull* (1933), and *David Harum* (1934) made Rogers the ideal exponent of native wisdom. His best films—*Judge Priest* (1934) and *Steamboat 'Round the Bend* (1935), both directed by John Ford, set Rogers's folksy characters against a well-observed background of rural Ameri-

Mr. Deeds Goes to Town *(Columbia, 1936). Eccentric greeting-card poet–turned–millionaire Longfellow Deeds (Gary Cooper, center) is hailed by the people after his triumphant sanity hearing.*

ca. The stories mixed humor, sentiment, and a touch of melodrama in expert proportions, and Rogers presided over them with affability.

One comedy released in the same year as *Steamboat 'Round the Bend* also offered a note of pleasing Americana, this time set in the rougher, burlier environment of the old West. *Ruggles of Red Gap* (1935), Harry Leon Wilson's story of a proper English butler transplanted to the American West, had been filmed twice before in 1918 and 1923, but this first sound version fully captured its whimsical charm. Under Leo McCarey's direction, Charles Laughton starred as Marmaduke Ruggles, the very model of an English butler, who, in the year 1908, is brought to the West by the vulgar, newly rich Americans Egbert and Effie Floud, played by the inimitable Charles Ruggles and Mary Boland (Egbert has won Ruggles in a poker game.) Unhappy at first in the rowdy western town where the citizens mistake him for an English lord, Ruggles comes to learn the true value of free enterprise and equality.

Sparked by Laughton's uncharacteristically restrained performance, *Ruggles of Red Gap* moves amiably through its humorous situations, without forcing their gentle humor or exaggerating a comic point. Confronting a society utterly different from his own ("Quite an untamed country, I understand"), Ruggles finds himself surrendering to its free and open spirit. By the time his former employer, the Earl of Burnstead (Roland Young, droll as always) comes to take him back to England, Ruggles is reluctant to return to his old life. In the expansive world of the American West, he has become, in Egbert's words, "a man whose decisions and whose future are in his own hands." We know that Ruggles has finally established his credentials as a new American when, in the movie's most famous scene, he recites Lincoln's Gettysburg Address to a saloon crowded with hushed, awed patrons. Laughton gives the lines a quiet, heartfelt reading that is most effective.

Ruggles of Red Gap *(Paramount, 1935). A bemused quartet (left to right: ZaSu Pitts, Charles Laughton, Charles Ruggles, Maude Eburne) in the Silver Dollar Saloon. A British butler turned American entrepreneur, Laughton's Ruggles later becomes a new man in the Old West.*

Amid the dark days of the Depression, one director's light shone like a beacon. While other directors traded in the chic sophistication of the well-to-do, Frank Capra lived among the common folk, extolling the bread-and-butter people who struggled for their place in a battered society. Especially in his social comedies of the thirties, he formulated a unique world where resourceful men and women, driven into a corner, could summon up what Capra called "necessary handfuls of courage, wit, and love" to emerge triumphant over corrupt lawyers, self-serving politicians, and native-born fascists. A deeply optimistic man, Capra was convinced that all the world's problems could be solved if we treated one another with warmth and kindness. Justice and right, he believed, would prevail over America's economic miseries, and even obliterate wars and dictatorships. In an age of despair, Capra held out hope.

Viewed in the light of our own time, Capra's philosophy seems like the musings of a well-meaning but naïve man who discovered a golden dream in his adopted country and refused to relinquish it. Indeed, there are moments in even his best films that make us wince with the "little people" stance adopted by Capra and his favorite writer, Robert Riskin. Yet a number of factors prevent Capra's movies from drowning in the milk of human kindness: the warm humor that continually bubbles to the surface; the energy and brisk pace of his direction; and the sturdy performances he elicits from his actors. It can even be said—and proven—that many of his comedies of the thirties (and forties, as well) are actually not as oppressively sunny as one might believe at first glance. While they may exult in the expected Capraesque endings (chicanery defeated, honesty triumphant), the heroes must travel to the very edge of despair before they can win the day. Think of Longfellow Deeds, in *Mr. Deeds Goes to Town*, willing to be judged insane in his misery, or Jefferson Smith, in *Mr. Smith Goes to Washington*, the victim of an insidious scheme to dishonor him, on the verge of collapse on the Senate floor. (The apogee of Capra's desolate characters, the suicidal George Bailey of *It's a Wonderful Life*, appeared in 1946.) If optimism ultimately prevails, pessimism still lurks in the background, a dark cloud intruding on the sunshine.

Light or dark, Frank Capra's films reveal a lifelong love of films and a smooth professionalism honed by many years of experience in the Hollywood mills. Born in Sicily, Capra emigrated to the United States with his family at the age of six. Eventually, he found his way into filmmaking, first as a gag writer for Mack Sennett and then as mentor and director to Harry Langdon, whose odd, childlike screen personality required special treatment. Fired by Langdon, who wanted to assume total control over his films, Capra moved to the "Poverty Row" of Columbia Studios, where his most prolific and rewarding period began. After directing second-level genre films and a few films of more than common interest (*American Madness*, 1932; *The Bitter Tea of General Yen*, 1933), Capra had his first (and unexpected) success with a movie called *Lady for a Day* (1933).

Adapted by Robert Riskin from a story by Damon Runyon, this pleasing fable combined Runyon's unique humor, in which disreputable characters revealed hearts of purest gold, with Capra's predilection for "little people" with big problems. The story focused on "Apple Annie" (May Robson), a salty old derelict who learns, to her dismay, that the daughter she has not seen for years and who thinks she is a society grande dame is coming to America with her wealthy fiancé and his father. Annie's raffish friends, led by Dave the Dude (Warren William), transform her into a swell for the occasion, and after a few disheartening setbacks, the ruse is carried off with the help of city officials. Amusing for all its heavy sentiment, *Lady for a Day* contains some of the ingredients that would go into Capra's later, more polished movies, especially the tacit acknowledgment of the Depression and the activism of people when one of them is threatened, in this case with exposure as a fraud.

Capra introduced his first true populist hero in *Mr. Deeds Goes to Town* (1936). Stirred by the nation's plight during the Depression years, he was eager to show that ordinary people with homespun virtues were more than a match for the greedy shysters, tycoons, and bosses. To make this point, Capra had Robert Riskin adapt a Clarence Budington Kelland story about a guileless young greeting-card poet named Longfellow Deeds, who triumphs over the powers of cynicism and corruption. To play Deeds, Capra chose Gary Cooper, one of the screen's best representatives of innate decency.

Deeds's ultimate victory made satisfying viewing in 1936, and indeed there is still much that is worthwhile, although admittedly simplistic, in Capra's film. The screenplay traces the evolution of Deeds from a small-town innocent to a disillusioned man who finally learns the price of living in the real world. Inheriting millions from his uncle, Deeds becomes an easy mark for John Cedar, (Douglass Dumbrille), the venal lawyer who controls the estate, and for Babe Bennett (Jean Arthur), a reporter who deceives him into becoming a media celebrity. When he learns the truth, and also confronts the bitter reality of the Depression, he tries to give all his money to the needy, only to be called insane and brought to court for a sanity hearing. Out of the depths of despair, he not only emerges triumphant but he is also reconciled with Babe, who has come to love him.

With not much subtlety, but with considerable warmth and humor, *Mr. Deeds Goes to Town* sets up the Capra dichotomy that was becoming familiar: Deeds, eccentric, honest, and pure of heart, versus the greedy people who mock him or want to use him. Deeds represents the anti-intellectual view that greater virtue can be found in common sense than in books or any form of culture. As long as his eccentricities provide fodder for Babe's newspaper stories, his "goodness" can be tolerated as a kind of joke in a cynical age. However, when he decides to give his money to form a cooperative for downtrodden farmers, he becomes a threat to the system and must be found mentally incompetent. In an audience-rousing climax, a depressed Deeds finally rallies to his own defense and, after being declared "the sanest man who ever walked into the courtroom," he is joyfully reconciled with Babe.

Frank Capra's abiding faith in the common folk permeated his next film, an adaptation of George S. Kaufman and Moss Hart's Pulitzer Prize–winning Broadway play, *You Can't Take It with You* (1938). On the stage, the play had concerned a wildly eccentric family that carried the principle of laissez-faire to extremes, with each member marching to his or her own private drummer. The plot hinged on the romance of the daughter of the house with her young boss, the son of a powerful Wall Street magnate. When the two families—his and hers—meet and collide, the result was comic catastrophe, but all was resolved happily by the final curtain.

Brought to the screen in a somewhat altered version by Robert Riskin, the Kaufman-Hart play became something else again, a Capraesque paean to individualism and brotherly love, as well as a ringing statement on the virtues of happy poverty as opposed to unhappy wealth. The engagingly scatterbrained Sycamore

family, presided over by amiable codger Grandpa Vanderhof (Lionel Barrymore), was retained, as was the plot line involving the romance of daughter Alice (Jean Arthur), the only sensible member of the family, with her boss Tony Kirby (James Stewart). Where the film version deviated widely from the play was in extending and enhancing the character of Tony's formidable industrialist father (Edward Arnold). In a clash of ideologies, the elder Kirby, with his lust for power, is now pitted openly against Grandpa Vanderhof and his philosophy of free-spirited individualism. This being a Capra film, it ends with a complete change of heart for the tycoon who is now relaxed enough, and democratic enough, to play a harmonica duet with Grandpa.

Fortunately, amid all the heavy-handed proselytizing, *You Can't Take It with You* retains much of the play's winning humor. The central sequence, in which the Kirbys arrive unexpectedly for dinner at the Sycamores and end up in prison after a fireworks explosion in the cellar, still works as lively knockabout farce, although even here the screenplay cannot resist a diatribe against Kirby and what he stands for. "You stupid idiot!" Grandpa shouts at him in a fit of temper. "You and your jungle and your sharp claws!" At a time when the country was only starting to emerge from the Depression, the film's philosophy ("You can't take it with you. So what good is it?") appealed enormously to audiences, as well as to the film industry, which rewarded it with an Oscar as the year's best film.

Capra's next film, *Mr. Smith Goes to Washington* (1939), proved to be one of his best and most successful efforts. Following the pattern of *Mr. Deeds Goes to Town*, this comedy-drama extolled the virtues of the ordinary man who can rise out of the ashes of defeat and triumph over the forces of corruption. Capra firmly believed this credo, which informs Sidney Buchman's screenplay concerning Jefferson Smith (James Stewart), the naïve, good-hearted, and intensely patriotic young man who is appointed senator from his state and is nearly crushed by the political machine that controls his district with an iron fist. The movie relates how Jeff, with the help of his loving, tough-minded assistant Saunders (Jean Arthur, once again in fine fettle), perseveres to restore his honor and topple the dangerously powerful empire of publisher Jim Taylor (Edward Arnold).

Essentially a drama laced with comedy, *Mr. Smith Goes to Washington* milks the basic situation for every last drop of heart-stirring emotionalism, from Jeff's first awed tour of Washington to his anguished filibuster before his fellow senators ("I'm going to stay right here and fight for this lost cause . . . !"). Yet somehow it all works, due to Capra's exceptionally adroit direction of an able cast that included

You Can't Take It with You *(Columbia, 1938). Frank Capra's adaptation of the Kaufman–Hart stage comedy featured (left to right) Mischa Auer, Jean Arthur, Edward Arnold, James Stewart, Ann Miller, and Mary Forbes.*

Claude Rains as the corrupted Senator Paine and Thomas Mitchell as a bibulous reporter. In the role that won him durable stardom, James Stewart is the very model of gawky earnestness that can turn into righteous fervor.

Most of the film's comic moments derive from the bumbling behavior of Jeff Smith, the lamb among the Washington wolves. His shyness with Senator Paine's daughter and his awestruck response to every Washington landmark are played for laughs, as is the weak-kneed ineptness of the state's Governor Hopper (Guy Kibbee), or the sheer bulk of Senator Paine's political sharpshooter, Chick McCann (Eugene Pallette), who, at one point, must extricate himself from a telephone booth. As in *Mr. Deeds Goes to Town*, Jean Arthur cuts through the heavy sentiment and the flag-waving with her wry, no-nonsense delivery. As she moves from caustic skeptic who throws Jeff to the reporters to a loving admirer who cheers him on from the Senate balcony, her unique voice crackles vibrantly.

Frank Capra's films after *Mr. Smith Goes to Washington* marked something of a falling off, although there are many who regard his 1946 film *It's a Wonderful Life* as his masterwork. In the altered world of the forties and beyond, Capra's style and his point of view began to seem like something of an anachronism, although his skill never deserted him. While flawed, his best films—*Meet John Doe* (1941), *It's a Wonderful Life, State of the Union* (1948)—continued to celebrate the basic decency and integrity of Americans and to attack would-be fascists and power-hungry politicians.

Mr. Smith Goes to Washington *(Columbia, 1939). Nearly at the end of his tether, filibustering young Senator Jefferson Smith (James Stewart) faces defeat. His adversary is Senator Paine (Claude Rains, left). Stewart's heartfelt performance earned him an Oscar nomination.*

By the end of the thirties, the war that raged in Europe and that would soon engulf America began to alter perspectives and change priorities. While a frivolous enterprise in the cosmic scheme of things, the movies began to take on a more important role than ever: as a tool for disseminating vital information (and also propaganda) and as a badly needed diversion from the grim struggle. Many members of the film industry took active roles in the conflict, either as fighting men and women or as purveyors of vital information on the war. (Frank Capra's wartime series of documentary films, *Why We Fight*, includes some of his best work.)

Film comedy itself was about to undergo a drastic change in the forties. Audiences would embrace a new breed of comedians: figures who abandoned the eccentric or grotesque garb of their predecessors, along with their playful mockery of morals, manners, and institutions. Sarcasm and hostility toward America's foibles were out, now that the nation was under attack. As America entered the war, comedy would begin to put on an entirely new face.

Part 2

KEEP 'EM LAUGHING

Movie Comedy in the Forties

A decade of war and human disaster, followed by hopes for a lasting peace . . .

As the decade begins, war rages throughout Europe. Nazi troops march into Paris and overrun Poland, Norway, and the Netherlands. On December 7, 1941, America enters the war after Japan attacks Pearl Harbor. During the next four years, costly defeats at Bataan and Corregidor are followed by hard-won triumphs at Midway and Guadalcanal. The Allied forces invade North Africa and battle their way into Italy. On the home front, the talk is about growing victory gardens and recycling tin and paper. In 1944, D-Day is launched, and Paris is liberated amid a joyful celebration. Germany surrenders in May 1945, and Japan follows in August.

The postwar years bring traumatic changes and adjustments, both here and abroad. For a while, America's economy suffers as millions of workers strike, disrupting important industries. On the international scene, statesman Bernard Baruch declares that "we are in the midst of a cold war." A year after Secretary of State Marshall unveils his Marshall Plan to help Europe, the Soviet's blockade of Berlin precipitates a massive American airlift. By the end of the decade, the cornerstone of the United Nations has been laid in New York City.

While the war and its aftermath dominate the decade, the forties also witness the completion of the monument on Mount Rushmore, the founding of the state of Israel, and the breaking of the sound barrier in aeronautics and the color barrier in baseball. On a more trivial note, these years introduce Bugs Bunny, Dannon Yogurt, ballpoint pens, and frozen foods. Audiences throughout the decade flock to see such films as *The Grapes of Wrath, Citizen Kane, Casablanca, Going My Way, The Best Years of Our Lives,* and *On the Town.*

The Miracle of Morgan's Creek *(Paramount, 1944). Consternation in the Kockenlocker household with (left to right) Betty Hutton, William Demarest, and Eddie Bracken. Preston Sturges dared to aim his poisoned darts at motherhood and other sacred topics.*

Chapter 6
The New Comedy Faces

By 1940, the world was changing alarmingly. War raged in Europe, and despite disclaimers by the government, the threat of the United States joining the fray loomed very large. Despite the message of hope offered by "The World of Tomorrow" at the New York World's Fair in 1939 and 1940, an unease hovered in the air, like a darkening cloud. It was not a time for mockery of human failings or shortcomings, which is often the best source of comedy. For a while at least, audiences would not respond to comedies that slashed at hypocrisy, pomposity, puritanism, and plain stupidity. If Americans had to stand together (and when war came, this was essential), comedy films could no longer be subversive, sardonic, or malicious.

In the democratization of American comedy, even the garb and the trappings that set the comedians apart from the rest of the populace were no longer in favor. Although they lingered on in the early forties, there was no longer a place for Groucho's fake mustache and swallowtail coat, or Harpo's horn, or Fields's top hat, or the ornate gowns that encased West's voluptuous figure. Now comedians began to look like everyone else, rather than creatures who had arrived on earth from some bizarre planet. In the war years, of course, they could be soldiers—*Buck Privates* who were *Caught in the Draft* and *Up in Arms*—or they could impersonate a salesman, or a detective, or a boxer, or any garden-variety of human. However, they were no longer clowns who came to the party to disrupt it, or to fleece the hostess of all her belongings or her sanity. They were now Everyman.

If this was the case, then what would be source of the humor? Where would the laughs come from if comedians merged with the crowd and could no longer be spotted by their appearance? The answer was simple, if not very satisfactory. The new comic figures would induce laughter by the way they behaved or, more accurately, through sheer bumbling ineptitude, failed to cope with crisis. In previous decades, the comedians found resourceful methods of coping with trouble. With the conspicuous exception of Bob Hope, the new comedians of the forties aimed

Buck Privates Come Home *(Universal, 1947). Bud Abbott and Lou Costello recall their old army days with top sergeant Nat Pendleton (right). The movie was a sequel to their enormously popular* Buck Privates, *released in 1941.*

98

for laughs by surrendering to trouble, or disaster, with little or no struggle—by responding to life's dilemmas with childlike helplessness. Many of the best-liked comedians of the forties won fans by behaving in ways that can only be termed infantile at best and disconcertingly feebleminded at worst. (The bellowed words "I'm a b-a-a-d boy!" became Lou Costello's trademark.) For a time, audiences were invited to laugh at comedians who either yammered with fright or dismay or exulted with delight at every turn of the plot.

One of the most popular of this new breed of movie comedian was a short, rotund veteran of vaudeville and burlesque named Lou Costello. With his tall, slim partner, Bud Abbott, Costello had been performing since 1931, playing the bumbling, childlike clown to Abbott's fast-talking straight man. Audience favorites on radio's "Kate Smith Hour," especially with "Who's on First?," the baseball routine they had perfected in their earlier days, the team also attracted attention in a Broadway revue entitled *The Streets of Paris*, as well as in night-clubs and on movie-house stage bills. Summoned to Hollywood, they made their film debut in a minor Universal musical comedy, *One Night in the Tropics* (1940). Only Abbott and Costello's appearance seemed to lift audiences out of their apathy, making it clear to Universal's executives that, in this team, they held a valuable property. The comics were assigned to star in an army comedy entitled *Buck Privates* (1941).

The result was sensational. Modestly produced and directed with no particular distinction by Arthur Lubin, *Buck Privates* somehow managed to find favor with movie audiences. Apart from its topical content—men were being drafted regularly into the army—and its batch of popular songs delivered by the Andrews Sisters, the film gave Abbott and Costello the opportunity to display some of the routines they had created during their years in vaudeville. Costello, forced into difficult situations by Abbott or by their tough top sergeant (Nat Pendleton), made a pathetically comic figure as he fumbled his way through a drill routine or found himself in a prizefight, with Pendleton as referee. He appeared to be more of an overgrown child than an adult, but audiences found him endearing and funny.

With *Buck Privates* an enormous success—it outgrossed *Citizen Kane* and *How Green Was My Valley*, even winning some admiring reviews—Universal hurried the team into a series of similiar movies, beginning with a haunted-house comedy, *Hold That Ghost* (1941) and followed inevitably by comedies that took them into other branches of the service (*In the Navy* and *Keep 'Em Flying*, also released in

1941). For the next few years, their box-office appeal remained largely unabated; in movie after movie, they repeated the basic formula involving Costello as the timid, childlike innocent who is badgered and manipulated by his partner into all sorts of serious trouble. Either the backgrounds changed (out West, Hollywood, Mars) or the team was paired with characters from Universal's horror films, such as the Frankenstein monster. As the routines became overly familiar, their popularity waned, and by the mid-fifties, their film career was drawing to a close.

Another comedian who, like Lou Costello, projected a kind of genial dumbness rose to prominence midway through the decade. After working as an entertainer from an early age, Brooklyn-born Danny Kaye had met and married an exceptionally clever writer named Sylvia Fine, who joined with producer Max Liebman in shaping his career. His performances in the Catskill Mountains resorts, bolstered by his additional talents as a mimic and a singer, brought him to roles in Broadway musicals, especially *Lady in the Dark*, in which he stopped the show with his tongue-twisting rendition of "Tchaikovsky." After starring in Cole Porter's stage musical *Let's Face It*, he was finally persuaded by Samuel Goldwyn to sign a long-term contract to make films.

His first movie for Goldwyn, a lavish Technicolor musical comedy called *Up in Arms* (1944), was a great success. Playing a jittery hypochondriac named Danny Weems who is drafted into the army, Kaye was called upon to dither with alarm at the prospect of serving as a soldier, express his adoration for Constance Dowling, who loves his best friend, Dana Andrews, and rush frantically about a troop ship when the girl comes aboard disguised as a sailor. In the improbable climax, Danny somehow manages to become a hero by capturing an entire Japanese regiment. All this hectic activity was accompanied by several large-scale musical numbers and a few songs, charmingly rendered by Dinah Shore as a girl inexplicably ignored by everyone.

Viewed many years later, Danny Kaye's feature-film debut (he had appeared earlier in short films) does not wear well. The character he plays is more off-putting than amusing, a nuisance whose antic behavior provokes irritation rather than affection. Fortunately, the movie pauses occasionally to permit Kaye to render several numbers in which he demonstrates his true gift as a performer of original patter songs. Early in the film, in a theater lobby, he runs through the entire plot of the movie everyone is waiting to see, playing all the roles and moving trippingly through the clever lyrics. Later, he sings his famous "Melody in 4F," a rapid-fire tribute to the draftee, which he had first performed on Broadway in *Let's*

Face It. In these specialty numbers, Kaye's talent is readily apparent; he falters only when he is required to create a credible character.

With the success of *Up in Arms*, Kaye was rushed by Goldwyn into another film, *Wonder Man* (1945), in which he played a dual role: a nightclub entertainer who is murdered by the mob and the entertainer's bookworm brother, who takes over his slain sibling's body. Once again, Kaye's specialty numbers, especially a hectic "Orchi Tchornya" (as a Russian baritone with a sneezing fit) outshone his attempt to play two disparate roles. In his next film, a remake of Harold Lloyd's *The Milky Way* entitled *The Kid from Brooklyn* (1946), Kaye starred as a dim-witted milkman who becomes a fighter. Despite his strenuous efforts, he failed to make the character likable: Exasperating as a clumsy milkman, he was even more obnoxious as a boxer whose prearranged victories go to his head.

Kaye's best work in films came after he left Samuel Goldwyn. (He returned only in 1952 for *Hans Christian Andersen*.) In 1949, he appeared in *The Inspector General*, in which he played a medicine-show helper in nineteenth-century Russia who is mistaken for a visiting dignitary. Loosely based on Gogol's classic story, the film gave Kaye a reasonably credible character to play, and although he was called on to behave in his usual manic fashion, he did not appear to be dull-witted, and he delivered his patter songs with enthusiasm.

Kaye's most successful film turned up in the mid-fifties. Consistently lively and elaborately made, *The Court Jester* (1956), placed the comedian in medieval England, where, as Hawkins, the champion of an infant heir to the throne, he becomes entangled with the intrigue at the court of the tyrannical King Roderick (Cecil Parker) by pretending to be the new court jester. The clever screenplay, written by Norman Panama and Melvin Frank, who both also directed, spoofed the conventions of the swashbuckler: the dual identities, the dashing hero, and the athletic duels. Many viewers remember with special fondness

Hawkins's desperate attempts to avoid drinking a brew poisoned by the necro-mancer Griselda (Mildred Natwick). ("The pellet with the poison's in the vessel with the pestle.") The remainder of Kaye's career was not auspicious, although he acted creditably in several straight roles.

Another popular comedian in the forties was Red Skelton, a brash buffoon

The Fuller Brush Man
(Columbia, 1948). Door-to-door salesman Red Skelton investigates a murder with Janet Blair.

whose stock in trade was knockabout humor that projected a kind of goofy amiability, rather than the infantilism of Lou Costello or Danny Kaye. After working for many years in vaudeville, burlesque, and circuses, Skelton finally found a niche in radio, where he perfected a number of comic characterizations (rube Clem Kadiddlehopper; Junior, the "mean wittle kid") that he would later take to television. He made his film debut in 1938 in *Having Wonderful Time*, playing the resident comic at a Catskills resort. Signed by MGM, he began appearing in comedies (*Whistling in the Dark*, 1941; *Whistling in Dixie*, 1942) and musicals (*Du Barry Was a Lady*, 1943; *Bathing Beauty*, 1944) that took advantage of his skill at performing slapstick and pantomime. If his comic routines sometimes lacked finesse, he succeeded in evoking laughter with a grinning clown's demeanor and a cheerful dumbness that never became excessive.

Later in the decade, in addition to appearing in remakes of earlier films (*The Show-Off*, 1946; *Merton of the Movies*, 1947), Skelton starred in one of his funniest comedies, *A Southern Yankee* (1948). In this Civil War farce, he played Aubrey, a bumbling bellboy who dreams of joining the Union Secret Service, then finds himself in the thick of the battle, impersonating a Confederate spy known as the "Gray Spider." Although the plot was merely a peg on which to hang Skelton's comedy routines, many of the film's gags were well executed, probably due to the advisory help of Buster Keaton, who was then working on the MGM lot. There are clear echoes of Keaton's Civil War comedy, *The General* (1927), especially in the chase sequences. Keaton may well have contributed the film's most inspired moment, in which Aubrey, trapped between Northern and Southern lines, wears halves of two jackets, blue and gray, which he displays to the cheers of both armies as he marches with their flags. In the early fifties, Skelton continued to mix comedies (*The Yellow Cab Man*, (1950) with musicals (*Three Little Words*, 1950; *Lovely to Look At*, 1952), occasionally adding a becoming note of restraint to his performances. When his film career began to fade, he moved successfully into television.

Among the film comedians who emerged in the forties, Bob Hope was the most original and the most successful. Like the others, Hope, at first glance, looked like an ordinary man. Unhandsome, with a ski-jump nose and jutting chin, he resembled a glad-hander at an Elks convention. However, when he strutted onto the screen, flashing his shark's smile, it was clear, at least in his own mind, that he was no ordinary fellow. His brazen manner told us that he fully expected to outwit every man, or to cause every woman to fall at his feet, swooning with adoration. Whereas Costello, Kaye, and Skelton usually quaked in fright at every assault on their dignity or their sanity, Hope plunged into the fray with a quip or a wisecrack at the ready.

What made us laugh, however, was not the supremely confident persona Hope tried to project, but the reality. In truth, the quips were not weapons but, rather, a shield against a hostile world bent on doing him in. Behind the character of the swaggering hero was a coward who fled unsuccessfully from danger. A good part of the laughter Hope generated was due to this discrepancy between the ladies' man he fancied himself to be and the boyish, ogling fools his characters truly were. The other part came from a simple fact: Many of Hope's gags, especially those in his best freewheeling comedies of the thirties and early forties, were extremely funny. It is true that many of them depended on the audience's familiarity with the offscreen Hope—his relationship with Paramount Studios, or his friendly rivalry with Bing Crosby. Most of his wisecracks, delivered in that inimitable voice, were amusingly impudent and brash, however. No viewer could catch him braying like Lou Costello or whinnying like Danny Kaye—Hope never played the jackass for his fans. In a sense, what made him a superior comedian of his time was that his humor, like that of W. C. Fields or Groucho Marx, whom he in no way resembled otherwise, was based on poking fun at the worst instincts of human beings. While we laughed at Fields's and Marx's misanthropy and chicanery, we also laughed at this vain, cowardly jackanapes.

Born in England, Bob Hope came to the United States at age four. After taking on many jobs in his early years, he launched a stage career that began in vaudeville and ended with featured appearances in such stage musicals as *Roberta* (1933) and the 1936 edition of the *Ziegfeld Follies*. After making a few short films in New York City, he moved into radio, where his quick gags and cocky personality pleased audiences. On the strength of that popularity, he was signed by Paramount to appear with W. C. Fields and Martha Raye in *The Big Broadcast of 1938* (1938). Joined by Shirley Ross, he rendered the witty and wistful song "Thanks for the Memory" as one of the very few highlights in a bewildering mélange of comedy and music. (The song later became his signature.) His films in the next few years were largely routine.

Hope boosted his status as a money-making Paramount star with the release of the 1939 comedy thriller *The Cat and the Canary*. A third version of the John Willard play—the other two appeared in 1927 and 1930—the movie adroitly mixed its scary "haunted house" elements, which were played without tongue in cheek,

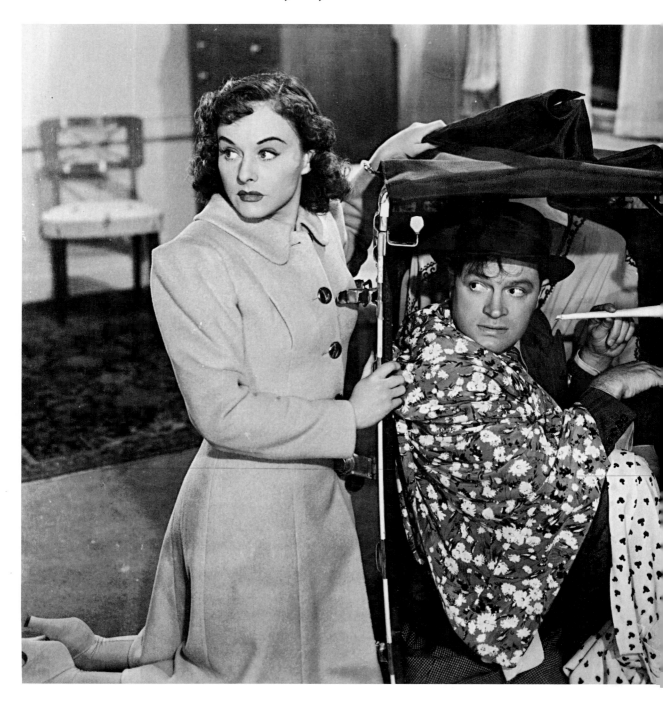

with Hope's comedy, which sought to smother his character's terror in a barrage of wisecracks. Stalking about a mysterious mansion, Hope drew laughs as he reacted nervously to sliding walls, dimming lights, and shrieks in the night. The film's popularity led to a similar mystery-comedy called *The Ghost Breakers* (1940), again from an old play previously filmed in 1922.

Hope's comedies over the next few years followed a successful pattern in which the comedian, a mass of quivering Jell-O beneath his confident exterior, joked his way out of perilous dilemmas to win the day—and the heroine. A number of the films touched lightly on the world situation: Hope coping with life in the army in *Caught in the Draft* (1941), or tangling with Nazi spies in *My Favorite Blonde* (1942) and *They Got Me Covered* (1943), or joining with other Paramount stars to boost wartime morale in *Star Spangled Rhythm* (1942).

With his indisputably contemporary style, Hope seemed an unlikely choice to star in a period comedy, but occasionally he was sent back in time to cavort in another era. Much of the humor derived from his blithe indifference to the period; his attitude—and many of his lines—were strictly 1940s. *The Princess and the Pirate* (1944), a brisk Technicolor spoof of swashbucklers, cast him as an itinerant ham actor who gets involved with buccaneers and a princess in distress (Virginia Mayo). The quips were continous, contemporary, and quite funny. In *Monsieur Beaucaire* (1946), very loosely based on the Booth Tarkington novel, Hope played the barber to France's King Louis XV, becoming embroiled in court intrigue. And in *The Paleface* (1948), one of Hope's best forties films, he turned up in the Wild West, joining with buxom Jane Russell as Calamity Jane to spoof the conventions of movie Westerns.

Among Hope's many films of the forties, few were as popular as the series of *Road* pictures he made with Bing Crosby and Dorothy Lamour. Originally scheduled as a

The Ghost Breakers
(Paramount, 1940). Not for the first or last time, Bob Hope finds himself in hot water. His partner-in-trouble is Paulette Goddard. The comedy-mystery showed Hope at his quipping best.

modest effort, the first *Road* film, *Road to Singapore* (1940), attracted large audiences who responded to its flippant, gag-laden humor and its carefree, anything-for-a-joke style. The pattern for the films was set from the start: Hope and Crosby appeared as friends and partners who find themselves in an exotic location, caught up in some perilous dilemma involving the sultry Lamour. Despite their

ostensible friendship, the two often showed a blatant disregard and even contempt for each other's well-being or safety as they quipped or sang their way through the slapstick situations. The road that started in Singapore also led to *Zanzibar* (1941), *Morocco* (1942), *Utopia* (actually Alaska, 1945), and *Rio* (1947), ultimately winding up in *Bali* (1952) and *Hong Kong* (1962). Viewed many years later, the *Road* comedies now seem largely like stale artifacts from a vanished era, with tired and only sporadically funny gags about Hope's gullibility and cowardice, or Crosby's efforts to con, humiliate, or even betray his "pal." Yet the flippant informality of the *Road* films does have its charm.

Hope's popularity remained strong for many years. By the sixties, however, his films were becoming increasingly weak, with a sense of strain overtaking the ease and the flair of his earlier movies. As he aged, his characterization of the aggressive but actually spineless braggart and womanizer seemed less and less appropriate. He fared well only when he played a recognizable character in a credible situation, as in Melvin Frank's *The Facts of Life* (1960), in which he excelled as a straying husband who runs off with married Lucille Ball. By the seventies, his film career was ended, and he turned exclusively to television and to personal appearances.

During his prime years in the forties, Hope had stood above the rest as a performer whose audacious, irreverent style on radio and in films contained a truer sense of the comic spirit than any of his contemporaries. He had found humor in playing not the dithering simpleton or the childlike clown but a crafty, energetic man who unabashedly hid his many weaknesses and flaws under a bushel of quips. In a sense he was like a wised-up Harold Lloyd, equally jaunty and confident but dispensing gags to hide his jitters, the way others swallowed pills to calm their nerves. For many years, especially after a series of calamitous films he completed in the late sixties, it was fashionable to denigrate Hope's film work, and his status in the pantheon of comedy. Yet in his best film period, he was an unfailing master at the art of provoking laughter.

Road to Singapore *(Paramount, 1940). Dorothy Lamour, Bing Crosby, and Bob Hope in the first of the extremely popular* Road *movies of the early forties. The movie's success surprised the studio and launched a number of sequels.*

Chapter 7
Working Girls and Boss Ladies
Romantic Comedy in the Forties

I n the thirties, the movie Cinderella had searched for her prince and often found him sitting on a park bench, an ordinary working stiff who offered her peanuts. If he turned out to be a genuine prince, his pockets stuffed with money, it was a happy surprise. The fun, the romantic excitement, lay in the search and the pursuit; the comedy stemmed from the maneuvers she had to make in order to win him. On the whole, these were working-class Cinderellas: secretaries in love with their bosses, shop girls dreaming of life among the swells, or gold diggers plotting to land a millionaire.

Not long after America entered the war in December 1941, the romantic-minded Cinderella began to change. Love still ruled the roost, but now she had more on her mind than dreams of a prince on horseback. With men off to do the fighting, women entered the work force, assuming responsibilities formerly relegated only to their husbands and boyfriends. Confronted with new challenges, America's women became more assertive, more aggressive. At least for the duration of the war, they began to believe that they were as fully capable as men, and sometimes even more capable, of handling jobs that required skill and know-how.

At the start of the forties, the pattern of the thirties was still evident in some romantic comedies (for example, Ginger Rogers dallied with a millionaire but decided to marry her working-class suitor in *Tom, Dick, and Harry*, 1941.) Gradually, however, as wartime concerns entered their lives, the romantic heroines took on a new coloration. Money no longer seemed a prime concern for them, and the playboys who were once their heart's desire largely vanished from the movies. Now the screen's working girls were much more a part of the real world, where finding a man was still important but not the only issue at hand.

There were even subtle changes in store for Jean Arthur, perhaps the movies' most prominent working girl of the thirties. Older but no less appealing, Arthur retained her style into the forties, but now there were more serious concerns than the

The More the Merrier *(Columbia, 1943). Connie Milligan (Jean Arthur) tries to work out a morning schedule with her new boarder Benjamin Dingle (Charles Coburn). Coburn's performance as a portly Cupid won him an Oscar.*

110

requisite romance. In George Stevens's *The Talk of the Town* (1942), matters involving law and dissent in society played a crucial role in the Irwin Shaw–Sidney Buchman screenplay. Arthur played Nora Shelley, a schoolteacher who becomes involved with two men: a distinguished professor of law named Michael Lightcap (Ronald Colman), who rents her house for the summer, and Leopold Dilg (Cary Grant), a self-professed anarchist falsely accused of murder, who hides from the police in the house.

Although much of the film is concerned with Nora's growing attachment to both men, the three-way romance often pauses to allow Lightcap and Dilg to discuss their disparate views on the law. The law, Dilg believes, is "a gun pointed at someone's head"; laws, he asserts, should be made out of common sense—out of what people actually do. Lightcap, on the other hand, is a stickler for observing the letter of the law, especially since he is about to be appointed as a justice of the Supreme Court. Investigating Dilg's case, Lightfoot comes to soften his stance about the law, while proving Dilg innocent. He wins the case but also loses Nora to Dilg. Undeniably serious in its intentions, *The Talk of the Town* still draws laughs, mostly from Nora's predicament with two men.

In addition to coping with the labyrinth of the law, Jean Arthur was required to deal with the special problems of wartime Washington in another (and better) George Stevens comedy called *The More the Merrier* (1943). Here, she played Connie Milligan, a working girl who, due to the capital's severe housing shortage, is obliged to rent half of her apartment to portly, elderly Benjamin Dingle (Charles Coburn, in an Oscar-winning performance). When Mr. Dingle rents half of *his* half of the apartment to Joe Carter (Joel McCrea), an army sergeant on special duty in Washington, the stage is set for romance, with Mr. Dingle as Cupid.

Much of the movie's fun comes from its satirical view of Washington's housing problems. Connie's predicament in sharing a small apartment triggers many laughs—early in the film her attempt to work out a morning schedule with Mr. Dingle turns into a comic shambles. Yet for all the spoofing, *The More the Merrier* remains a romantic comedy at heart. With Mr. Dingle's encouragement, Connie and Joe Carter start to behave amorously. Their growing mutual attraction leads to one of the best-remembered romantic scenes in forties comedy, in which, seated on the front steps of Connie's house, the two move into a love scene. As Joe kisses her throat and shoulder, Connie tries desperately—and futilely—to ignore his seduction and speak about mundane matters. A scene handled with such unforced romantic charm makes the film's farcical closing section, with much scrambling about and shouting, all the more disappointing.

Working Girls and Boss Ladies

In the climate of the early forties, such actresses as Jean Arthur and Claudette Colbert, who had pursued romance and riches in comedies of the thirties, never even gave riches a thought as they searched for romance. Working girl Colbert, in fact, went directly to salt-of-the-earth Fred MacMurray in two Mitchell Leisen–directed comedies, *No Time for Love* (1943) and *Practically Yours* (1945), without stopping to check his bank account.

Clearly, a new kind of woman was rising to prominence in films. With so many men in the armed forces, it was inevitable that their jobs would be filled by women, not only in the factories but in the executive suites, as well. Women who had never had the chance to rise in the ranks found themselves in take-charge positions, often with men as their subordinates. It was a wartime phenomenon that the movies could hardly fail to notice and absorb. For a while, the screen was populated with women whose jobs were most important in their lives. Of course it was not Hollywood's intention to reverse the myth of male superiority that had been so firmly established in its films, and so these boss ladies were sure to find by film's end that money and power were of little consequence without romance, and that femininity existed beneath their iron corsets.

An actress who appeared most prominently in boss-lady roles was Rosalind Russell, whose career in the thirties had consisted mainly of playing refined society women. (She called them "Lady Mary" roles.) After *The Women* and *His Girl Friday* established her as an assertive comedienne, she began appearing in films that called on her to be the smartly attired career woman who withered the opposition or disarmed a suitor with a glance or a wisecrack. Too busy for romance, but too womanly to ignore it completely, the Russell boss lady crystallized the change in attitudes toward women in films.

After appearing as a judge who becomes amorously involved with reporter Walter Pidgeon in *Design for Scandal* (1941), Russell left MGM to star in her first true boss-lady role for Paramount. In Mitchell Leisen's *Take a Letter, Darling* (1942), she played advertising executive A. C. MacGregor (apparently, two initials add authority and status), who hires Fred MacMurray as her secretary. Her real intention is to calm the suspicious wives of her clients by having MacMurray act as her nighttime escort. When an important client turns out to be unmistakably female, A.C. loses her poise and shows signs of jealousy. Not surprisingly, she also loses her take-charge stance and finds romance instead. Ill-matched with MacMurray (his diffidence clashes with her stridency), Russell still manages to keep the featherweight story afloat. Although her career-

lady roles varied little in subsequent years, she carried them off with aplomb.

Taking their cue from Rosalind Russell, other actresses who had seldom played comedy found it advantageous to take on roles as independent women: Joan Crawford as another initialed executive, M. J. Drew, in *They All Kissed the Bride* (1942), and Bette Davis as a high-powered magazine editor in *June Bride* (1948). On occasion, even Myrna Loy shed her wifely concerns of the thirties to play a strong-minded career woman; in Irving Reis's *The Bachelor and the Bobby-*

Soxer (1947), she was a sober-sided judge who finds herself drawn unexpectedly into a romance with bachelor Cary Grant.

In the space of only five years, another starring actress, Jean Arthur, made the leap from Washington working girl in *The More the Merrier* to Washington congresswoman in Billy Wilder's sardonic comedy *A Foreign Affair* (1948). Written with an acid-dipped pen by Wilder, Charles Brackett, and Richard Breen, the film cast Arthur as highly prim but capable Phoebe Frost, the most determined (and only female) member of a delegation sent to the American sector of Berlin to investigate military morale. Instead, she become romantically attached to Captain John Pringle (John Lund), an officer who has made bombed-out Berlin his own profitable domain. Pringle's true intention is to keep the congresswoman from investigating his mistress, Erika von Schluetow (Marlene Dietrich), a sultry nightclub singer and a former consort of Nazi bigwigs. By the time the newly liberated Phoebe realizes that she has been Pringle's patsy, it is too late: She has fallen in love with him.

A harshly cynical film, *A Foreign Affair* works best as a view of postwar Berlin, an impoverished and corrupt city overrun with black marketeers and desperate citizens trying to make ends meet, all under the thumb of the harried and sometimes indulgent U.S. occupation forces. Wilder draws such a portrait of hopelessness and despair—gray clouds hovering over bombed-out buildings—that it is something of a surprise that he manages to elicit any laughter at all. Yet

A Foreign Affair
(Paramount, 1948).
Cabaret singer Marlene Dietrich and congresswoman Jean
Arthur are ill-matched
prisoners at a Berlin
police station. Billy
Wilder's film took a
wickedly funny look
at this battered city
after the war.

some scenes are maliciously funny: the congressional committee being welcomed to Berlin; a tipsy Phoebe insisting on singing the Iowa state song at the seedy Lorelei nightclub, or the raid on the club, with Phoebe and Erika von Schluetow as the oddest of couples in the police station.

During the man shortage of the war years, single women assumed a more aggressive role in film comedy. (Married women always held the upper hand.) The demure shop girls and hopeful secretaries of the thirties were replaced by more assertive working women. Strong-minded females placed their broad, padded shoulders on the wheel of business and industry. For a while, the screen was replete with lady mayors, judges, and top-ranking executives who could measure up to any man.

Or so it seemed. In fact, the true message of the romantic comedies of the war years was quite the reverse. Women may have entered the work force out of necessity, and the working girls and boss ladies may have linked arms to do the best possible job, but it was evident that their ultimate happiness did not stem from production quotas but from romance. In reality, the need for a man that obsessed the single thirties heroine had not changed all that much in the forties. Film after film condemned the career woman for thinking that intelligence and ability were possible substitutes for love.

Flash forward a half century, and one comes upon a drastic change that reflects new attitudes in society. In the 1988 comedy *Working Girl*, directed by Mike Nichols, heroine Tess, played by Melanie Griffith, no longer needs to sacrifice her career for a man. By the closing credits, she has not only won a top-level position after much tricky manipulation but she also has captured the lover of her nasty boss lady. It may still be movie fantasy, but in the new era, unlike earlier times, Tess can have it all.

Chapter 8
Wedded Bliss
Marital Comedy in the Forties

As the forties got under way, the marital comedy that had been a staple in the thirties continued unabated, but only for the first two years before the United States entered the war. (During the war years, marriage was a tender link binding the fighting man to home and hearth rather than a subject for comedy.) In 1934, Nick and Nora Charles had sparked the notion that marriage could be a pleasant affair of give-and-take, a viable relationship between two adults who shared physical attraction and a sense of humor. Still, the *Thin Man* mysteries in which they were featured depended not only on the couple's witty banter but also on the mystery that Nick was obliged to solve. Marital comedies with nary a corpse in sight required a different set of complications. And in the early forties, with these comedies appearing regularly, there was no shortage of such complications.

When not carrying out their sleuthing chores in the *Thin Man* series, Myrna Loy and William Powell costarred in several briskly entertaining comedies on marital matters. In W. S. Van Dyke's *I Love You Again* (1940), a farfetched premise was made amusing by their skill. Powell starred as a suave con man who is astonished to learn that he has been a victim of amnesia—for nine years he has lived as a dull small-town resident with a bored wife (Loy). Seeing the chance to bilk the townspeople, he decides to pose as the honest citizen he used to be. The catch is that he falls genuinely in love with the wife he doesn't remember. Most of whatever fun there was came from Powell's strenuous efforts to behave respectably, despite his larcenous instincts. He strikes a comical figure as he trudges through the woods with his Boy Rangers, or discovers his alter ego's enthusiasm for taxidermy. A year after *I Love You Again*, the team reunited for *Love Crazy* (1941), with somewhat less felicitous results.

Another team that had appeared to advantage in the thirties as a married couple was happily reunited at the start of the new decade. Irene Dunne and Cary Grant, who had helped to turn *The Awful Truth* into a durable pleasure by their

Skylark *(Paramount, 1941). Below deck on a rocking boat at sea, Claudette Colbert precipitates a comic disaster in the film's funniest scene. She played a dissatisfied wife who has a brief fling with a bachelor.*

artful performances, returned to costar in Garson Kanin's comedy *My Favorite Wife* (1940). Although in no way as witty or as smoothly executed as its predecessor, the film had more than enough charm and sparkle to keep audiences amused.

Drawing on the familiar "Enoch Arden" theme that was the basis for other films and plays, the screenplay by Samuel and Bella Spewack focused on Nick Arden (Cary Grant), who, on the day of his marriage to Bianca (Gail Patrick), learns that his first wife, Ellen (Irene Dunne), whom he has long thought died in a shipwreck, is actually alive and ready to return to her role as wife and mother. She is also secretive about her years on a desert island with a muscular Adonis named Steve, played by Randolph Scott. Nick's desperate attempt to deal with two wives, while suppressing his suspicions about Ellen, was the source of most of the film's humor. To the surprise of nobody at all, his marriage to Bianca is annulled, and he is welcomed back by Ellen.

Since Nick's dilemma is the center of the movie, much depends on Grant's performance, and *My Favorite Wife* is virtually a primer on this actor's comic technique. With his usual finesse, he plays against his extraordinary good looks, suave appearance, and much-imitated voice, making us laugh at seeing so debonair a man reduced to a dithering fool. Yet even when he is playing slapstick, he retains enough of his intelligence and lightly mocking wit to earn our admiration instead of our irritation. Grant never merely plays the frenetic clown in the style of Danny Kaye or Jerry Lewis. We have only to watch him in *My Favorite Wife* as he sees Ellen for the first time. Standing in an elevator about to ascend, he spots the wife he had given up for dead, and his body tilts completely to one side as he gazes with shock through the closing door.

The most popular, and also most effective, acting team to express married (and romantic) love in the forties made its first appearance early in the decade. By 1940, Spencer Tracy's rugged Irish face, forthright manner, and unaffected acting style had made him a popular star. On the other hand, Katharine Hepburn, who had been considered "box-office poison" for many years, had only recently returned to audience favor when she appeared in the film version of her Broadway play *The Philadelphia Story* (1940). The success of that film had brought her back in demand, and for her next MGM project, she purchased an original screenplay by Ring Lardner, Jr., and Michael Kanin, chose George Stevens to direct it, and requested Spencer Tracy as her leading man. The movie was *Woman of the Year* (1942).

Wedded Bliss

It marked the start of an extraordinary collaboration on-screen, as well as a lifelong friendship off the screen. We cannot know their reaction when they first met. The legend has it that Hepburn remarked, "I fear I may be a little too tall for you, Mr. Tracy," whereupon producer Joseph Mankiewicz countered, "Don't worry, he'll cut you down to size." However, we can see the instant rapport between their characters when, as feuding writers for the New York *Chronicle*, they come together for a truce in the publisher's office. As political columnist Tess Harding and sports writer Sam Craig, they are polar opposites in interests and attitudes—she is an ardent feminist, deeply involved in world issues, while he occupies a man's world where a crony can say, "Women should be kept illiterate and clean, like canaries." Yet Tess and Sam share an immediate sexual attraction that is palpable in their glances and remarks. Inevitably, courtship is followed by marriage, and when their differences emerge once again, they separate, but not for long.

The early scenes of *Woman of the Year* trace their growing attachment and their efforts to come to terms with their opposite lifestyles. Sam takes her to a baseball game, where she finally succumbs to its boisterous spirit; she invites him to a party of VIPs, where he is at a total loss. Still, romance is the true game, and when Tess and Sam begin to share obliquely their feelings for each other in a restaurant booth, the stars create a sequence of incomparable charm and wit. Their faces in profile as they gaze raptly at each other, Hepburn and Tracy seem to be expressing an emotion that, for a fleeting moment, transcends the characters they are playing.

Dissension begins even on their wedding night when a defecting European scientist and his friends converge on their apartment, and Sam counters by inviting *his* raffish friends. As time passes, their marriage is marred by her constant absence for important meetings and events, and although she makes a few stabs at domesticity, her working life takes precedent. Things come to a head on the night of the dinner at which she is to be given an award as Woman of the Year. They quarrel bitterly, and Sam declares, "The outstanding Woman of the Year isn't a woman at all." Their estrangement ends after Tess, taking his words to heart, makes a disastrous attempt at being the domesticated homebody Sam seems to prefer. "Why can't you be Tess Harding Craig?" he asks her, and it appears that she will now try to balance her married life and her career.

While *Woman of the Year* earns its place in film annals as the first teaming of Hepburn and Tracy, its point of view remains rather ambiguous. In spite of the feminist sentiments uttered by Tess and her aunt (Fay Bainter), the film betrays an unmistakable bias in favor of Sam Craig and his longing for a true "wife." Sam's salt-of-the-earth bluntness is often contrasted favorably with Tess's highfalutin airs; in fact, the movie seems to suggest that intelligence in a woman as attractive as Tess may be something of a handicap. Still, Hepburn's performance is unfailingly expert and earned her a fourth Academy Award nomination as Best Actress. She lost to Greer Garson's noble *Mrs. Miniver*, but the screenplay did receive an Oscar.

After reuniting Hepburn and Tracy in a turgid melodrama entitled *Keeper of the Flame* (1942), MGM waited several years to return them to comedy in *Without Love* (1945), a film version of the Philip Barry play in which Hepburn had starred on Broadway. Never very substantial and depending largely on the witty banter between the two principal characters, the film was a pleasant bauble nonetheless. The play had been fashioned expressly for Hepburn, and Donald Ogden Stewart's screenplay followed suit, giving her character the nervous, quicksilver manner and verbal affectations ("By gum!") that the actress seemed to favor. She played Jamie Rowan, a Washington widow who enters into a platonic marital arrangement with Pat Jamieson (Spencer Tracy), a scientist who moves into her home to work on a secret government project with her assistance. Claiming to be against love (she had the best of it, he the worst), they agree to maintain only a serious working relationship. Of course by the film's end, they are involved romantically.

Since any half-alert audience will recognize from the start that the two actually care for each other, the only fun to be had in *Without Love*, apart from their disparaging chatter about love, is to watch them trying to avoid it. Much is made of Pat's penchant for walking in his sleep, which brings him into Jamie's bed and leads to her inevitable misunderstanding. The conflict between them, however, is virtually nonexistent and only the potent Hepburn-Tracy combination keeps the film afloat under Harold S. Bucquet's direction.

Following their appearance in Frank Capra's *State of the Union* (1948), a political comedy derived from the Howard Lindsay–Russel Crouse stage play, Tracy and Hepburn costarred in *Adam's Rib* (1949), their final—and best—collaboration for the decade. An exceptionally witty and adroit comedy, it cast Tracy and Hepburn as Adam and Amanda Bonner, happily married lawyers who find themselves on opposite sites of a headlined case. Assistant District Attorney Adam has been charged with prosecuting a woman (Judy Holliday) accused of attempting to kill cheating husband Tom Ewell and his mistress, Jean Hagen. Amanda, believing fervently that a woman should have the same rights as a man in defending herself

and her family against an intruder, takes the woman's case. The resulting brouha-ha tears the Bonner marriage apart, for a while.

Around this clever premise Ruth Gordon and Garson Kanin spun a perceptive and funny screenplay with provocative overtones that still echo more than four decades later. In a sense, *Adam's Rib* is one of the earliest feminist comedies; Amanda Bonner is a pioneer women's libber, an independent-minded woman cast in the modern mold. Early in the film, she affirms, "Lots of things a man can do, and in society's eyes it's all hunky-dory. A woman does the same things—the same, mind you—and she's an outcast." An amused Adam can only give her a condescending reply: "You just sound so cute when you get cause-y."

As the accused, Doris Attinger, goes to trial, the courtroom fireworks between Adam and Amanda constitute the heart of the film. In her insistence that women should have equality under the law, Amanda goes to theatrical lengths, bringing in women of different callings, one of whom, a circus strongwoman (Hope Emerson), lifts a startled Adam from the floor. Soon Adam is angrily accusing Amanda of "shaking the tail of the law." More relevant to their marriage, however, is Amanda's new belligerent stance. "All of a sudden I don't like being married to what's known as a new woman," Adam shouts in a climactic scene. His is the battle cry of every man at the dawn of the feminist movement: "I want a wife—not a competitor!" It takes considerable maneuvering before their endangered marriage is on the right track again.

Under George Cukor's astute direction, *Adam's Rib* seldom falters, and a good part of the reason is the splendid cast in support of the leads. In her star-making role (she had appeared earlier in small parts), Judy Holliday is a revelation. Simultaneously funny and touching, she creates a desperate, neglected wife whose thoughts, and even speech patterns, move to their own private rhythm. (Asked about her straying husband, she replies, "He used to do that a lot. Not come home.") Notable performances are also contributed by Tom Ewell, Jean Hagen, and David Wayne as the Bonners' slightly effete songwriting neighbor.

Coming at the end of the decade, *Adam's Rib* makes a fascinating comparison with *Woman of the Year*, released seven years earlier. In both films, Hepburn plays a strong-minded, achieving woman whose attitudes and opinions alienate her from her more traditionally minded husband, Spencer Tracy. *Woman of the Year* begins with Hepburn's sharp-tongued put-down of Tracy and the sports world, and ends with her frantic attempts to prove to him that she can be as domestic as the next woman. Nearly a decade later, *Adam's Rib* begins with the couple as equals in their marriage and their profession and closes with their reconciliation after a stormy near-breakup. And how are they reconciled? Not by proving that Amanda Bonner should give up the law and return to the kitchen, but by Adam's using a ploy commonly used by women: He pretends to shed tears at their parting, and a touched Amanda takes him back. In any contention between the sexes, the film is saying, there are no male or female stratagems, only stratagems that succeed. Men and women can be equals in war and in peace. *Adam's Rib* does not go all the way on the side of feminism—Amanda still seems a little shrill, or, as Adam puts it, "cause-y." But the film did make considerable strides from the earlier days of *Woman of the Year*.

Adam's Rib was not only a film highlight of 1949 but also a rarity, crowning a decade that had seen relatively few marital comedies after 1941. The war years had witnessed wrenching separations of husbands and wives, and the postwar period had required painful, often difficult readjustments; many films (*The Best Years of Our Lives*, for example) had dealt dramatically with these matters. In the first two years of the decade, however, there had been a number of variations on marital themes in comedy films that seemed to take place in a world apart, where real life rarely intruded. These films were, in a sense, a continuation of those of the thirties, offering a few more years of escapist fantasy before the dream was shattered by war.

For whatever reason, quite a few marital comedies in the early forties attempted to titillate audiences with stories about marriages in name only, marriages that were euphimistically called "kiss-less." Of course, the situation was changed (or so it was strongly hinted) just before the closing credits. *Hired Wife* (1940) had crisply efficient secretary Rosalind Russell marrying boss Brian Aherne for business reasons, then scheming to eliminate the competition so that she can be much more than a secretary to him. *The Doctor Takes a Wife* (1940) involved bachelor girl and best-selling author Loretta Young (her book is called *Spinsters Aren't Spinach*), who must pretend to be married to physician Ray Milland. And *This Thing Called Love* (1941) even ran into censorship problems by "daring" to suggest that a frustrated husband (Melvyn Douglas) might actively attempt to seduce his "kiss-less" bride (Rosalind Russell).

During this period, marriages made in movie heaven could crash against the rocks for a variety of reasons. Two screenwriter favorites remained: rampant jealousy and severe neglect. The green-eyed monster reared its ugly head on more than one occasion. In W. S. Van Dyke's *The Feminine Touch* (1941), the ubiquitous

Rosalind Russell played the wife of a pompous professor (Don Ameche), who teaches him that a wife actually can be flattered by having a jealous husband, a familiar conceit in Hollywood's movie-marriage lexicon. *You Belong to Me* (1941), directed by Wesley Ruggles, tried to extract humor from the unreasoning jealousy of wealthy playboy Henry Fonda toward his doctor wife, Barbara Stanwyck. Unfortunately, his behavior becomes so asinine—he knocks down one of her male patients—that the irritation replaces laughter.

In some marital comedies, the wife rebelled at being neglected or taken for granted by her distracted or indifferent husband. Such was the case in Ernst Lubitsch's moderately diverting *That Uncertain Feeling* (1941), in which wife Merle Oberon takes drastic measures to regain the interest of husband Melvyn Douglas, and in Mark Sandrich's fairly jaunty *Skylark* (1941), adapted from Samson Raphaelson's Broadway play. In *Skylark*, Lydia Kenyon (Claudette Colbert) finally leaves executive husband Tony (Ray Milland) when his ambition looms larger than their marriage. Characterized in Allan Scott's screenplay as something of an insensitive boor, Tony finally comes to his senses, but not before Lydia has enjoyed a harmless fling with a carefree bachelor

A Letter to Three Wives *(Fox, 1949). Linda Darnell, Ann Sothern, and Jeanne Crain get the bad news—one of their husbands has run off with another woman. Joseph L. Mankiewicz's witty, intelligent screenplay won an Oscar.*

played by Brian Aherne. The premise is slender, but Colbert helps by bringing her customary intelligence and crisp acting style to the movie.

Occasionally, screenwriters strained to conceive a novel approach to marriage in jeopardy. *Mr. and Mrs. Smith* (1941) came up with the notion that, due to a legal mistake, Anne and David Smith (Carole Lombard and Robert Montgomery) are not really married at all. When David hesitates briefly at the prospect of remarrying Anne, she tosses him out of the house and falls into the waiting arms of David's law partner, Jeff (Gene Raymond). David now has the unenviable task of winning Anne back. The situations in Norman Krasna's screenplay are reasonably amusing, but what makes the movie unusual is its director, Alfred Hitchcock. In his first American comedy after years of directing suspenseful melodramas, Hitchcock is proficient enough, moving his actors through their paces with ease but with no special distinction.

By the mid-forties, marital comedies were in short supply, and even in the postwar years, comedy films were much more inclined to deal with the domestic problems of couples trying to cope with a new world rather than with questions of divorce or estrangement. The rush to normalcy included finding appropriate living space (*Apartment for Peggy*, 1948), or building a new home (*Mr. Blandings Builds His Dream House*, 1948). Whereas children had been largely absent in marital comedies of the early forties, postwar comedies began to stress family values and concerns in such films as *Sitting Pretty* (1948), *Family Honeymoon* (1948), and *Father Was a Fullback* (1949).

However, one outstanding marital comedy of the period hearkened back to the recurrent theme of the straying husband. *A Letter to Three Wives* (1949) began with an intriguing premise: On a fateful afternoon, three country-club wives receive a letter from a friend informing them that she has run off with one of their husbands. During the afternoon, each wife muses over her marriage, wondering whether hers is the one that has been shattered. Flashbacks reveal the married status of each couple: gauche Deborah Bishop (Jeanne Crain) and Brad (Jeffrey Lynn); radio writer Rita Phipps (Ann Sothern) and teacher George (Kirk Douglas); and gold-digging Lora May Hollingsway (Linda Darnell) and hard-boiled Porter (Paul Douglas). After much unspoken trepidation, the straying husband is revealed, albeit ambiguously, as Porter, but he returns to his wife to resume their scratchy but loving relationship.

In addition to its clever premise, *A Letter to Three Wives* offered elements that had been in scant supply for years. Its screenplay by Joseph L. Mankiewicz (who also directed) contained substantial amounts of wit, intelligence, and satire. A veteran Hollywood writer and producer, Mankiewicz had added directing to his credits in the late forties with such films as *The Ghost and Mrs. Muir* and *The Late George Apley* (both 1947). These were fairly polished entertainments, but with *A Letter to Three Wives*, Mankiewicz revealed a verbal dexterity and sophistication that had all but vanished since the days of Ernst Lubitsch and his collaborations with Samson Raphaelson. Mankiewicz lacked Lubitsch's mesmerizing visual skill, but he compensated with dialogue and characterizations that were refreshingly adult.

Although the segments involving the Bishops and the Phippses have amusing moments, the best section of *A Letter to Three Wives* concerns the battling Hollingsways, Lora May and Porter. These are two well-matched people in the marital battle arena: He is a wealthy, rough-hewn businessman, and she is a tough girl from "the wrong side of the tracks," sharp-tongued, knowing, and utterly brazen in her campaign to seduce Porter into marriage. Mankiewicz portrays the on-again, off-again nature of their relationship perceptively—at the same time that Porter understands her game ("It's an old act, but you're good at it!"), he finds that he cannot resist her. When we see them at the beginning of the film, their marriage has hardened into mutual contempt. Their hostility has become so pervasive that they are unable to recover the feeling they once had for each other, until the shock of possible separation sets them back on the right path. Expertly played by Linda Darnell and Paul Douglas, the Hollingsways contribute enormously to making *A Letter to Three Wives* a first-rate comedy. Mankiewicz's screenplay and direction for *A Letter to Three Wives* both received Academy Awards.

In the years after *A Letter to Three Wives*, movie husbands would continue to stray, or wax jealous, or fight to keep their marriages from unraveling. However, for a while at least, in a new climate, Porter, George, and Brad were the last of a vanishing breed.

Chapter 9
Footlights to Film

I n the constant need to find fresh material to fill the screen, the studios often turned to the theater. Like a best-selling novel, a hit play could provide a guaranteed audience, or at least a hard-core audience of moviegoers who had heard or read about the play and were curious to see how it was transferred to film. Usually, the play was "opened up" to allow for the larger resources of motion pictures. Sometimes the film version of a play diluted the material because of censorship problems, an inferior screenplay, or inappropriate casting. On rare occasions, the film improved on the play in many ways. The film adaptation of the George S. Kaufman–Edna Ferber play *Stage Door*, released in 1937, comes to mind. It eliminated the play's sour remarks about Hollywood, as well as a tiresome romantic subplot, and built up the role of Jean Maitland to accommodate Ginger Rogers's crisp, unaffected acting style.

Film adaptations of plays turned up repeatedly in the thirties, many of them comedies. Another Kaufman–Ferber play, *Dinner at Eight* (1933), with its ripe mixture of brittle comedy and emotional drama, provided the basis for an all-star movie from MGM, which also offered adaptations of Rachel Crothers's *When Ladies Meet* (1933), Mark Reed's *Petticoat Fever* (1936), and Clare Boothe's *The Women* (1939). A number of adaptations of stage comedies came from Warner Bros.; among them were *Three Men on a Horse* (1936), derived from George Abbott and John Cecil Holm's play about a timid greeting-card "poet" (Frank McHugh) with a talent for picking winning horses; *Tovarich* (1937), based on Robert E. Sherwood's adaptation of Jacques Deval's comedy concerning married Russian émigrés (Charles Boyer and Claudette Colbert) who are penniless in Paris; and *Brother Rat* (1938), adapted from the John Monks, Jr.–Fred F. Finklehoffe play about raucous doings at the Virginia Military Institute.

With the arrival of the forties, Warners continued to draw on the stage for many of its comedy films, to a much greater extent than any other studio. Particularly in the first half of the decade, Jack Warner and his producers displayed a

My Sister Eileen *(Columbia, 1942). In their ramshackle basement apartment, two sisters from Columbus, Ohio (Rosalind Russell and Janet Blair) face the unknown perils of life in New York City.*

130

penchant for buying plays that they believed would make popular films. Curiously, however, the studio seemed to approach the stage material with little finesse, broadening the situations to emphasize the physical comedy over the dialogue and encouraging the actors to play as if they were participants in a marathon race rather than characters in a believable story. A number of the films turned comedy in the direction of farce, and if farce was actually part of the original material, the movie version played it at a pace that left the actors and the audience exhausted instead of exhilarated.

A case in point was Warners's adaptation of Joseph Kesselring's stage comedy *Arsenic and Old Lace.* Made in 1941 but not released by the studio until 1944 because of contractual obligations, the film took a play that was hardly a model of subtlety in the first place and sent it careening wildly in all directions. The intention seems to have been to distract the audience from the fact that it was watching a comedy about multiple murder by submerging the ghoulishness in nonstop farcical action. The result was often amusing but also rather disconcerting, a black comedy taking place at a time when mass murder was the sanctioned policy of the German government.

The premise was simple: Drama critic Mortimer Brewster, played by Cary Grant, discovers on the day of his marriage that his two sweet old maiden aunts Abby and Martha (Josephine Hull and Jean Adair, repeating their stage performances) are quietly poisoning homeless old men who come to their Brooklyn home, and burying them in the cellar. Into this homicidal home comes Jonathan Brewster (Raymond Massey), Mortimer's presumed brother and a sadistic killer with his very own body count. As the mad Brewsters contend for further corpses, other characters converge on the scene, including Mortimer's bewildered new wife, Elaine (Priscilla Lane), another Brewster (John Alexander), brother to the darling aunts, who believes he is Teddy Roosevelt, and Jonathan's aide-de-homicide, "Dr." Einstein (Peter Lorre).

With scant opportunity to bring in his familiar humanism, director Frank Capra tries to rein in the all-out frenzy, but it spirals out of control. Although many of the lines are funny (Mortimer: "Insanity runs in my family. It practically gallops!"), the humor is eventually dissipated by the strenuous pace and by Cary Grant's wildly undisciplined performance as Mortimer. As the addled aunts, Josephine Hull and Jean Adair are the film's treasures—the former a plump, waddling joy as she dispenses good cheer with every fatal sip of wine; the latter the very soul of gentility as she comments on their special elderberry brew: "One of our gentlemen found time to say 'How delicious!'" The film, however, lacks the polish and the precision of superior farce.

A cluster of stage adaptations emerged from Warners in the early forties. With its many satirical references to the contemporary theatrical and literary scene, the George S. Kaufman–Moss Hart play *The Man Who Came to Dinner* (1941) seemed at first an odd prospect to attract viewers in middle America. Shorn of some of its malicious humor, the film version still managed to evoke laughter by dropping a sharp-tongued celebrity named Sheridan Whiteside (Monty Woolley, recreating his stage role) into the home of an unsuspecting Ohio family after he breaks his hip on their doorstep. (Nobody questions why he isn't taken to a hospital.) Known to the public as a sentimental and generous man (modeled on the popular writer and raconteur Alexander Woollcott), Whiteside is actually a self-absorbed, meddlesome misanthrope who disrupts the household and deliberately wrecks the romance of his secretary, played by Bette Davis. He is also visited by some of his renowned friends, including flamboyant actress Lorraine Sheldon (Ann Sheridan), effete British playwright Beverly Carlton (Reginald Gardiner), and the rambunctious Banjo (Jimmy Durante). These characters were based on, respectively, Gertrude Lawrence, Noël Coward, and Harpo Marx, all close friends of Woollcott's. In due time, the rascally Whiteside sets things right for everyone.

Partly a play à clef and partly a comedy of invective (Whiteside's insults are still widely quoted by fans of the play and movie), *The Man Who Came to Dinner* is enormously entertaining in spite of the blunted wit. Monty Woolley contributes the pearliest moments under William Keighley's direction. Whether badgering marvelous Mary Wickes as his unnerved nurse Miss Preen ("You have the touch of a love-starved cobra!") or firing his poisoned arrows at everyone in his vicinity ("Dr. Bradley is the greatest living argument for mercy killing"), he makes an indispensable Whiteside, tossing off his lines with lip-smacking relish. Bette Davis plays his secretary, Maggie Cutler, with becoming restraint (only her laughter seems forced), while Jimmy Durante bellows his way enthusiastically through the role of Banjo.

Although Warners' adaptation of the James Thurber–Elliott Nugent play *The Male Animal* (1942) also tended to coarsen the material by encouraging the actors to play too broadly, it generated a number of laughs. Henry Fonda (complete with spectacles to indicate his intellectualism) starred as Tommy Turner, professor at Midwestern University, who becomes the center of a campus controversy by want-

Life with Father
(Warner Bros., 1947).
The Day family,
headed by Father
(William Powell) and
Mother (Irene Dunne)
take off on a spin
about New York City
in 1880s. Trivia note:
Look for Arlene Dahl
in the Delmonico's
scene.

ing to read "radical" Bartolomeo Vanzetti's letter to his students. His problems also increase when his wife, archly played by Olivia de Havilland, basks in the attentions of an old beau, ex-football hero Joe Ferguson (Jack Carson). There are amusing moments, notably at a rally where the frenzy of college football is nicely satirized. Yet the movie now seems hollow and forced, despite strenuous effort by director Elliott Nugent, who also coauthored the play and originated the role of Tommy Turner on Broadway. Once again, it appears as if the studio did not trust the original material, and so felt that it needed to be made more emphatic for popular consumption. The same fate befell other Warners stage adaptations, such as *George Washington Slept Here* (1942) and *The Doughgirls* (1944).

Not every stage adaptation to appear in the forties came from the Warners studio. Columbia, which had introduced the scatterbrained family of *You Can't Take It with You* to moviegoers in 1938, brought another group of lively eccentrics to the screen with a film version of the Broadway hit *My Sister Eileen* (1942), adapted by Ruth McKinney, Joseph Fields, and Jerome Chodorov from McKinney's autobiographical short stories. In this fast-paced comedy, Rosalind Russell and Janet Blair played the Sherwood sisters, Ruth and Eileen, who come to New York's Greenwich Village to seek their fortune, Ruth as a writer, Eileen as an actress. Their basement flat becomes a way station for all sorts of odd characters, but after an assortment of crises, everything works out well, and Ruth even finds romance with Brian Aherne, the debonair editor of *Manhatter* magazine.

Briskly directed by Alexander Hall, *My Sister Eileen* boasts spirited performances by a game cast. It is Rosalind Russell, however, who sparks the proceedings with her energetic portrayal of the cerebral, sharp-tongued Ruth. By this time, the actress had proved her mettle in comedy, chomping her way through *The Women* and holding her own with Cary Grant in *His Girl Friday*. In *My Sister Eileen*, she must walk a fine line between being abrasive and sympathetic, and she succeeds admirably. Whether commenting sardonically on their seedy flat, which is dangerously near a subway under construction, or dancing wildly with a group of Portuguese sailors—she has been assigned to write a news story about them—Russell soars through the movie with unquenchable exuberance.

While Warners dominated the area of stage adaptations with a heavy hand, it could occasionally find a way to bring a Broadway play to the screen with full respect for its style and intention. After a lengthy, record-breaking run following its Broadway debut in November 1939, the studio finally turned Howard Lindsay and Russel Crouse's play *Life with Father* into a film in 1947. A slender but warmly affectionate, ingratiating memoir of Clarence Day, Jr.'s life with his family, especially his overbearing father, in New York City of the late 1880s, the play had charmed audiences for years with its gentle humor. The screenplay by Donald Ogden Stewart retained the play's charm, focusing on the despotic Father Day (William Powell) as he bellows and swears his way through every situation to the dismay—and also loving tolerance—of his wife, Vinnie, played by Irene Dunne. Photographed in glowing Technicolor under Michael Curtiz's direction, *Life with Father* evoked a bygone era with unhurried ease, finding room for Father's dilemma—apparently he was never baptized—or, more seriously, for Mother's threatening illness. Another period comedy, *The Late George Apley*, based on the George S. Kaufman–J. P. Marquand play and Marquand's novel, also opened in 1947. Ronald Colman starred as the snobbish, autocratic Boston Brahmin who learns the error of his ways.

Films such as *Life with Father* and *The Late George Apley* matched the temperament of the late-war and postwar years, when moviegoers longed for a return to domesticity and family values after the long ordeal. During the war years, the theater had offered a number of amiable, lightweight comedies that had little or nothing to do with the conflict, and when they were adapted to the screen in the mid- and late forties, war-weary audiences enjoyed watching them. Film versions of such plays as *Kiss and Tell* (1945), *Junior Miss* (1945), *Snafu* (1945), and *Dear Ruth* (1947) dealt with problems no more threatening or unsettling than the romantic tribulations and family misunderstandings of teenagers or young marrieds.

In the decades that followed, filmmakers continued to draw on the theater for new material to feed the ever-hungry movie machine. Popular musicals, in particular, could be expanded from the stage into spectacular films that took full advantage of vast studio resources. Few decades, however, turned to the theater as often as the forties, particularly in the war and immediate postwar years when many screenwriters were serving in the armed forces or only just returning to civilian life. Successful Broadway plays offered ready-made, surefire material for the screen, and it scarcely mattered that the material sometimes failed to survive the move from one medium to another. Still, there were pleasures to be had by audiences who had never seen a Broadway comedy and who could now revel in their wit and gaiety.

Chapter 10

The Great Originals

Amid the proliferation of standard comedies in the forties—the gag-laden farces with Bob Hope and Red Skelton; the lighthearted excursions into romance, marriage, and divorce—a few filmmakers allowed us to enter into their own private comedy world, where people behaved and even spoke with the unique stamp of their creators. Their work was refreshingly original but not entirely new. Several already had established their reputations in earlier years and continued to offer their very own comic vision in the new decade. Actually only one filmmaker, a bold mountebank named Preston Sturges, seemed to have leapt full-grown into the forties as a writer-director with a unique style and point of view. But even he had started to develop his offbeat comic perspective as a writer in the thirties.

Charlie Chaplin, perhaps the filmmaker with the most original comic vision of all (Buster Keaton is the only possible other contender), had been dormant for four years when he returned in 1940 with his first fully sound film, *The Great Dictator*. In *Modern Times* (1936), he had satirized the dehumanization of man in an industrialized society. Now, with the dark shadow of the Nazis looming over the world, Chaplin decided to attack Hitler and his totalitarianism with his only weapon: laughter. *The Great Dictator* not only ridiculed the little man with the black mustache but also called on everyone to resist the evil he represented.

Still, Chaplin was an entertainer and comedian, and the film, when it is not drowning in sentiment or groping for profundity, contains comic sequences that are utterly inspired. Chaplin plays the dual role of an unnamed Jewish barber and Adenoid Hynkel, the dictator of Tomania, who are look-alikes. In the Jewish ghetto, the barber resists the Tomanian storm troopers and protects young Hannah (Paulette Goddard) from persecution. At the same time, Hynkel plots to invade neighboring Austerlich, which requires him to entertain Benzino Napaloni (Jack Oakie), the dictator of Bacteria, who also has designs on Austerlich. Through a complicated series of events (more complicated than the usual Chaplin plot), Han-

Heaven Can Wait *(Fox, 1943). His Excellency (Laird Cregar), otherwise known as Satan or the Devil, welcomes Henry Van Cleve (Don Ameche) to the nether regions. Director Ernst Lubitsch offered a satirical view of manners and morals over four decades.*

nah flees to safety in Austerlich and the barber is mistaken for Hynkel. After leading the Tomanian armies into Austerlich, he is asked to make a victory speech.
Instead, he uses the opportunity to deliver a deeply felt talk on peace and brother-
hood. Apart from its flaws, *The Great Dictator* offers further proof of Chaplin's dazzling virtuosity. An unquestionable highlight of his Hynkel impression is the celebrated ballet with a large balloon representing the planet Earth. His leaps and
twirls as he balances the globe on his fingertips are graceful, funny, and the
expression of ambition gone mad.

Coming seven years after *The Great Dictator*, Chaplin's next film, *Monsieur
Verdoux* (1947), sparked a storm of controversy over its bitterly misanthropic point
of view. A cynical variation on the Bluebeard story, the film focused on a refined
and dapper bank teller with a crippled wife and child, who, after losing his job,
earns his living by courting and marrying wealthy women under a pseudonym and
then murdering them. Ultimately, he is apprehended and sentenced to death, but
not before he can express his views to a priest. His crime, he attests, is no worse
than the mass murders committed in the world every day by weapons of destruction. ("One murder makes a villain. Millions a hero. Numbers sanctify.")

Although *Monsieur Verdoux*, subtitled *A Comedy of Murders*, is now regarded
more favorably than when it was originally released, it is an extremely uneven film,
poorly cast in most of the roles apart from Chaplin, and staged with Chaplin's
usual indifference to the physical production. The film approaches the heights only
in the inspired casting of Martha Raye as Annabella, one of Verdoux's wives. A
splendid low comedian, Raye turns Annabella into a wondrously vulgar virago
whom Verdoux cannot seem to kill, despite his strenuous efforts. Finally, in the
movie's funniest scene, he tries—and fails—to drown her in a lake. With Raye as an
apt foil, Chaplin makes this scene a brilliant demonstration of the vanishing art of
slapstick.

Another major figure who brought his unique approach to filmmaking into the
forties was director Ernst Lubitsch. By 1940, his shimmering visual style and sly,
lightly sardonic approach to his material had established him as one of the screen's
most sophisticated filmmakers. Working with such sympathetic writers as Samson
Raphaelson and Billy Wilder, he had established his own milieu, in which a touch
of rue mingled with the romance and the laughter.

Lubitsch's first film for the decade proved to be one of his finest, the masterly
comedy-drama *The Shop Around the Corner* (1940). In a warmer mood than usual,
Lubitsch touched on life's small joys and sorrows, drawing on another exquisitely

fashioned screenplay by Samson Raphaelson (based on a play by Nikolaus Laszlo). The story is based on a slender conceit: Klara (Margaret Sullavan) and Alfred (James Stewart), antagonistic clerks in a Budapest gift shop, are unaware that they are each other's pen pal, sharing their feelings and ideas through the mail. Love eventually blossoms by the time they realize the truth. A subplot involves the shop owner, Mr. Matuschek (Frank Morgan), who has come to believe that his beloved wife is having an affair with Alfred. (The actual culprit is another clerk, the unctuous Mr. Vadas, played by Joseph Schildkraut.)

Around this frail plot (it served as the basis for later screen and stage musicals), Lubitsch spins a web of enchantment. Very little of consequence occurs, and yet the film succeeds in involving us deeply in the lives of the principals and their colleagues at Matuschek and Company. The wistful hope and longing of Klara and Alfred as they muse over their "beloved friend" of the letters, or their understated pain as they cope with reversals in their lives, have a rare poignancy and sweetness. Alfred Kralik is not an extraordinary man, but as James Stewart plays him in a style that had not yet become patented, he is thoroughly engaging. The actor makes us smile as he confides in his friend Pirovitch (Felix Bressart), "Just a lovely average girl, that's all I want," or he touches us as he reads aloud his unexpected letter of dismissal with quiet sorrow. Best of all is his scene with Klara in the restaurant, where she has come to meet her dearest pen pal, not knowing that Alfred is the man. Stewart plays this scene with a delicacy that combines hesitancy, apprehension, and a flickering hope. Margaret Sullavan matches him throughout the film, using her throaty voice and air of vulnerability to create a rounded portrait of a romantic-minded woman.

Two years later, Lubitsch returned to the more familiar terrain of biting satirical humor with *To Be or Not to Be* (1942). On the assumption that no topic, however grim, is immune from the healing balm of laughter, he directed a screenplay by Edwin Justus Mayer that mocked the obtuseness and cruelty of the Nazis as they stormed through Europe. This alone would not have provoked controversy—laughing at the enemy was one way of diminishing its size—but Lubitsch chose to set the story in Nazi-occupied Poland and to make the country's anguish part of an essentially comic story. The result was a mixture that baffled or angered many critics and viewers in 1942; they were unable to make the leap from a shot of Warsaw in ruins to the hectic activity of farce. In truth, even five decades later, the film's veering from melodrama to satire can be disconcerting. Jack Benny and Carole Lombard costarred as a married team of popular Polish actors who become dangerously involved with the underground at the time of the Nazi occupation.

For his next film, *Heaven Can Wait* (1943), Lubitsch returned to the past, evoking the sweet gentility and sentiment of *The Shop Around the Corner* but adding many of the satirical touches of which he was so fond. Using Technicolor for the first time, he recreated an idealized New York City to tell the four-decades story of Henry Van Cleve (Don Ameche) as he goes from being an infant fought over by his mother and grandmother to becoming an old roué with an eye for young women. Samson Raphaelson's witty screenplay (from a play by Lazlo Bus-Fekete) begins on a note of fantasy: Henry comes to Hell, where he is certain a sinner such as he belongs, to be interrogated by the Devil himself, here called His Excellency (Laird Cregar). As Henry recounts his story, we witness flashbacks to various crucial birthdays, and we meet the important people in his life, especially his adored wife, Martha, played by Gene Tierney, and his irreverent grandfather, Charles Coburn.

As Henry's narrative moves through the years, *Heaven Can Wait* pokes gentle and sometimes malicious fun at various targets, including the fatuity and priggishness of turn-of-the-century New York society and the vulgar brashness of the nouveau riche. The latter group is represented hilariously by Martha's parents, the Strables of Kansas, played with noisy relish by Marjorie Main and Eugene Pallette. A pair of blunderbusses who have apparently loathed each other for years, the Strables wage an endless war for one-upmanship. In the movie's funniest scene, they are seated at either end of a long table, seething over possession of the daily comic strips and sending their harassed servant back and forth with angry communiqués. *Heaven Can Wait* never tops this glorious sequence of low comedy, and the film tends to sag a bit after the Strables' departure.

By far the most original comedy filmmaker of the forties was a man whose life was as eccentric as the world of charlatans, blowhards, and victims he created on the screen. In the early forties, at a time when America was rallying its forces in defense of liberty and movies were celebrating the virtues and ideals that were in jeopardy, Preston Sturges wrote and directed films that dared to poke fun at these very same virtues and ideals. Some of his targets were fair game—politicians are always a good source of hilarity—but what could be said about his irreverent, ferocious attacks on such topics as motherhood, hero worship, and romance? Surprisingly, most film critics (with a few defections along the way) and many moviegoers (but by no means all) welcomed Sturges as a refreshing new voice. One simple reason is that his films were extremely funny, and even the most bruising satire can generate laughs when couched in the frantic slapstick that Sturges enjoyed so much.

The son of a Chicago stockbroker and a woman who founded a successful cosmetics business, Sturges grew up under the wing of his mother, who fancied herself as something of an aesthete. Determined to make her son an "artist," she subjected him to so much "culture," dragging him from museum to opera house, that he developed a lifelong aversion to its worst excesses. For a while, he worked in his mother's cosmetics firm, where he invented the first nonsmear lipstick. Later, after years of inactivity, he decided to try his hand at playwriting. His second play, *Strictly Dishonorable*, was a Broadway success, but his next three plays were failures. He moved to Hollywood, where his notable screenplays included *The Power and the Glory* (1933), a fascinating forerunner of *Citizen Kane*, and his sparkling comedy *Easy Living* (1937).

Sturges's first chance to direct a film came with *The Great McGinty* (1940), a political comedy for which he had written the screenplay. Anxious to try his hand at directing, he offered to sell the screenplay for a minimal amount—providing he could direct the film. Recognizing a good bargain, the studio agreed. The result was a movie that established Sturges's reputation as an original writer-director (he was awarded the Oscar for Best Original Screenplay) and also introduced his inimitable style of combining social criticism with flat-out slapstick.

A rowdy send-up of political chicanery set in the early years of the century, *The Great McGinty* shows clear signs of an original mind at work. The film traces the rise and fall of one Dan McGinty (Brian Donlevy), who relates his story while tending bar in a banana republic. Beginning as a hungry tramp, he takes on the job as strong-arm man for New York City's most powerful political boss (Akim Tamiroff), then rises to become the town's mayor and a pawn of the boss. Ultimately, in Sturges's sardonic commentary on our political system, he is elected governor. His downfall comes when he marries a righteous woman (Muriel Angelus), who encourages him to fight the boss's corrupt machine. McGinty ends up in prison in a cell next to the boss's, but a successful prison break leads to his new bartending job—where the bar owner turns out to be the boss.

Political comedies were not unknown by 1940, but few of them had ever succeeded to any great extent. Where *The Great McGinty* excelled was in the pungency of Sturges's dialogue, and the distinctive turns of phrase that became one of his trademarks. Educating his burly protégé in the way of politics, the boss explains, "This is the land of opportunity. Everybody lives by chiseling everybody else." Further instruction for McGinty comes from the boss's chief aide (William Demarest), who tells him, "If you didn't have graft, you'd have a lower class of people in politics."

Following *The Great McGinty*, which received mostly admiring reviews from surprised critics, and a lightweight, sporadically amusing comedy called *Christmas in July* (1940), Sturges brought his unique style as a writer-director to the realm of romantic comedy with *The Lady Eve* (1941). Given his quirky mind, there was no way that Sturges could create a conventional boy-meets-girl story, and as expected, the movie tosses convention to the winds. Here, the boy is Charles ("Hoppsy") Pike (Henry Fonda), wealthy scion of the Pike's Ale business, whose sole interest is snakes, and the girl is Jean Harrington (Barbara Stanwyck), an attractive cardsharp who initially sets out to fleece Hoppsy and ends up by falling for him. Her father, "Colonel" Harrington (Charles Coburn), is her accomplice. When Hoppsy learns of her trickery, he abandons her, claiming to have known all along about her scheme. Furious, Jean concocts an elaborate plan for revenge, impersonating a captivating British girl she names Lady Eve Sidwich. Her goal is to seduce a bewildered Hoppsy into marriage, then desert him. Her ruse works, but by this time, she truly loves Hoppsy, and they seem to be heading for a happy relationship.

Merely stating the not always believable plot line of *The Lady Eve* cannot do justice to the clever twists and turns of dialogue and situation that Sturges concocts for the film. The early portions in which Jean and her father scheme to "hook" the "poor fish" Hoppsy are perhaps the most diverting, with the Colonel pronouncing their creed ("Let us be crooked but never common") and Jean working her feminine wiles on this snake-loving millionaire. (He is nearly overcome by her perfume in an amusingly erotic scene.)

After Jean and Hoppsy quarrel and part company, the film moves to its less satisfactory section, in which she impersonates the Lady Eve. The ruse strains credulity, but Sturges keeps viewers royally entertained by adding touches of beautifully timed slapstick (especially Hoppsy's series of pratfalls when he encounters Jean-Eve), and by bringing in several marvelously eccentric new characters. Eugene Pallette excels as Hoppsy's crochety father, clanging dish covers together like cymbals when he finds no breakfast at his table, and Eric Blore turns a cardsharp named Sir Alfred McGlennan Keith into a funny caricature of genteel thievery. In the leading roles, Barbara Stanwyck and Henry Fonda bring a

deft touch to the film's best-remembered scene in which Eve tells Hoppsy increasingly lurid stories about the men in her past. Each time, as she starts to relate the details, the train goes into a tunnel and the roar of the train punctuates her confessions.

Early the following year, Paramount released Sturges's most unusual (and also one of his most problematic) movies, *Sullivan's Travels* (1942). At a time when war was raging in Europe and America was just entering the fray, Sturges felt that it was essential to justify his preoccupation with frivolous matters in his comedies. He also wanted to poke fun at pompous filmmakers who insisted on injecting "sig-

The Lady Eve *(Paramount, 1941). Cardsharps Charles Coburn (left) and his daughter, played by Barbara Stanwyck, work on victim Henry Fonda. Observing in the background is William Demarest, Fonda's suspicious bodyguard.*

Sullivan's Travels
(Paramount, 1942). Film director John L. Sullivan (Joel McCrea) starts his odyssey to learn about poverty, among other things. His butler warns him: "Only the morbid rich would find the subject interesting."

nificance" and "realism" in their movies. The result was an odd, disconcerting, but also brilliant mixture of slapstick comedy and serious, even grim drama that resembled no other film in that tumultuous year, and few films afterward.

Joel McCrea played the leading character, a movie director named John L. Sullivan, who is tired of working on trivial comedies and now wants to make dramas that will reveal the "sociological and artistic potentialities of the medium." Over

studio objections, he hits the road as a tramp, where he meets a hungry, despondent girl (Veronica Lake) who takes up with him. (She is never given a name.) After a number of adventures, including his first encounter with the "reality" of a hobo colony, Sullivan decides to give money to the needy poor. Through a twist of fate, however, Sullivan undergoes a nightmarish experience in which he loses his identity and finds himself accused of his own "murder" and sentenced to hard labor in a vicious prison. When he is finally released, he decides to produce only comedies: "There's a lot to be said for making people laugh. Did you know that's all some people have? It isn't much but it's better than nothing in this cockeyed caravan!"

Sullivan's Travels is an uneven film; its shift of mood from comic to serious is often bewildering, and the scenes in the later portions, where Sullivan comes up against the stark reality of the hobo colony (the ravaged faces of the tramps, the cramped quarters) are staged by Sturges with a heavy hand. Not surprisingly, the earlier sections are much more persuasive, especially the wild chase in which the nervous studio people, traveling in a bus, race behind the hot-rodder who has given Sullivan a lift. Resembling a Keystone comedy with sound, the sequence becomes a comic symphony of sirens, screeching brakes, and near-collisions.

Sturges's next comedy, *The Palm Beach Story*, released late in 1942, has many admirers, most of whom retain fond memories of the slapstick train sequence involving the boisterous Ale and Quail Club. A madcap marital comedy with many Sturgesian twists of plot and character, the film starred Claudette Colbert as Gerry, wife of a jobless architect and inventor named Tom (Joel McCrea). Tired of being broke and annoyed by his unreasoning jealousy—she also is convinced that she is simply no good for him—Gerry leaves him. On the train to Palm Beach, she becomes the adopted mascot of the Ale and Quail Club, a group of rowdy hunters who romp through the train with their dogs or fire their guns at random. She also meets wildly eccentric billionaire John D. Hackensacker III (Rudy Vallee), who falls for her. Tom pursues Gerry to

John's Palm Beach estate, where she introduces him as her brother, Captain McGloo. On hand to complicate matters is John's amorous, much-married sister (Mary Astor), a princess by her last marriage, who immediately sets her cap for Tom. After much frantic activity, Gerry and Tom are reunited.

Despite some diverting sequences, *The Palm Beach Story* fails to satisfy fully, mainly because the principal characters of Gerry and Tom lack appeal: For all her professions of loyalty, she seems to be a mercenary woman with ambiguous motives for leaving her husband, and he is merely bland. Most of the humor stems from the secondary characters, who are true creations of Sturges in their offbeat behavior. John D. Hackensacker III is a classic fool; as embodied by Rudy Vallee in the first of his many roles as a wealthy dimwit, he makes asininity hilarious. Even funnier is Mary Astor's princess, an outrageous creature who tells Tom, "I grow on people—like moss." When he notes that she never thinks of anything but "Topic A," she retorts, "*Is* there anything else?"

After making *The Great Moment*, an odd, uncharacteristic film concerning W. T. G. Morton, the discoverer of anesthesia—it remained unreleased until late 1944—Sturges returned to top form with *The Miracle of Morgan's Creek* (1944). His boldest effort to date, this hectic satirical farce dared to take aim at some of America's most cherished illusions, at a time when such illusions were essential to wartime morale. The myth held that the nation's young women waited faithfully for their men to return from battle, sustained by visions of marriage and motherhood, in that order. Audaciously, *The Miracle of Morgan's Creek* upset the apple cart by relating the dilemma of a small-town girl who becomes pregnant one fateful evening by a soldier she cannot even identify. To keep her reputation, she wheedles the hapless 4-F who loves her into tying the knot. Energetic Betty Hutton played the party girl, Trudy Kockenlocker, who pays a high price for her love of a good time. Saddled with a constantly irate father—a classic performance by William Demarest—who happens to be the town constable, Trudy has to find a husband quickly. She settles on Norval Jones (Eddie Bracken), a stammering bumpkin who has always adored her. Many frantic sequences later, everything is more or less resolved, with Trudy admitting that she genuinely loves Norval, who has gone through a comic hell on her behalf. And then, to the amazement of the immediate world, Trudy gives birth—to sextuplets! It is difficult to understand how the closing legend could have passed the censors: "Some are born great, some achieve greatness, and some have greatness thrust upon them."

The Miracle of Morgan's Creek is not consistently amusing—some of the plot turns show signs of strain, and after a while Eddie Bracken's dithering Norval grates on the nerves. Few comedies of the forties, however, are as dense with wicked satirical touches or moments of inspired lunacy. Sturges's view of small-town people is not exactly idyllic: Trudy's father, the redoubtable Constable Kockenlocker, is no benign paterfamilias. He harbors deep suspicion about daughters in general and Trudy in particular ("If you don't mind my mentioning it, Father, I think you have a mind like a swamp!" younger daughter Diana Lynn tells him.) His suspicions turn out to be accurate. Norval is no amiable "aw-shucks" small-town suitor but an angst-ridden hysteric who breaks out in spots under stress. Even the townspeople bear the Sturges stamp: At a dance for visiting soldiers, one member of the band is a swinging matron with a sizzling horn. Despite its shortcomings, *The Miracle of Morgan's Creek* stays in the mind as Preston Sturges's Bronx cheer to small-town America.

Sturges continued his jaundiced view of small-town life with his 1944 film *Hail the Conquering Hero.* His most complex and well-sustained satire, it also aimed at other familiar Sturgesian targets, including mindless hero worship, wartime hysteria, the gentle tyranny of motherhood, and the sort of politics that turns lies into campaign promises. Eddie Bracken returned as the star, this time playing Woodrow Lafayette Pershing Truesmith, another hapless 4-F, whose father, Hinky Dinky Truesmith, was a famous marine hero. Taken under the wing of a group of marines when he bemoans his fate, Woodrow is dragged kicking and screaming into a deception—he is returned home as a war hero. Swept away by enthusiasm over his borrowed uniform and medals, Woodrow is nominated to replace his town's corrupt mayor. Ironically, the townspeople love him even after he confesses to lying to them.

Hail the Conquering Hero is the most successful example of Sturges's ability to combine deftly timed slapstick with pungent social satire. The town's reception for Woodrow turns into a sharply observed model of disorganization as four bands battle furiously to gain the upper hand, the organizer (a deliriously funny Franklin Pangborn) gives way to hysteria as everything goes wrong ("Oh, death, where is thy sting?"), and the town's bombastic mayor (Raymond Walburn) delivers a florid speech with "deep humility." By the time they are ceremoniously burning his mother's mortgage, Woodrow is in a state of total panic and the town's delirium is out of control. Woodrow's reluctant entry into politics gives Sturges another chance to spoof a favorite target: Once again, the small-town politicians are blowhards and opportunists with little regard for their constituents.

Annoyed by Paramount's interference in his films, Sturges chose not to renew his contract and moved into independent production. It proved to be an unwise decision—his subsequent movies were not successful, either creatively or financially. Only *Unfaithfully Yours,* produced at Fox in 1948, has survived the years as another example of his unique style. A clever, darkly comic film with an original premise, the movie starred Rex Harrison as Sir Alfred De Carter, a famed conductor who has come to believe that his lovely wife, Daphne (Linda Darnell), has been cheating on him with his secretary, Tony (Kurt Kreuger). In a series of fantasy sequences, each shown as he conducts his orchestra, Sir Alfred plots various ways of killing his wife and implicating her "lover." He bungles his one real attempt at murder, only to learn that his wife is innocent, after all. An unjustly neglected comedy, *Unfaithfully Yours* contains elements familiar from previous Sturges films: the odd turns of phrase, the bursts of slapstick, and the unexpected characterizations, such as Edgar Kennedy's music-loving detective.

At the peak of his satirical powers in the first half of the forties, Preston Sturges brought a unique voice to films, one that was briskly American in its brashness, irreverence, and sharp-edged wit. Like the greatest filmmakers, he constructed a world inhabited by people who could exist only in his fertile imagination. Eccentric, impudent, and laughable, these mountebanks, con men, rubes, and rascals marched across the screen to their very own beat and often spoke in their very own rhythm, but Preston Sturges always called the tune. By the mid-forties, the tune was fading, but for a while, it was like no other. A mischievous iconoclast, Sturges never failed to laugh at that "cockeyed caravan" called life.

Hail the Conquering Hero *(Paramount, 1944). Woodrow Truesmith (Eddie Bracken) is propped up by his marine pals, Freddie Steele and William Demarest. Forced to pretend that he is a war hero, hapless Woody nearly loses his girlfriend, his reputation, and his mind.*

Chapter 11
Back Home Again

In the years following the war, as Americans began a new life free of conflict outside their borders, the motion picture industry turned inward. It seemed an appropriate time not only to look at the problems that resulted directly from the war, especially the dilemmas faced by returning soldiers, but also to examine some of the ills that had been festering even before America entered the conflict. Filmmakers discovered that they could combine social responsibility with success at the box office, giving rise to such provocative movies as *Pride of the Marines* (1945), which traced the painful rehabilitation of a blinded marine, and *The Best Years of Our Lives* (1946), which eloquently examined the plight of returning veterans. Topics that barely had been hinted at in films were now openly discussed—*Gentleman's Agreement* (1947) came to grips with the blight of anti-Semitism, while such films as *Home of the Brave* (1949) and *Lost Boundaries* (1949) touched on questions of racial prejudice.

In many cases, comedy also turned inward, as if to reassure moviegoers that the old verities of home and hearth still existed despite the disruption of the war. In addition to the usual number of romantic or marital comedies, or the knockabout farces starring popular comedians, many cozy domestic comedies appeared in the late forties and early fifties. They found their humor in the dilemmas that confronted families in their everyday lives as they gathered in their living rooms (bedrooms then were for sleeping) or moved through the quiet and ordered streets of suburbia or small towns (cities were the province of *film noir*). While the social dramas and *noir* melodramas took us into the dark corners where trouble and danger lurked, the sunny domestic and family comedies of the postwar years trafficked in promise and hope.

During the thirties and forties, 20th Century–Fox had specialized in family entertainments, offering cheery movies starring Shirley Temple, Alice Faye, and Betty Grable. In the postwar years, the studio was not about to lose its franchise as it turned out a number of domestic comedies in the same vein. Efficiently played

Miracle on 34th Street *(Fox, 1947). Celebrating Christmas are (left to right) John Payne, Maureen O'Hara, little Natalie Wood, and Edmund Gwenn. Gwenn's performance as the old gent who claims he is really Santa Claus won an Oscar.*

and directed, these films bore little resemblance to the real world; in their litter-free streets and dirt-free homes, they personified the American dream as seen through the camera eye. Audiences flocked to see these films, pleased to have their illusions restored after having them crushed by the war. It hardly mattered that other, dramatic films sent a conflicting message about the state of the nation.

Fox struck one especially rich vein of gold with its 1947 release of an engaging comedy, *Miracle on 34th Street.* A contemporary fable concerning a genial old man who insists that he is *really* Santa Claus, the film warmed moviegoers with the sort of good cheer Hollywood always liked to dispense. Veteran actor Edmund Gwenn played the white-bearded Kris Kringle, who is hired by Macy's department store for its Thanksgiving Day parade and then proceeds to cause an uproar by claiming to be authentic, and by innocently sending Macy's customers to its competitors. Along the way, he foments a romance between young divorcée Maureen O'Hara, who organizes the Macy's parade, and lawyer John Payne, and he also restores the childish innocence of the divorcée's too-sensible little daughter, played by Natalie Wood. At a hearing to determine his sanity, it is decided for various reasons (some of them self-serving) that he may indeed be Santa Claus.

Under George Seaton's direction, the film moves with ease and charm, and his screenplay (from a story by Valentine Davies) succeeds in modifying the built-in sweetness with a few satirical thrusts at the commercialization of Christmas and that ever-popular target, psychiatry. Edmund Gwenn won a Best Supporting Actor Oscar for his expert performance, which never slipped into sentimentality, and Seaton and Davies won Oscars for their screenplay and original story. Gwenn turned up the following year in another pleasing George Seaton film, *Apartment for Peggy* (1948), this time playing a world-weary professor who finds new meaning in his life when he agrees to rent his attic to young veteran William Holden and his ebullient, pregnant wife, Jeanne Crain.

That same year, Fox released a home-and-hearth comedy that enjoyed a huge success and gave a new direction to the film career of an unlikely star. Walter Lang's *Sitting Pretty* (1948) built its story around a slim but amusing premise: Seeking a baby-sitter, a suburban couple (Maureen O'Hara and Robert Young), to their own astonishment, find themselves hiring a haughty, acerbic, and monumentally efficient gentleman named Lynn Belvedere (Clifton Webb), who moves in with them. A self-proclaimed genius and a master of everything, Mr. Belvedere disrupts the couple's lives and causes ripples of dismay when he turns out to be the author of a best-selling novel about the sometimes indiscreet activities in the neighborhood. Naturally, he resolves all dilemmas, and, his air of superiority fully intact, he moves on to his next triumph. From the moment Webb's Mr. Belvedere enters the movie, he dominates every scene, whether he is putting people in their place or dumping oatmeal on the head of the couple's baby in retaliation for being splattered.

Films such as *Sitting Pretty*, along with other Fox domestic comedies such as *Mother Is a Freshman* and *Father Was a Fullback* (both 1949), gave filmgoers a sense of order and serenity that had been missing in their lives in the turbulent war years and immediate postwar period. In a sense, they were entirely fraudulent, glossing over the social disruptions that were forming beneath the surface. Yet they were also immensely popular, none more so than MGM's *Father of the Bride* (1950), perhaps the ultimate expression of the prevalent attitude toward home and hearth. Adapted by Frances Goodrich and Albert Hackett from Edward Streeter's novel and given polished direction by Vincente Minnelli, this immensely likable film signaled the entry of the fifties into the fantasy world of the American family.

Father of the Bride brought willing viewers into the lives of the Banks family—gruff but lovable Stanley (Spencer Tracy), his serenely beautiful wife (Joan Bennett), and their children, especially their ravishing twenty-year-old daughter (Elizabeth Taylor). On the surface, the vision was perfect: well-kept rooms in a comfortable, unostentatious house, where father and daughter call each other "Pops" and "Kitten." (Father wears a suit and tie on every occasion, no matter how casual.) Beneath the surface, however, was the sort of sensibility that soon would become the province of television situation comedies: the father as the hapless victim of gentle female tyranny, reduced to a quivering wreck by a sweetly condescending wife and a daughter trembling on the brink of womanhood. The movie began and ended with a battered and weary Stanley Banks surrounded by debris after his daughter's wedding. Behind all the laughter was a distinct hint of melancholy at seeing a man of substance temporarily reduced to ruin.

Still, there was considerable laughter in *Father of the Bride*, and its easygoing, lightly satirical air guaranteed audience satisfaction. The entire film was built around the events preceding the marriage of daughter Kay, including Stanley's interrogation of the prospective bridegroom (Don Taylor), in which he talks mostly about himself; his overwhelming encounters with the caterers, decorators, and workmen involved in the wedding ceremony and reception ("An experienced caterer can make you ashamed of your house in fifteen minutes"), and the temporary spat

between Kay and her fiancé, resolved in a flood of tears. The chaos mounts until Stanley has a surrealistic nightmare (actually the movie's best sequence) in which he ends up a pitiable figure in rags. Of course there are compensations for Stanley, none more compelling than the vision of his daughter in her bridal gown. In a role that requires him to be variously irascible, tender, jealous, baffled, and humiliated, Spencer Tracy gives a brilliant performance that earned him an Oscar nomination.

The great success of *Father of the Bride*—it was also nominated as Best Picture—led to an enjoyable sequel the following year, entitled *Father's Little Dividend* (1951). Once again, the film focused on a single event, here the happy arrival of Stanley Banks's first grandchild. Vincente Minnelli returned to lead the cast through the hectic activities surrounding the birth of the baby, none of them unexpected but also freshly observed and quite funny. If the film now seems to be an improvement over the original, it may be because the principal character is less of a sacrificial lamb being trussed up for the kill and more of a recognizable human being preparing to face the joys and perils of grandparenthood.

By 1950, it was abundantly clear that fifties audiences, including those who were watching the small screen, wanted the comfort and reassurance of domestic life. ("I Love Lucy" premiered in October 1951.) Never mind the Korean conflict that raged from 1950 to 1953, or the social ills that continued to plague U.S. cities. For a while at least, American entertainment brought viewers a comedy world in which Santa Claus was real, wives were incurably zany but nice, and fathers marched down the aisle with their radiant daughters to a happy ending. It was certainly a pleasant world, but like the breathtaking multimirror view of Elizabeth Taylor near the end of *Father of the Bride*, it was basically unreal.

Sitting Pretty *(Fox, 1948). Lofty baby-sitter Lynn Belvedere (Clifton Webb) takes over the household of Robert Young and Maureen O'Hara. Mr. Belvedere's popularity spawned a few more films built around his character.*

Part 3

MARKING TIME
Movie Comedy in the Fifties

A decade of war in Korea, racial unrest and upheaval at home, and Monroe and McCarthyism . . .

The early years of the decade find America and the United Nations steeped in the Korean "police action" following the Communist attack by North Korea on South Korea. The intervention of Chinese troops complicates the conflict, but in late November of 1951, a temporary truce is forged between the United Nations and North Korea. By July of 1953, the fighting in Korea has ended.

At home, Senator Joseph McCarthy's 1950 allegations of Communist infiltration into the government are causing an uproar. A panel of senators concludes that his allegations are false, but his accusations persist. In 1954, the Army-McCarthy hearings on television enthrall American viewers; later that year, the Senate votes to condemn McCarthy for abusing his colleagues.

Also on the home front, the decade sees dramatic progress in civil rights for all Americans. Following the landmark *Brown v. the Board of Education* decision, the Supreme Court announces, in 1955, its directives for ending school segregation "with all deliberate speed." By the end of 1956, the city of Montgomery, Alabama, finally complies with a Supreme Court ruling declaring segregation on buses unconstitutional. Noteworthy events during the decade: the detonation of the H-bomb, the world's first thermonuclear device, on a tiny atoll in the Marshall Islands . . . the investigation of crime in America by Senator Kefauver and his committee . . . the creation of the first effective polio vaccine by Dr. Jonas Salk . . . and the admission of Alaska and Hawaii into the Union as the nation's forty-ninth and fiftieth states.

The fifties see the arrival of Smokey Bear and the comic strip "Peanuts," of "I Love Lucy" and Disneyland, of Hula Hoops and *TV Guide*. These are also the years in which Elvis Presley and Marilyn Monroe loom large in the public eye. Among the decade's hit movies are *All About Eve, From Here to Eternity, On the Waterfront, Rebel Without a Cause,* and *Ben Hur.*

The Seven Year Itch *(Fox, 1955). Marilyn Monroe and Tom Ewell in a much-publicized scene from Billy Wilder's adaptation of the Broadway play. The movie was as gossamer-thin as Monroe's summer dresses, but it had amusing moments.*

Chapter 12

Jerry and Judy

I n the early years of the fifties, some of the popular comedians of the previous decade still flourished. Their comedic style varied little from other years, but audiences seemed to prefer it that way; it brought a sense of comfort and tradition. In such films as *The Lemon Drop Kid* (1951), *My Favorite Spy* (1951), and *Son of Paleface* (1952), Bob Hope continued his winning record of offering gag-heavy farces that traded on his brash, quipping personality. *Son of Paleface* was the best of the group, an enjoyable comedy sparked by Frank Tashlin's direction, which frequently had the actors moving in the slam-bang style of an animated cartoon. It was only in the last years of the decade that Hope's films began to decline, becoming increasingly tired, strained, and, worst of all, unfunny.

While other comedians of the forties, such as Red Skelton, Abbott and Costello, and Danny Kaye, appeared in movies that played on their long-established personae, new comic figures were beginning to make their presence known in the fifties. In 1949, the comedy team of Dean Martin and Jerry Lewis had made its film debut in *My Friend Irma*, adapted from the popular radio series. Playing supporting roles to Marie Wilson's dim-witted Irma (with Diana Lynn as her long-suffering friend Jane), the team won most of the critical attention—Martin as the romantic crooner and Lewis as the zany comic, with squeaky voice, eccentric movements, and an air of well-meaning idiocy. The two had met in 1946 when they were small-time entertainers and had forged an act that was enthusiastically received in nightclubs and theaters across the country. Their reception in *My Friend Irma* led to a sequel, *My Friend Irma Goes West* (1950), and then to a series of popular starring vehicles.

The pattern of their films remained largely the same: Martin and Lewis cavorting through wildly slapstick situations, with Lewis as the pivotal comic figure, shrieking and yammering his way into and out of trouble, his arms and legs moving spastically, his face distorted with anxiety or bewilderment. In repose, he appeared to be a pleasant if none-too-bright young man; in the midst of a dilem-

Jumping Jacks *(Paramount, 1952). A startled Jerry Lewis prepares for his first parachute jump. Lewis's zany impression of a bumbling misfit found favor with many moviegoers in the fifties.*

ma or a crisis, however, he seemed like a defective mechanical toy spiraling out of control. At first, Paramount starred the team in service comedies (*At War with the Army*, 1951; *Sailor Beware*, 1952; *Jumping Jacks*, 1952) that allowed Lewis to play the naïve recruit who tangles unwittingly (and also witlessly) with military authority. Many viewers, especially children, found his antics hysterically funny, but there were others (including some critics) who were taken aback or offended by his seeming impression of a retarded young man with a serious nervous disorder. Watching him wail and bellow his way through his films, one might wonder how he would have fared without sound; in *Sailor Beware*, for example, during the navy physical, he behaves in a manner much like Harpo Marx—he swallows a thermometer and seems to have no heartbeat or blood pressure. The climactic scene in which he is forced to take charge of steering a submarine is reminiscent of Buster Keaton. Yet his protesting whines and loony manner often induce winces rather than laughter.

Occasionally, a Martin-Lewis film attempted to give the story line a more realistic base and even a touch of poignancy. In Hal Walker's *That's My Boy* (1951), the Harold Lloyd–like plot had Lewis as the gawky, anxiety-ridden son of college football hero Eddie Mayehoff, who is expected to follow in his father's footsteps. Of course by the film's end, he has repeated history. Most of the amusement came from Mayehoff's impression of a domineering (but all-American) blunderbuss, although Lewis managed some expert slapstick in the climactic football game. *The Stooge* (1953) went even further in creating a credible framework for Martin and Lewis—here Lewis portrayed a Brooklyn comic who works as a stooge for the egotistical Martin and sees him usurp the success that is rightly his. Lewis also revealed a flair for broad satire in one of the few funny moments in *The Caddy* (1953), in which he impersonates an upper-class dandy who renders a clever song called "The Gay Continental."

As their popularity continued well into the fifties, Martin and Lewis turned to old films for their material, reshaping them to accommodate their by-now patented comedy style. *Scared Stiff* (1953) loosely reworked the haunted-house tomfoolery of Bob Hope's 1940 comedy, *The Ghost Breakers*, while *Living It Up* (1954) drew on the sardonic *Nothing Sacred* (1937), with Lewis playing Carole Lombard's role of the small-town yokel who becomes a national celebrity when he is diagnosed wrongly as suffering from a terminal case of radium poisoning. In yet another sex reversal, Lewis took on Ginger Rogers's role in *The Major and the Minor* (1942), playing a noisy dimwit who dons a sailor suit to masquerade as a thirteen-year-old enrolled at a fashionable boarding school. Renamed *You're Never Too Young* (1955), the new version eliminated most of the saucy wit of the original film.

Following *Pardners* (1956), derived from an old Bing Crosby musical called *Rhythm on the Range* (1936), the team had an acrimonious parting. Martin moved on to become a passable actor in comedy and dramatic roles and Lewis began a new career as a solo comedian in tailor-made vehicles. Such movies as *The Delicate Delinquent* (1957) and *Don't Give Up the Ship* (1959) gave free rein to the character he had created earlier: the hopelessly inept schlemiel whose behavior under stress ranges from infantile to moronic. The plot seldom mattered; sequences were constructed to allow Lewis to exercise his skill with slapstick, pantomime, and impersonation.

Alone or in tandem with Dean Martin, Jerry Lewis was one of the most popular (if not *the* most popular) film comedians of the fifties. His loyal fans expected—and received—a healthy dose of knockabout humor as Lewis tangled unsuccessfully with life's small and large complications. In his best films, the element of surprise—a sudden sight gag, an inspired moment of comic mayhem—could reduce audiences to helpless laughter. Yet his comic persona never seemed instinctive as it did with Groucho Marx, W. C. Fields, or even Bob Hope; it always appeared to be grafted onto this pleasant-looking, normal-seeming young man who suddenly exploded in paroxysms that were usually more alarming than funny. In a crucial way, Lewis resembled other leading comedians of the forties and fifties (Lou Costello and Danny Kaye in particular) who seemed temporary residents in an ephemeral comedy world—guests at a party who have been asked to entertain for the evening—rather than the permanent inhabitants of a self-created comic domain.

The fifties were not an especially innovative period for film comedy. While Martin and Lewis cavorted on the screen, and the old reliable figures such as Hope and Skelton continued to ply their trade, there were only a few performers who could strike an entirely original note: those rare actors whose comic persona could not be duplicated. One was a surprise: a not-young, sophisticated former Broadway entertainer named Clifton Webb, who amused moviegoers with his impressions of lofty, effete men of the world. Another was almost equally unlikely: a pleasantly plump, nasal, and altogether inimitable actress named Judy Holliday.

Holliday had achieved success by a circuitous route—nightclubs to films to Broadway and back to films—that began in the early forties with a group of performers called the Revuers. Fresh and exceptionally clever, the Revuers included

Betty Comden and Adolph Green, who were destined to become giants in musical theater and films. The group went to Hollywood, where they were seen fleetingly in a Fox musical called *Greenwich Village* (1944). Holliday remained at Fox briefly, turning up in small roles in a few movies, then returned to New York, where she first attracted attention in a play called *Kiss Them for Me*. When it came time to replace Jean Arthur in the Broadway-bound production of Garson Kanin's comedy *Born Yesterday*, she was chosen for the plum role of Billie Dawn. Opening in February 1946, the play earned her enthusiastic reviews and stardom. After a lengthy run, she went to Hollywood to play an important part in *Adam's Rib*, in which she made audiences and critics sit up and take notice with her unique personality and paradoxical smart-as-a-fox dumbness.

Meanwhile, the screen rights to *Born Yesterday* went to Columbia Pictures, and for several years, the studio's burly head, Harry Cohn, sought the actress who could play Billie in the film version. Finally, while Holliday was filming *Adam's Rib*, she was given the chance to make a screen test for a highly reluctant Cohn, who thought of her as overweight and homely. Bolstered by the enthusiastic support of Katharine Hepburn, Garson Kanin, and George Cukor, who was set to direct *Born Yesterday*, Holliday won the role of Billie Dawn. The result was film stardom for a decade and an Academy Award in 1950 as Best Actress.

In retrospect, four decades later, it is difficult to surmise how anyone but Holliday could have been considered to play Billie. As the ex-showgirl turned mistress to ruthless, truculent junk king Harry Brock (Broderick Crawford), Holliday rivets our attention the moment she steps onto the screen. (One might say even *before* she appears, when she bellows "WHAT?" to Brock's summons.) Unabashedly vulgar and ignorant, she seems out of place in the hurly-burly of Washington politics. But as she blossoms under the tutelage of writer Paul Verrall (William Holden), an innate intelligence, honesty, and even wit begin to emerge, and rising above Brock's brutal treatment, she becomes a vibrant woman who can expose and destroy his corrupt activities. We can even believe that Paul Verrall would fall in love with the transformed Billie.

Born Yesterday *(Columbia, 1950). Judy Holliday won fame and an Oscar for repeating her triumphant stage performance as dumb-as-a-fox Billie Dawn. Her costars were Broderick Crawford and William Holden.*

Although she had played the role many times onstage, Holliday was able to bring fresh nuances to the role. There is, of course, that one-of-a-kind voice, a combination of street-grown savvy and dumb-blonde ingenuousness. It can turn a simple query into a cue for laughter—she asks the senator's wife, "Ya wanna wash your hands or anything, honey?"—or it can bring a hint of pathos to a simple declaration—"I'm stupid and I know it," she tells Paul Verrall. Her bluntness is endear-

The Marrying Kind *(Columbia, 1952). A skillful blend of comedy and drama, the film starred Aldo Ray and Judy Holliday as a couple on the verge of divorce, who review their lives together.*

ing—when she finds Paul attractive, she goes straight to the point: "Are you one of those talkers," she asks him, "or would you be interested in a little action?"

Born Yesterday has its undeniable flaws: It slackens noticeably after Billie becomes "educated"—there are too many pious pronouncements about democracy, morality in government, and so forth—and the male leads are not entirely satisfactory: Crawford is too brutish and lacks the charisma that Paul Douglas brought to the role onstage, and Holden is a shade too old for Verrall. Yet when Holliday is present (which happily is most of the time), the film entertains. The indelible moments are all hers: her gin game with Brock, in which her incessant singing leads an exasperated Brock to shout "WILL YOU?" at the top of his lungs; her quietly defiant response of "Drop dead!" after he has forced her to submit to his will; and her unalloyed delight in learning more every day about the workings of government. Guided by George Cukor, Holliday invests the role with warmth and humanity.

Her success in *Born Yesterday* prompted Columbia to reunite her with Cukor in another film—but one entirely different in style and intention. Recognizing her rare ability to blend brashness and vulnerability, Garson Kanin and his wife, Ruth Gordon, who were responsible for *Adam's Rib*, wrote a screenplay entitled *The Marrying Kind* (1952) expressly for her. Holliday played Florence Keefer, an ordinary middle-class woman on the verge of divorcing her husband, Chet (Aldo Ray), a postal worker. A kindly judge (Madge Kennedy), believing that they are making a mistake, asks them to review their marriage. Flashbacks reveal their early happiness with two children, their large and small problems, and the tragedy—the drowning death of their son—that shattered their lives. Events are seen from contrasting viewpoints, and at the end, there is a promise of reconciliation for the couple. *The Marrying Kind* proved to be one of Holliday's best films: a deft mixture of comedy and drama that benefited from Holliday's special qualities and also from the earthy personality of her gravel-voiced costar, Aldo Ray, in his second film.

Holliday continued her association with George Cukor and Garson Kanin (this time without Ruth Gordon) for her 1954 comedy *It Should Happen to You*. Holliday had the role of Gladys Glover, an average New York girl who decides to make a name for herself by placing her name (and nothing else) on a billboard overlooking Columbus Circle. The ploy works: She becomes a celebrity in demand by the media, and she also causes panic in the advertising agency that usually rents the space. Her personal life is also changed: She meets, falls in love with, quarrels with, and finally reconciles with a photographer named Pete Shepherd (Jack Lemmon). At the film's close, she goes back to being plain Gladys Glover.

America's mania for celebrities, no matter how small their achievements, was not a new topic in films (*The Gilded Lily*, 1935; *Nothing Sacred*, 1937, for example), but *It Should Happen to You* gives it an amusing spin. What makes the film more than a merely pleasant spoof, however, is Judy Holliday. Although her Gladys is naïve and not very bright, Holliday gives her a charm and a sweetness that makes the character irresistible. The film is also notable for introducing Jack Lemmon to

It Should Happen to You *(Columbia, 1954). Anxious business executives try to persuade a stubborn Gladys Glover (Judy Holliday) to give up the billboard on which she's placed her name. At Judy's left: Peter Lawford.*

the screen. His fresh-faced good looks and direct, open manner made him an appealing leading man for Holliday's dumb-smart city girl, and his rapport with her was complete. Unfortunately, when they were reteamed immediately for Mark Robson's *Phffft!* (1954), the result was an only mildly amusing comedy about a divorcing couple.

Holliday's next film, *The Solid Gold Cadillac* (1956), cast her in a role that had been performed on Broadway by a much older actress, the veteran Josephine Hull. In Abe Burrows's adaptation of the George S. Kaufman–Howard Teichman play, she

was Laura Partridge, a seemingly simple but actually sly and straight-talking young woman who attends a stockholders' meeting of International Products and confounds the board of directors with her blunt questions. To divert any further investigation of their corrupt activities, the board members give Laura a token job with the company. Laura also becomes involved with Ed McKeever (Paul Douglas), the company's founder and now a powerful Washington consultant. Joined by McKeever, with whom she has fallen in love, Laura succeeds in ousting the board and taking over the company. She also wins McKeever's heart. Although its satirical bite is not very deep, consisting of a few amiable jabs at venal business practices, *The Solid Gold Cadillac* is an entertaining comedy, competently directed by Richard Quine.

Sadly, Holliday's next movie—and the next-to-last film before her untimely death—was one of her weakest. Another in the cycle of domestic comedies in the fifties, *Full of Life* (1957) concentrated on the marriage of Nina and Tony Rocco (Holliday and Richard Conte) and the uproar created by two events: Nina's first pregnancy and the intrusion into their home of Tony's flamboyant Italian father, Vittorio, played by opera basso Salvatore Baccaloni. The screenplay ran through the familiar dilemmas of pregnancy, but gave more time to the noisy antics of the father, who ranted at every opportunity. Presumably, audiences were expected to find him an endearing eccentric, but he came across as an insensitive and tyrannical boor. Under Richard Quine's direction, *Full of Life* worked strenuously to be amusing and warmhearted, but this time not even Holliday's expertise could lift it above the routine.

Holliday's most frequent director, George Cukor, offered this summary of her very special quality: "Her comedy had a subtle, hidden quality that, to express it as physically as possible, made you think that you alone had heard her, that if she had lowered her voice even a trifle you would not have heard her, and that what she said would have been gone forever." It is this rare quality of intimacy, combined with an uncanny ability to blend comedy and pathos, often in the same sequence, that makes us remember her so many years after she left the scene.

Chapter 13
The Graying of Romance
Romantic and Marital Comedy in the Fifties

Roman Holiday
*(Paramount, 1953).
Audrey Hepburn, as
Princess Anne, pre-
pares to meet the
press. Hepburn's deli-
cate beauty appealed
to audiences, and her
performance as a Cin-
derella in reverse
won her an Academy
Award.*

In the war and immediate postwar years, women had taken on a more aggressive stance, encouraged by their newly important roles in the work force. In film, especially romantic comedy, this translated into the assertive career women and boss ladies of the forties who disclaimed romance but who ended up in the hero's arms in the last reel. Unlike the wistful Cinderellas of the thirties, these women often pursued goals other than men and marriage. There was a difference as well in their Prince Charmings: Instead of the playboys and working stiffs of the thirties, the romantic heroes of the forties were men who could meet the boss ladies on their own level, executives and professionals who knew that those broad-shoul-dered dames really longed to be kissed. The best romantic comedies of the forties had sparkle and wit, but they were not terribly romantic.

By the start of the fifties, it was time for romance to return, time again for the dewy-eyed Cinderellas who wanted moonlight and roses. In films, there was a resurgence of domestic and family comedies, sparked by the need for normalcy, or what passed for normalcy. Yet there was also a need for the sort of film in which love and laughter were blended joyfully. In the thirties, Ernst Lubitsch had created such films, adding his own touch of wry sophistication. Two decades later, they were coming back, especially in the work of Lubitsch's disciple, Billy Wilder.

However, if Cinderella was on the comeback trail, she was headed for a grayer Prince Charming. In place of the young men who won the heroine in previous years, the proletarian Fred MacMurray or the filthy rich Ray Milland, the romantic comedies of the fifties offered, on the whole, leading men who were well past the first blush of youth.

Audiences were perfectly willing to accept that actors such as Clark Gable, Gary Cooper, and Spencer Tracy, who had actively pursued their leading ladies in

the thirties, were still attractive enough, and agile enough, to do the very same in the fifties. In most cases, the heroines remained as young and starry-eyed as before. There was no shortage of young leading men to play romantic leads—Van Johnson and Rock Hudson were only two of many. Yet in a number of romantic comedies, the hero played October to the heroine's April or May, the mature Prince to her blossoming Cinderella.

The most representative movie Cinderella of these April-October romances of the fifties was the slender, lithe, and exquisitely lovely Audrey Hepburn. A Belgian-born actress who had appeared briefly in several British films, Hepburn had scored a triumph on Broadway in an adaptation of Colette's *Gigi.* On the basis of that success, she was chosen to appear opposite Gregory Peck (thirteen years her senior) in William Wyler's romantic comedy *Roman Holiday* (1953). She played a Cinderella in reverse—the princess of a mythical country who is on a state visit to Rome. Bored and exasperated by her lonely life, Princess Anne flees her gilded prison into the heart of the city, where she finds adventure and romance with a newspaperman (Peck) named Joe Bradley. In the end, she leaves him to return to her responsibilities as a princess.

Smoothly directed by William Wyler, *Roman Holiday* is a bauble that succeeds in being both a charming, bittersweet romance and an eye-catching tour of the Eternal City. As Anne sheds her bonds, changing her coiffure and her clothing to match her incognito status, she comes to know Rome, and, luckily, so does the audience, as she enjoys a wild motorcycle ride through its streets, or dances on a barge tethered on the Tiber. Hepburn is also a visual treasure, especially in her princess finery, and her enchanting performance of a naïve and wistful girl won her an Academy Award as Best Actress.

In her next film, *Sabrina* (1954), Hepburn played a true Cinderella: a working-class girl who dreams of a prince, finds herself in the rarefied world of the rich, and then, through circumstances, comes to marry a prince, after all (but one far from the prince of her dreams). Adapted by Billy Wilder, Ernest Lehman, and Samuel Taylor from Taylor's Broadway play *Sabrina Fair,* the film marked Hepburn's first collaboration with director Wilder. *Roman Holiday* had been a romantic fable made magical by Hepburn and Rome, but under Wilder's influence, Hepburn's elfin charm was mixed for the first time with traces of cynicism and melancholy. Its story of love among the rich, for all its wit and gaiety, includes an attempted suicide (as does Wilder's *The Apartment,* made six years later), as well as behavior that can be described as snobbish at best and nasty at worst.

Sabrina *(Paramount, 1954). Sabrina (Audrey Hepburn) shares a romantic idyll with David (William Holden), the man of her youthful dreams. Later, she will realize that she prefers his older brother, Humphrey Bogart.*

Hepburn was Sabrina, daughter of the chauffeur to the wealthy Long Island Larrabees, who harbors a secret love for David Larrabee (William Holden), the much-married younger son. Sent off to a Paris cooking school after attempting suicide, Sabrina returns an enchanting and confident girl. David finds her fetching, despite the fact that he is about to be married again. Alarmed that his prearranged marriage for David may be in jeopardy, conservative older brother Linus (Humphrey Bogart) decides to court Sabrina himself. Despite the disparity in their ages—he calls himself "Joe College with a touch of arthritis"—Linus finds himself falling in love with Sabrina, and she with him. After a few false starts, they are happily together.

A Cinderella tale in which the prince has been wrongly viewed as the frog, *Sabrina* keeps its slim story moving briskly by tossing bright banter about like so many bouquets. Yet behind the sparkling dialogue, there is a slightly acidulous taste: Unable to have David, Sabrina tries killing herself by inhaling carbon monoxide; Linus schemes to get David married to a local society girl, with no regard for anyone's feelings or intentions; and, worst of all, he plans to trick Sabrina into leaving with him on a boat to Paris, then desert her abruptly. He ends up with Sabrina, but it is difficult to tell why from the character as written and as played by Bogart in one of his rare indifferent performances. Thirty years older than Hepburn, he seems sorely miscast as Linus, tired, heavy-handed, and unconvincing in his transformation from disapproving elder brother to ardent lover. As in *Roman Holiday*, Hepburn embodies elegance and charm, and her performance earned her a second Academy Award nomination.

Hepburn and Billy Wilder were happily reunited three years later in the delightful romantic comedy *Love in the Afternoon* (1957). The most Lubitschian of Wilder's films—in essence an homage to Lubitsch's sophisticated comedies of the thirties—the movie recalled the master's winking view of romance. In style and execution, even in its Paris setting and the presence of Maurice Chevalier, it echoed the films in which dashing roués, demure ingenues, straying wives, and jealous husbands engaged in a roundelay of amorous games.

As in *Sabrina*, Hepburn played a starry-eyed innocent who falls in love with a man considerably older and more sophisticated than she. A music student in Paris, her Ariane Chavasse, the daughter of a private detective (Chevalier), finds herself enthralled by a wealthy American womanizer named Frank Flannagan, played by Gary Cooper. Flannagan, who is being tracked by Ariane's father on behalf of a jealous husband, is enchanted but baffled by this mysterious gamine and makes a strenuous effort to seduce her. Ariane tries to play by his amoral rules, but her genuine love for him persists, while he resists falling in love with her. A moment before they are to be separated, he surrenders to his feelings and sweeps her up in his arms.

Although the film is actually little more than a delicious soufflé, the screenplay by Wilder and I. A. L. Diamond (their first collaboration) has sufficient charm and wit to keep it from collapsing. The evident difference in age between the high-living millionaire and the romantic-minded music student easily might have created a distasteful situation, but the script wisely makes a point of it. (Ariane: "I don't care much for young men. I never did.") There are so many slyly amusing touches that one hardly notices that the story is actually lighter than air: A three-piece gypsy orchestra, ready to create a romantic atmosphere, follows Flannagan wherever he goes, or a Paris policeman shows total indifference to the murderous threat of a jealous husband. One scene in particular, in which Flannagan attempts to seduce Ariane in his hotel room, plays like a virtual pastiche of Lubitsch, with the camera focusing largely on the closed door as Flannagan plies his prey with food, drink, and gypsy music.

For whatever reason, story lines concerning the amorous—or merely titillating—relationships between young girls and older men continued to turn up throughout the fifties in romantic comedies. In his late forties, Cary Grant was cast opposite young Jeanne Crain in Joseph Mankiewicz's verbose but interesting comedy-drama *People Will Talk* (1951). Although hardly decrepit at forty-four, David Niven was obliged to play an older man—a suave roué—to Maggie MacNamara's "professional virgin" in Otto Preminger's *The Moon Is Blue* (1953). The girl, however, preferred young bachelor William Holden in this mildly controversial adaptation of F. Hugh Herbert's Broadway play. Another Broadway comedy, George Axelrod's *The Seven Year Itch*, found its way to the screen in 1955 under Billy Wilder's direction; it wove an extremely slender tale of middle-aged "summer bachelor" Tom Ewell, who fantasizes his way through an innocent assignation with Marilyn Monroe, the light-headed, voluptuous girl who lives upstairs.

By the decade's end, the screen's longtime principal purveyor of male charisma still retained enough box-office appeal to undertake the leading role in a romantic comedy. In his late fifties, Clark Gable was cast opposite thirty-four-year-old Doris Day in George Seaton's moderately enjoyable comedy *Teacher's Pet* (1958). He played a crusty newspaper editor who becomes infatuated with an attractive journalism instructor (Day) and enrolls in her class under false pretenses. Gradually, despite their divergent views on journalism and life, he woos her successfully. Although George Seaton does not have the light touch required for a comedy of this stripe, the screenplay by Fay and Michael Kanin (which received an Academy Award nomination) has its bright and perceptive moments.

In addition to the many May–December romances of fifties comedy, there were some films that dealt with relationships between couples who were no longer young. Several of the aging male stars who dallied with young girls also found costars who were reasonably close to their own age. The humor evolved from the sexual games undertaken by more seasoned players. One rather slender example, Stanley Donen's *Indiscreet* (1958), involved a still-dapper Cary Grant as a suave diplomat whose romance in London with a famous actress (Ingrid Bergman) goes through various permutations before ending happily. Adapted by Norman Krasna from his play *Kind Sir, Indiscreet* was a lighthearted exercise for two attractive stars, but too frivolous and insubstantial to make any real impression.

Inevitably, the foremost exponents of mature romance in film comedy remained Spencer Tracy and Katharine Hepburn. The rapport that had been so evident earlier in *Woman of the Year* and *Adam's Rib* extended into the fifties in an amiable comedy entitled *Pat and Mike* (1952), directed by George Cukor. Once again, the comedy stemmed from the attraction of two opposite poles: she as Pat Pemberton, a brittle physical-education instructor who becomes a professional sports star; he as Mike Conovan, a rough-hewn sports promoter who manages her career. Their scratchy relationship eventually blossoms into love.

Curiously, the Ruth Gordon–Garson Kanin screenplay marks several steps backward from the more or less feminist attitude of their script for *Adam's Rib*. When we first meet Pat, she has a condescending, judgmental beau (William Ching) who completely unnerves her when he attends her golf tournaments. Under Mike's management, her security returns, and she becomes a leading contender in tennis as well as golf. But when she becomes aggressive with the crooks with whom Mike has an uneasy partnership, he rages at her for taking charge. ("I like a he to be a he, and a she to be a she!") Only when she softens her stance and pretends to be dependent on him does he forgive her. As in *Woman of the Year*, where she tried to be the domesticated "little woman," Hepburn must demean herself to win Tracy.

Still, *Pat and Mike* pleases with bright dialogue and cleverly realized characters. Spencer Tracy's Mike Conovan is clearly a refugee from a Damon Runyon story, a hard-bitten but soft-centered man who knows a good thing when he sees one. As Pat walks away from him, his admiration is blunt: "Nicely packed, that kid.

Not much meat on her, but what's there is *cherce!*" Once Pat is free of the influence of her obnoxious boyfriend, her confidence returns, and for a while the assertive woman returns, parrying with Mike in one of those man and woman skirmishes that the team made so delightful.

Five years later, when they were reunited for *Desk Set* (1957), Hepburn and Tracy were on a more even keel than before; this time, no humiliating charade was required for her to win Tracy's affection. Romance, however, seemed almost incidental—more to the point was the business conflict that set the plot in motion. In this adaptation of William Marchant's play, Hepburn appeared as the head of the research library for a broadcasting company, and Tracy played the engineer who arrives to computerize her operation. By the time they have fallen in love, she has demonstrated the superiority of the human mind over the machine and proven, for the first time in the Hepburn-Tracy canon, that she need not sacrifice her independence to his masculine whims. Competently directed by Walter Lang, *Desk Set* is a trivial film, an appetizer served up as a main course, but it is mildly diverting.

While the many romantic comedies of the fifties that involved either mature love affairs, or affairs of older men with younger women, were not entirely devoid of passionate feeling, neither did they generate much sexual heat, or suggest in any precise way that a bedroom was the site for anything else but sleeping. Yet by the end of the decade, it was clear that a new approach to romantic comedy was in the offing. Although the film industry, still governed by its Production Code and the pressures of the Legion of Decency, continued to monitor the content of movies, there was a general feeling that it was possible to extend slightly the boundaries of what was permissible. Producers agreed tacitly that an audience could be titillated without being offended.

By the sixties, there would be an influx of film comedies that took a winking and even leering attitude toward sexual relationships. One romantic comedy, released in the fall of 1959, appeared to lead the way. Viewed more than three decades later, *Pillow Talk* seems laughably tame, yet its approach to the game of seduction and its view of a virginal heroine ripe for bedding down were regarded as surprisingly bold. Today, that film's attitude toward women would be regarded as antediluvian, yet in its time, the script was widely admired for its wit and sparkle, and it even won Academy Awards as Best Original Story (Russell Rouse and Clarence Greene) and Best Screenplay (Stanley Shapiro and Maurice Richlin).

For all of its glittering artificiality, *Pillow Talk* does offer a workable premise for comedy: Jan Morrow (Doris Day), a chic and successful interior decorator, shares a party line with Brad Allen (Rock Hudson), a Broadway composer who pursues women aggressively. When Jan lodges a formal complaint against Brad's hogging of their party line, he exacts his own kind of revenge: He impersonates a shy Texan whose sweetness and sincerity release Jan's long-dormant libido. Jan is furious when she learns the truth, but by this time, they realize that they truly love each other.

Under Michael Gordon's direction, Doris Day and Rock Hudson exhibited a rapport and a modest, if not sharply honed, comedy sense that would make them one of the most popular acting teams of the sixties. Some of the situations are cleverly contrived, as when Brad plays the "aw shucks" Texan for Jan's benefit, or when Jan worries about Tex's interest in fabrics and recipes. What makes this bauble significant, however, is its new, near-salacious attitude toward sexual matters. Jan's presumed sexual repression is made the butt of Brad's jokes and sardonic comments ("Don't take your bedroom problems out on me!" he tells her), and Brad's insatiable womanizing—he uses and discards women like so many Kleenex tissues—is viewed as vastly comic. When he first sees Jan, he ogles her as the camera moves up and down her body. The camera, in fact, often serves

Pillow Talk *(Universal, 1959). It seems mild now, but this romantic comedy with Doris Day and Rock Hudson was considered a freshly "adult" view of the battle between the sexes. Day and Hudson became a popular costarring team.*

as a kind of voyeur: In one scene, a split frame shows Jan and Brad soaking in their respective bathtubs. As they talk romantically, each places one foot against the middle of the frame, so that they appear to be touching. Few films until that time would have attempted such a scene.

The great success of *Pillow Talk* could hardly go unheeded by filmmakers, and in the sixties, a flood of sexually oriented comedies reached the screen as Production Code restrictions were relaxed. As the leading romantic actors of the forties and fifties moved into character roles or retirement, a new kind of actor—more sexually aggressive and threatening—began to emerge to fill the void. In place of Clark Gable and Cary Grant, whose graying presences could still be seen on occasion, films offered Dean Martin, Tony Curtis, and, unlikely as it may seem, Walter Matthau.

For a while at least, the fifties presented a largely benign and mature view of romance. Films such as *Pillow Talk* suggested that something new was blowing in the wind.

Like the romantic comedies, many marital comedies of the fifties dealt with couples who were veterans of the war between the sexes. The films starring Judy Holliday—*The Marrying Kind, Phffft!,* and *Full of Life*—had involved couples who were relatively young as they faced the rewards and tribulations of married life. A number of others, however, were concerned with mature husbands and wives who were finding out, after living together for a while, that the state of matrimony could easily become a battle zone. In most of these films, as opposed to the ordinary, middle-class background of the Holliday movies, the couples led privileged lives.

The reasons for marital dissension were as different as the films themselves, and sometimes they were original enough to make for a reasonably diverting movie. Mitchell Leisen's *The Mating Season* (1951) concerned the marriage of socialite Gene Tierney and ambitious lawyer John Lund, whose mother turns out to be a down-to-earth, plain-speaking working-class woman, played with comic finesse by Thelma Ritter. The complications that ensue when Mama is mistaken for a servant generated a good number of laughs, while commenting obliquely on America's social strata. There was also some amusement in Edmund Goulding's multipart comedy *We're Not Married* (1952), if only in watching Ginger Rogers and Fred Allen as a squabbling radio couple, married for many years, who discover through a legal error that they have never been wed at all. Their nasty bickering off the air, contrasted with the sweetness and light for their faithful public, had somewhat more bite and humor than the other four episodes of the film, mainly due to the dour-faced Allen's acerbic style.

Some marital comedies involving mature couples found their inspiration in past successes. Vera Caspary, who had contributed the story to *A Letter to Three Wives*, virtually repeated herself by writing the story and coauthoring the screenplay for *Three Husbands* (1951); this time, the story concerned three men (Howard da Silva, Shepperd Strudwick, and Robert Karnes) who learn that one of their wives has had an affair with a recently deceased playboy (Emlyn Williams). Other reworkings of past properties included *Let's Do It Again* (1953), a lackluster remake of *The Awful Truth*, with Jane Wyman and Ray Milland, and *Designing Woman* (1957), loosely based on the Katharine Hepburn–Spencer Tracy comedy *Woman of the Year*. The latter film offered Gregory Peck in a rare comedy role as the sports writer who falls in love with and marries a woman from a different social level, this time a chic fashion designer played by Lauren Bacall. George Wells's Oscar-winning screenplay had at least a measure of wit, and Vincente Minnelli directed with an even hand.

By the last years of the decade, it was evident that the more permissive climate that had started to affect the romantic comedy was doing the same for the relatively few comedies about marriage. The result, at first, was hardly auspicious. Gene Kelly's *Tunnel of Love* (1958), for example, transformed the Joseph Fields Broadway play and Peter de Vries novel into a labored film built around a single joke: After an infertile Westport couple (Richard Widmark and Doris Day) contact a child-adoption agency, the husband comes to believe that he has somehow impregnated the attractive woman (Gia Scala) who is investigating the couple as prospective parents. Reduced to a dithering idiot when he learns that the baby they will receive from the agency may well be his own, the husband tries to keep the secret from his adoring wife. On this misunderstanding, the film builds a series of farcical situations that lack taste, humor, and style.

Clearly, with Doris Day fighting to retain her virginity in *Pillow Talk*, or grappling with temperature charts in *Tunnel of Love*, a new attitude was emerging in romantic and marital comedies. It would reach fruition in the sixties.

Chapter 14

Tongue-in-Cheek
Satires and Farces in the Fifties

P aradoxically, while fifties comedies stressed domesticity and family ties, or focused on mature romances, the decade also witnessed a return to the sort of irreverent satire that had been prevalent in the thirties. With only a few exceptions, the fifties satires lacked the sharp edges and brazen tone of earlier years (there was something oddly inhibiting about the wide screens and garish Technicolor of the fifties), but there was still the sense that certain topics were fair game for broad spoofs and parodies or even, on occasion, for the cutting edge of authentic satire.

Although television had not yet fully impinged on the national consciousness in the early fifties, a few films took aim at this burgeoning (and increasingly dangerous) rival to the movie industry. A satirical 1951 comedy entitled *Callaway Went Thataway* offered a genial but hardly piercing spoof of early television Westerns. Fred MacMurray and Dorothy McGuire starred as advertising people, in business and in love, who are called on to locate a facsimile of one Smoky Callaway, a one-time Hollywood Western hero who has long faded from the scene. The couple finds a startling look-alike for Smoky in a cowpoke named "Stretch" Barnes (Howard Keel). The attempt to turn Stretch into a Western star sparked some cleverly satirical touches. ("You only got to have two expressions," Stretch is told, "hat off and hat on!") Complications ensue when the real Callaway, a nasty drunkard also played by Howard Keel, returns to claim his due.

Another fifties comedy, Claude Binyon's *Dreamboat* (1952) not only poked fun at television but also reached back in time to spoof the excesses of moviemaking in the silent era. Clifton Webb starred as a lofty English professor who is revealed to have once been a dashingly romantic silent-screen star named Bruce Blair, whose old films are becoming popular again on television. In his attempt to stop them from being shown, he comes up against his old but well-preserved leading lady (Ginger Rogers) and the huckster (Fred Clark) who is making a killing with the

All About Eve (Fox, 1950). Stage star Margo Channing (Bette Davis, right) faces Eve (Anne Baxter), the girl who will prove to be her nemesis. Visible in the background are Celeste Holm, George Sanders, and Marilyn Monroe.

ancient films. The parodies of these films were broadly funny, while perpetrating the hoary myth about the florid acting style of the silent era.

No branch of the lively arts was immune from satire during this period. The legitimate theater, which, in the past, had been lightly mocked for its retinue of snobs, poseurs, and sycophants, received its wittiest, most incisive treatment in the classic 1950 comedy *All About Eve*. Joseph L. Mankiewicz, who, a year earlier, had sounded off on various topics in his screenplay for *A Letter to Three Wives*, now took on the stage to portray the temperaments and idiocyncrasies of a group of theatrical people, and those who spin in their orbit.

Mankiewicz's screenplay for *All About Eve*, from a story by Mary Orr, would hardly qualify as a realistic view of the modern American theater. Instead, it offers a kind of heightened realism in which the characters, witty and knowing, often speak in aphorisms, wisecracks, and glimmers of perception (sometimes even about themselves). The story line is simple: Margo Channing (Bette Davis), a celebrated but volatile, insecure actress, is deceived by Eve Harrington (Anne Baxter), a girl who seems to be a pitiable, worshipful fan of Margo's but who is actually a treacherous schemer out to replace her, both onstage and in life. Eve also disrupts the lives of Margo's trusting friends. She claws her way to the top, only to be taken down by Addison De Witt (George Sanders), the acid-tongued critic who considers her his personal possession, a monster he created. At the end, another girl is scheming to replace Eve at the top of the ladder.

As in *A Letter to Three Wives*, Mankiewicz's dazzling dialogue for *All About Eve* outshines his rather conventional direction. In a sense the modern-day equivalent of Restoration comedy, the film bristles with lines that have become part of movie lore, including Margo's warning of storm clouds gathering at her party ("Fasten your seat belts, it's going to be a bumpy night!") and Addison De Witt's introduction of his dull-witted but ravishing companion (Marilyn Monroe): "Miss Caswell is an actress, a graduate of the Copacabana School of Dramatic Arts." Mankiewicz's penchant for intruding his personal point of view can become tiresome when it is unrelated to the film (as in *People Will Talk*), but in *All About Eve*, his theatrical characters are appropriate spokespeople for his ideas on the lively arts.

The acting throughout is impeccable. In the role originally intended for Claudette Colbert, Bette Davis gives one of her finest performances; her Margo is a fierce, scathingly witty woman, terrified by the inroads of age and then finally reconciled to the future. (This time, her flamboyant acting style works for the character rather than overpowering it.) George Sanders also gives one of his best performances, using his cultured voice and his air of arrogant superiority to turn Addison De Witt into a perfectly comprehensible monster. As Margo's devoted, outspoken maid, Birdie, Thelma Ritter gets many of the film's best lines: Listening to Eve's sad story, her good instincts and common sense make her suspicious—when Eve finishes her tale of woe, Birdie comments, "What a story! Everything but the bloodhounds snappin' at her rear end!" Anne Baxter often has been criticized for her performance as Eve, but in fact, her blandness is right for the role, concealing the treachery that lies behind that unruffled demeanor and honeyed voice.

The bewhiskered cliché that film is a visual medium may well be true, and yet *All About Eve* indicates that spoken dialogue need not only advance the plot or develop a character; it can also give us the civilized pleasure we usually expect in the theater. This film may not be "cinematic," but at a time when witty dialogue in films is in short supply, it reminds us that a film can please by doing as much for our ears as for our eyes. In its year of release, *All About Eve* clearly pleased: It won the Academy Award as the year's best film, and Oscars also went to Joseph Mankiewicz for his direction and screenplay, and to George Sanders for his incisive performance as Addison De Witt.

In addition to the films that spoofed the excesses of the lively arts, there were fifties comedies that scattered their fire over a wide range of subjects. Curiously, 20th Century–Fox, which turned out many of the cozy domestic comedies of the period, also produced more than a few of the scattershot satires that were popular in the fifties. Howard Hawks's *Monkey Business* (1952), for one, poked fun at the outer reaches of scientific experimentation and, more specifically, at the search for eternal youth that seems to preoccupy men and women in every era. A wild slapstick comedy written by the prolific I. A. L. Diamond, Charles Lederer, and Ben Hecht, the film cast Cary Grant as Barnaby Fulton, a bespectacled, absentminded research chemist (shades of *Bringing Up Baby*!) who is seeking to discover a serum that will rejuvenate. When the experimental serum accidentally gets into the lab's water supply, by way of a mischievous chimpanzee, everyone who drinks the water is reduced to behaving like a teenager. Among those affected are Barnaby's loving wife, Edwina (Ginger Rogers).

More frenetic than funny, *Monkey Business* draws scattered laughs by having adults, especially serious-minded adults, act like Hollywood's idea of teenagers. (Howard Hawks delights in deflating men of learning, as witness *Bringing Up Baby* and *Ball of Fire*.) One sip of the formula, and a youthful Barnaby, complete with crew cut and loud new wardrobe, can be seen careening about town in a hot rod, accompanied by his boss's voluptuous blond secretary (Marilyn Monroe on the verge of full-fledged stardom). Edwina, too, reverts to childhood, which in her case makes her seem faintly feebleminded. Very little of this antic nonsense is really amusing, although there is one well-remembered moment in which Barnaby's boss (reliable Charles Coburn) hands secretary Monroe a letter and says, "Find somebody to type this," then adds, by way of explanation, "Anybody can type."

Fox's penchant for voluptuous blondes (Betty Grable reigned as queen of the lot in the forties) reached its apogee in the fifties with Marilyn Monroe. Although writers would extol her comedic gifts after her premature death, she actually demonstrated only minimal acting ability in such early Fox films as *Niagara* (1953) and *How to Marry a Millionaire* (1953). In the latter film, the first comedy to be filmed in the wide-screen Cinema-Scope process, she played one of three New York models who set out to snare

rich husbands. (Betty Grable and Lauren Bacall played the others.) Apart from her dumbness, the single joke about Monroe's character of Pola was her extremely poor eyesight. The film's glittering production failed to conceal the fact that Nunnally Johnson's screenplay was really threadbare and old hat.

Just as Marilyn Monroe had replaced Betty Grable (who had replaced Alice Faye) as Fox's resident blonde, big-bosomed Jayne Mansfield turned up in the mid-fifties as a virtual clone of Monroe. Interestingly, there was a significant difference among the blondes of each decade. Whereas, in the forties, Betty Grable had projected a cheerful and knowing brashness, her successors, Monroe and Mansfield,

How to Marry a Millionaire *(Fox, 1953). On the prowl for rich husbands, Marilyn Monroe, Betty Grable, and Lauren Bacall chat with wealthy William Powell. Over the years, Hollywood reworked the gold-digger theme many times.*

almost invariably appeared to be dull-witted to the point of stupidity, mere sex objects ripe for teasing and humiliation. While Grable never elicited laughter at her own expense, Monroe and Mansfield openly invited leers and mockery. Mansfield's two Fox films of the fifties are cases in point. Laced with off-color jokes and sexual innuendos, *The Girl Can't Help It* (1956) and *Will Success Spoil Rock Hunter?* (1957) both benefited from the cartoonlike comic energy director Frank Tashlin brought to his best films. Yet it is difficult to dismiss the overall tone of ogling vulgarity.

Another fifties comedy that aimed its arrows at various targets had its origins in a hugely popular novel. Patrick Dennis's book *Auntie Mame* purported to be the author's reminiscences of his rowdy, outrageous, and loving aunt, who had raised him. Adapted to the stage with Rosalind Russell as the star, the story found its way to the screen in 1958. Not unexpectedly, it was a popular success: a diverting if sprawling entertainment that gave Rosalind Russell one of her best roles.

Under Morton Da Costa's unsubtle direction—he also directed it for the stage—the Betty Comden–Adolph Green screenplay for *Auntie Mame* took the irrepressible Mame through a series of episodes as she tries to raise her orphaned nephew, Patrick (Jan Handzlik as a youngster, then Roger Smith as the grown-up Patrick) with love and a free spirit. Various characters enter her hectic life, including her catty actress friend Vera Charles (Coral Browne); a dowdy secretary, Agnes Gooch (Peggy Cass), with a few surprises up her sleeve; and Mr. Babcock (Fred Clark), a peevish lawyer who disapproves of Mame's antics. Mame dominates them all, and as her fortunes rise and fall over the years, she teaches Patrick some basic lessons about tolerance, bigotry, individuality, and life itself. More of a series of blackout sketches than a coherent story, *Auntie Mame* uses sledgehammer strokes to get its effects. Yet despite its lack of finesse and the obviousness of its satirical targets, the movie does succeed in earning some laughs. And Rosalind Russell makes Mame an enchanting woman by investing her eccentricities with warmth and generosity.

Occasionally, a fifties comedy appeared that, while clearly satirical in intent, defied classification or pigeon-holing. One such comedy was John Huston's undeniably eccentric film *Beat the Devil* (1954), which baffled or irritated most moviegoers and more than a few of its participants. Still, it established itself as a cult film soon after its release. A sly parody of the sort of den-of-thieves melodrama represented by *The Maltese Falcon,* the movie boasted impressive credits: a notable director in John Huston, a screenplay written by Huston and Truman Capote, with rumored contributions by others, and a sterling cast headed by Humphrey Bogart, Jennifer Jones, Gina Lollobrigida, Robert Morley, and Peter Lorre. Yet from all reports, the project seems to have gone fatally awry. Apparently, the screenplay was patched together each day, with nobody sure of what was happening or whether the tone should be comic or melodramatic. The film was completed in disarray, with dissatisfaction or dismay on all sides.

The result, for all to see, was a most peculiar, yet frequently funny movie, a shaggy-dog tale that amuses one moment with patches of off-the-wall dialogue, then bewilders with scenes of disconcerting flatness. The group of international rogues that assembles on the coast of Italy, headed for a crooked deal to buy uranium-rich land in Africa, is made up of Billy Dannreuther (Humphrey Bogart), a kind of free-lance consultant on bribery; Petersen (Robert Morley), a falsely jovial fat man not unlike Sydney Greenstreet; a blond-haired German (Peter Lorre), inexplicably named O'Hara; and several other disreputable types. Also present is Dannreuther's beautiful Italian wife, Maria (Gina Lollobrigida). The fortunes of this motley crew are altered drastically when they meet an ersatz British aristocrat (Edward Underdown) and his blond wife, Gwendolen (Jennifer Jones), who happens to be a

pathological liar. Before the ironic ending, marital partners are exchanged, the group finds itself caught in the middle of an Arab uprising, and, after finally arriving in Africa, Petersen and his cohorts are arrested when they are incriminated by Gwendolen. A sort of aberration in fifties comedy, *Beat the Devil* is not very good—among other things, it suffers from a patently miscast Bogart and Jones—but viewed in the right frame of mind, its unexpected twists of plot and quirky dialogue can be disarming.

Amid the many satirical comedies of the fifties, there were a number of films that poked fun at America's military establishment. With the war beginning to recede in memory, filmmakers found it more acceptable to recall the lighter side of military service, the comic mishaps and predicaments that occur whenever civilians are turned arbitrarily into members of the armed forces. There had been military comedies during the war years—films such as *Caught in the Draft* (1941) and *See Here, Private Hargrove* (1944)—but many more were turned out in the fifties, most of them cheerfully light-headed and enjoyable in their depiction of a bumbling hero at odds with military regulations.

Inevitably, the ever-popular U.S. Army provided many opportunities for humor in such service comedies as *Up Front* (1951), *Off Limits* (1953), and *No Time for Sergeants* (1958). The funniest of these comedies was *Operation Mad Ball* (1957), which succeeded in turning a slim premise into hilarious farce. In the kind of rowdy, take-charge role at which he excelled, Jack Lemmon played Private Hogan, chief arranger and organizer at an army hospital in Normandy at the close of World War II. His nemesis is Captain Lock, portrayed with manic malevolence by comedian Ernie Kovacs. Hogan's goal is to defy the obnoxious Lock by planning "the maddest mad ball in the history of the United States Army" at a nearby inn. Before this formidable goal is realized, Hogan and his cohorts undergo all sorts of slapstick adventures, staged at a galloping pace by director Richard Quine.

More than one service comedy in the fifties honored America's long-standing defiance of bullying authority by pitting a modest but assured military man against his obnoxious and overbearing superior. Perhaps the best example of this, and one of the best military comedies of the period, was the 1955 adaptation of the long-running Broadway play *Mister Roberts,* which, in turn, had been derived by Joshua Logan and Thomas Heggen from Heggen's novel. Here, to balance the familiar antics of a ship's crew, facing long inactivity and a truculent captain (James Cagney) at the height of World War II, the screenplay offered several reflective and even touching interludes. Starring in his first film in six years, Henry Fonda repeated his memorable stage role as Lieutenant (jg) Doug Roberts, a thoughtful, well-loved officer aboard the unwieldy cargo ship *Reluctant,* who defies the captain while yearning to join the fighting.

Directed by Mervyn LeRoy after John Ford resigned due to illness, *Mister Roberts* captures the frustration and desperate high jinks of the ship's crew as they sail "between the islands of Tedium and Apathy, with side trips to Monotony." These antics make up the bulk of the film: The crew's riotous return from its first liberty ashore in months; the sailors' discovery, through binoculars, of the nurses on the nearby island; and the destruction of the ship's laundry, engineered by the lecherous, irrepressible Ensign Pulver (Jack Lemmon in an engaging Oscar-winning performance). Overshadowing all the good-natured buffoonery, however, is the quiet figure of Mister Roberts, sensitive to the needs of the men while suppressing his own.

A mid all the cozy, lightweight domestic comedies and broad satirical farces that turned up in the fifties, leaving no indelible impression, there was one film that succeeded in closing out the decade with a singular triumph. Throughout the years, Billy Wilder had offered his unique mix of vinegar and champagne: vinegar in such sardonic, trenchant views of humanity as *Sunset Boulevard* (1950) and *Ace in the Hole* (also known as *The Big Carnival,* 1951); champagne in the sparkling romance of *Sabrina* (1954) and *Love in the Afternoon* (1957). And then Wilder, in a burst of inspiration, directed a film that proved to be not only his funniest comedy but also one of the durable treasures of sound comedy. For no particular reason, it was called *Some Like It Hot* (1959).

Cowritten by Wilder and I. A. L. Diamond (their first collaboration after *Love in the Afternoon),* *Some Like It Hot* is an uproarious mix of slapstick, satire, and romance, a one-of-a-kind comedy that wickedly mixes some decidedly noncomic elements into its heady brew. Set in Hollywood's perennial view of the Roaring Twenties—a world of gangsters and molls where sudden death is as common as jazz and illegal booze—the story revolves around Joe (Tony Curtis) and Jerry (Jack Lemmon), down-in-the-mouth musicians who are inadvertent witnesses to the St. Valentine's Day Massacre in a Chicago garage. Terrified, they flee to Florida as members of an all-girl band, calling themselves "Josephine" and "Daphne." To eventually seduce the band's well-endowed singer Sugar Kane (Marilyn Monroe), Joe masquerades as an impotent millionaire, while Jerry is courted by a near-imbecilic *true* millionaire named Osgood Fielding III (Joe E. Brown). Comic chaos breaks

SL(331-10) 88

Some Like It Hot *(United Artists, 1959). Millionaire Osgood Fielding III (Joe E. Brown) insists on marrying "Daphne" (Jack Lemmon), despite every obstacle. When "Daphne" reveals his true sex, Osgood's response is one of the great classic lines.*

loose when the Chicago mob, headed by "Spats" Columbo (George Raft), turns up at the hotel where the band is working. In the end, Joe wins Sugar in his own person, and Jerry is still trying to cope with an amorous Osgood, who insists on marrying "Daphne."

Caught up in the film's virtually nonstop fun, a viewer can hardly be blamed for failing to notice that the screenplay actually touches on some serious matters, including transvestism, impotence, alcoholism, and gangland murder. Yet the material is so cleverly wrought, and Wilder's direction is so astute, that one is swept up by the hilarity. Sugar Kane may be, in essence, a sad, vulnerable, badly abused alcoholic, but when the voluptuous Sugar wiggles into an upper berth with the agonized Jerry in drag, or tries amorously to awaken the sleeping libido of her "impotent millionaire," we respond with laughter. Joe may be a bully with Jerry—he treats him much like Bing Crosby treats Bob Hope in the *Road* movies—and he may behave treacherously with Sugar, but when he pulls off his earrings at the very last moment before his rendezvous with Sugar, or rises fully clothed from a bubble bath to vent his rage at Jerry, we forgive his selfish ways and join in the fun.

Apart from any unsavory elements, *Some Like It Hot* is replete with memorable moments: our first glimpse of "Josephine" and "Daphne" at the train station, gamely trying to cope with high heels ("How do they walk on these things? How do they keep their balance?"); Jerry going from elation to ticklish hysteria as Sweet Sue's girls crowd into his berth; or the band's arrival at the Florida hotel, as a porchful of lecherous old millionaires rock in unison. The sequence on Osgood's yacht, in which Joe professes impotence as a challenge to Sugar, is one of the film's funniest. Warming to the occasion, Joe tries to impress gullible Sugar with his status as a world-class sportsman. Water polo is dangerous—"I had two ponies drown under me," he admits solemnly.

The film's cast could not be bettered. As Joe, Tony Curtis discloses a flair for comedy that had seldom been evident before, and Marilyn Monroe gives Sugar a touch of melancholy that tempers her flaunted sexuality. (She always gets "the fuzzy end of the lollipop.") Joe E. Brown's dim-bulb millionaire is a brilliant creation; his tango with "Daphne"—their solemn twirling alone on the ballroom floor—is an inspired send-up of that dance. Yet Jack Lemmon towers above them all in a performance that is surely one of the imperishable joys of film comedy. The heartiest laughs belong to him: his stunned first view of Sugar ("like Jell-O on springs"); his reaction to recognizing Joe in his millionaire garb (one foot poised in the air, he freezes on the spot with his back to the camera); or his gleeful euphoria after a night on the town with Osgood. Lemmon's performance is such a remarkable achievement that it seems almost a shame that the famous last line of the film ("Well, nobody's perfect.") falls to Osgood rather than Jerry–"Daphne."

The fifties had not been a banner year for comedy. Yet *Some Like It Hot* ended the film decade with a glorious demonstration of comic skill—and a roaring good time for everyone. More than three decades after its release, viewers are still enjoying the rowdy adventures of "Josephine" and "Daphne" down among the sheltering palms.

Part 4

A TURNING POINT
Movie Comedy in the Sixties

A decade of achievements in space and of rebellion and alienation amid a controversial war in Vietnam . . .

In the sixties, man reaches for the stars and comes close to the age-old dream of conquering space. In 1961, Navy Commander Alan B. Shepard, Jr., becomes America's first man in space, and in the following year, John H. Glenn, Jr., is the first American to make an orbital flight, whirling three times around the Earth before splashing down. Four years later, astronaut Edward White II becomes the first American to walk in space. By the end of the decade, astronauts Neil Armstrong and Buzz Aldrin take "one giant leap for mankind" by landing on the moon.

Yet this decade of achievement is badly scarred by the Vietnam War and upheavals at home. In May of 1961, President Kennedy orders four hundred Special Forces soldiers and one hundred military advisers to South Vietnam. By the mid-sixties, while the war in Vietnam rages, waves of antiwar protests sweep the country. As the war deepens, the massive opposition increases. In 1969, as President Nixon launches his plan of "Vietnamization," the largest antiwar demonstration in Washington's history draws an estimated 250,000 people.

The sixties are also a time of traumatic events that shake the country. In 1963, President John F. Kennedy is assassinated in Dallas, and five years later his brother, Senator Robert Kennedy, is also killed, as is the Reverend Martin Luther King. During the decade, King has been the spearhead for racial change and upheaval, making his famous "I have a dream" speech in 1963.

The sixties also enjoy their share of cultural phenomena: Chubby Checker and the twist . . . the invasion of America by England's Beatles . . . the proliferation of hippies and flower children . . . Woodstock, where 400,000 people gather to attend a concert. Across America, people line up to see such movies as *Psycho, West Side Story, Bonnie and Clyde,* and *The Graduate.*

Dr. Strangelove or: How I Learned to Stop Worrying and Love the Bomb *(Columbia, 1964). German scientist Dr. Strangelove (Peter Sellers) tries to keep his arm from rendering the Nazi salute automatically. Sellers played two other characters in this blistering apocalyptic comedy.*

Chapter 15

All Kinds of Love

Romantic Comedy in the Sixties

With the arrival of the sixties, the sense of change and upheaval that would reach fruition in the later years of the decade had already begun to take hold. In the movies, it resulted in the growing feeling that frankness and even boldness in the choice of subject matter would be tolerated by the moviegoing public, and that a more audacious attitude toward matters usually handled discreetly would not necessarily violate the powerful Production Code of the Motion Picture Association of America. In 1968, the Production Code was replaced by a self-regulatory system involving ratings. Two years earlier, the Catholic Church's Legion of Decency had changed its name to the National Catholic Office for Motion Pictures, taking a more progressive attitude than it had in the past. All this signaled to the filmmakers that it was now possible to be more straightforward and even more salaciously explicit about depicting sexual matters on the screen.

Not that the familiar themes of the more constricted fifties had faded away entirely. There were still a number of movies that concerned romance between mature people, or May-November love affairs that ended in either nuptial bliss or separation. Now pushing sixty, Clark Gable starred in Melville Shavelson's *It Started in Naples* (1960) as a gruff, disenchanted bank manager who returns to Italy fifteen years after the war's end to claim his brother's child, and, instead, finds romance with the boy's fiery and beauteous aunt, Sophia Loren. A mature Ingrid Bergman also dabbled in a romance involving disparate ages in Anatole Litvak's bittersweet 1961 release, *Goodbye Again*. In this film adaptation of Françoise Sagan's novel *Aimez-vous Brahms?*, she played a prosperous, middle-aged, Parisian interior decorator who, against her better judgment, begins an affair with a young American, Anthony Perkins. The actress would have to wait until the end of the decade to find romance with a more appropriate partner (Walter Matthau) in the

The Apartment *(United Artists, 1960). Rising executive "Bud" Baxter (Jack Lemmon) shows an interest in elevator operator Fran Kubelik (Shirley MacLaine). Billy Wilder's acidulous comedy won a Best Picture Oscar.*

1969 adaptation of the Broadway comedy *Cactus Flower*. In this instance, she won him away from a younger competitor, played by Goldie Hawn in her first major role.

For all this discreet romancing between older or ill-matched couples, it was evident, early on in the decade, that the keynote to romantic comedy would lie in its more explicit approach to sexual matters. The sixties even began with a major comedy that touched on a topic that only had been hinted at coyly in other years: the sexual games played by married executives in the everyday business world. In *The Apartment* (1960), Billy Wilder, whose fifties comedies had been influenced by the romantic aura surrounding Audrey Hepburn, returned to his more sardonic and satirical style. In keeping with the changing tenor of the times, here was a film in which the central character is a kind of casual pimp for his business colleagues and the heroine is a suicidally inclined girl desperately in love with an unmitigated heel. Around these less than savory characters, Wilder, who directed and coauthored the screenplay with I. A. L. Diamond, managed to fashion a sharp-witted romantic comedy.

Jack Lemmon starred as C. C. ("Bud") Baxter, an ambitious office worker who, on the promise of advancement, agrees to lend his bachelor apartment to higher-ranking colleagues for sexual assignations. Bud is in love with elevator operator Fran Kubelik (Shirley MacLaine), who turns out to be the discarded mistress of Jeff Sheldrake (Fred MacMurray), a womanizing married executive in the company. In the end, Bud regains his integrity and pride and also wins Fran's admiration and love.

Despite the high degree of polish and observant wit in the screenplay, and the praise it received at the time of its release (it also won the Oscar as the year's best film), *The Apartment* leaves an unpleasant residue. Until he changes his ways, Bud Baxter is not a particularly attractive character—in fact, he seems spineless and opportunistic, groveling before his cheating superiors to get ahead. Although an engaging comic actor, with a dithering, flustered style of his own, Jack Lemmon cannot make his character entirely palatable. Shirley MacLaine is on firmer ground—her trademarked combination of perkiness and vulnerability helps to make her Fran Kubelik reasonably sympathetic. Their scenes together are the best in the film: memorable encounters between a lonely man and a wounded girl. After her attempted suicide, their relationship deepens; she learns about his own vulnerability and despair, while his love for her grows stronger. The sight of Jack Lemmon beaming happily as he strains their spaghetti with a tennis racket is one of the pleasurable images of the period. *The Apartment* has many conspicuous virtues, yet this time Billy Wilder's essentially sardonic view of life overwhelms the comedy.

Shirley MacLaine's rounded portrait of the lovelorn heroine in *The Apartment* made her an ideal candidate to portray women who were neither virginal nor promiscuous but merely spirited and amiably eccentric. Her characters always appeared ready to speak their minds and express their feelings, and in the next few years, her roles in such films as *All in a Night's Work* (1961) and *Two for the Seesaw* (1962) reflected the more open attitude toward sexual matters that was beginning to emerge in the sixties. By the time of Billy Wilder's *Irma La Douce* (1963), she was able to come full circle from the melancholy Fran Kubelik of *The Apartment* to the life-embracing Parisian streetwalker of the title. In adapting the French play by Alexandre Breffort that had become a hit Broadway musical, Wilder and his collaborator I. A. L. Diamond managed to retain much of the saucy humor without offending the censors. (They also excised all of the songs.)

In the early sixties, romantic comedies continued to replace a smile with a leer, giving some performers a chance at appropriate new roles. An actor such as Dean Martin, released from his partnership with Jerry Lewis since the mid-fifties, seemed an apt choice to star in the burgeoning number of sex comedies. A competent light comedian, Martin suggested sexual danger or at least sexual mischief with his off-hand style, hooded eyes, and lecherous smile. Such films as Daniel Mann's *Who's Been Sleeping In My Bed?* (1963) and Billy Wilder's *Kiss Me, Stupid* (1964) never missed the opportunity to place him in risqué situations, surrounded by compliant women. The humor, however, was usually more depressing than titillating.

Throughout the sixties, comedy after comedy offered a rather unflattering vision of an America seemingly populated with panting, overheated bachelors and cheating, sexually unfulfilled husbands in relentless pursuit of the next conquest. In some cases, the pursuit seemed to occupy most of their waking hours. In Michael Gordon's *Boys' Night Out* (1962), bachelor James Garner convinces his married friends to buy a cooperative apartment so that they can secretly share the favors of buxom blonde Kim Novak. It turns out that the joke is on them: Novak is actually a sociology student doing research for a doctoral thesis entitled "Adolescent Sexual Fantasies in Adult Suburban Males." Bud Yorkin's *Come Blow Your Horn* (1963), adapted from Neil Simon's first Broadway success, also became a springboard for a bachelor's fantasies. Frank Sinatra starred as an insatiable girl-chaser who introduces younger brother Tony Bill to the myriad pleasures, mostly sexual, of the high life in New York City. Leaning too heavily on the fragile structure of the play, Yorkin caused it to collapse under the weight of a barrage of lame gags.

With the possible exception of Dean Martin, no actor in the sixties seemed to work as assiduously at pursuing and seducing women as Tony Curtis. Ironically, after demonstrating his ability to inhabit rather than walk through a role in such late fifties films as *Sweet Smell of Success* (1957), *The Defiant Ones* (1958), and, of course, *Some Like It Hot,* Curtis saw fit to spend much of his time during the decade playing swinging bachelors in light-headed farces. For years, he appeared to be mired in the prevailing "aren't we being wicked" approach of many sixties filmmakers, leering his way through such meretricious films as *Goodbye Charlie* (1964), *Boeing Boeing* (1965), and *Not with My Wife You Don't!* (1966).

Curtis also found his way into one of the more aggressively suggestive comedies of the period, *Sex and the Single Girl* (1964). Using only the title of Helen Gurley Brown's best-selling book, the movie cast him as a scandal-magazine writer who blasts the widely read tome of a demure research psychologist (Natalie Wood)—can you guess its title?—then proceeds to stalk her amorously, hoping to wear down her maidenly reserve. On the sidelines are Henry Fonda and Lauren Bacall as Curtis's battling neighbors. Some of the dialogue contributed by novelist Joseph Heller and David R. Schwartz has satirical bite—among the inevitable targets are sex, marriage, money, and advertising—and director Richard Quine keeps the cast spinning, but too often the strain to be devilishly wicked is all too evident.

Natalie Wood's role as the seemingly knowing, book-smart girl who is really a lamb at large in the sexual jungle was typical of many of the heroines of the period, all of whom seem to be embodied by the increasingly popular Doris Day. However, there were other heroines of sixties romantic comedy who were ready and even eager to enjoy sexual adventures in the new permissive climate. Jane Fonda, who had made her film debut as a sweet young coed in *Tall Story* in 1960, quickly heated up her image in such movies as *Walk on the Wild Side* (1962) and *The Chapman Report* (1962). By the time she came to Peter Tewksbury's

Sunday in New York (1963), adapted from Norman Krasna's Broadway play, she could play with ease the romantically naïve heroine who is willing to have her virtue tested by an amorous fellow (Rod Taylor) on a rainy afternoon in New York. In *Any Wednesday* (1966), based on Muriel Resnik's play, she was the mistress of a married executive (Jason Robards, Jr.) who must cope with her lover's efferves-

Breakfast at Tiffany's *(Paramount, 1961). In the film's last moment, Paul Varjac (George Peppard) and Holly Golightly (Audrey Hepburn) embrace in the rain. Hepburn was enchanting as the amoral "wild thing" living a quicksilver existence in New York City.*

Lover Come Back
(Universal, 1962).
Doris Day cheers on
her horse as Rock
Hudson watches her
admiringly. Doris is
being duped—Rock is
a rival advertising
executive posing as a
shy inventor. Guess
how it all ends.

cent wife (Rosemary Murphy) and a new—and more appropriate—suitor (Dean Jones).

Perhaps the most telling commentary on the "bolder" new approach to romantic comedy in the sixties came with the casting of Audrey Hepburn as Holly Golightly, the amoral, madcap, but inwardly vulnerable party girl of Blake Edwards's *Breakfast at Tiffany's* (1961). In her first years on the screen, Hepburn had portrayed dewy-eyed damsels whose innocence enchants and ultimately wins over such mature men as Humphrey Bogart and Gary Cooper. But in *Breakfast at Tiffany's*, she played a farm girl who has deliberately given herself over to the hedonism of the day, brazenly welcoming the attentions of men who can meet her price. Of course in the end, the decency and sweetness of the earlier Audrey shines through—she is revealed as an innocent at heart, who mourns her dead brother, adores her cat, and loves the young writer (George Peppard) who finds her both exasperating and entrancing.

By now, the attitude and even the decor of *Breakfast at Tiffany's* have dated badly, but George Axelrod's screenplay, a softened, less unsavory version of Truman Capote's novella, still contains its funny, poignant, and authentically romantic moments. Holly's wild party in her brownstone apartment, peopled with bizarre types; her brief encounter with her gentle Texas husband (Buddy Ebsen), who knows her as Lulamae Barnes; and her romantic excursions with the writer through city streets that seldom looked more inviting—these sequences override the film's flaws. Hepburn herself leaves the most indelible impression—one recalls with pleasure the enchanting vision of Holly seated at a window as she sings the Oscar-winning "Moon River," by Johnny Mercer and Henry Mancini, or as she races through a downpour in the film's final scene, anxiously searching for her cat, and then rushing to embrace George Peppard.

In sixties romantic comedy, not every heroine was avidly seeking sexual encounters, or living the hedonistic existence of a Holly Golightly. Doris Day, who had closed out the previous decade trying to avoid being bedded down by Rock Hudson in *Pillow Talk*, continued her virginal battle into the sixties. In fact, in light of the changing mores, her primness and her indignation when the hero turned amorous became something of a running joke appropriated by comedians. Time and again, she would react to being placed in a compromising position by crossing her eyes and emitting a squeal of maidenly fury.

Apart from her ironclad virginity, however, Doris Day was, in fact, a somewhat underrated comic actress. Within her limited range, she could express a

refreshing candor and a pert, unforced charm. Given a superior screenplay, as in *Lover Come Back* (1962), she could demonstrate the reasons for her enormous popularity. Here, under Delbert Mann's direction, she played Carol Templeton, a hardworking executive for an advertising agency, who shares a party line with Jerry Webster (Rock Hudson), a rival, none too ethical advertising man and insatiable womanizer. Angered by Carol's bringing him up on charges before the Advertising Council, Jerry seeks revenge by inventing a nonexistent product called "Vip," and challenging Carol to get the account. When his scheme backfires, he is forced to impersonate the inventor of "Vip," characterizing him as a woman-shy introvert who would like an unsuspecting Carol to launch his sexual initiation. By the time Carol learns the truth and plots her retaliation, the two are genuinely in love. Apart from some easy swipes at the advertising game, the Stanley Shapiro–Paul Henning screenplay has a brightness that may not qualify as wit but that comes reasonably close.

Day's virginity came under siege again in her next film, *That Touch of Mink* (1962), but this time, the result was less amusing. Again under Delbert Mann's direction, she played Cathy Timberlake, a jobless computer operator who is swept off her feet by wealthy business tycoon Philip Shayne (Cary Grant). Against her better judgment, she agrees to accompany him on a trip to Bermuda. Her nervous state, however, causes her to break out in a rash, and she does no better by fortifying herself with liquor. Finally admitting that she wants nothing less than marriage, she decides to make Philip jealous by going off to Asbury Park, on the New Jersey seashore, with a clerk (John Astin) who has been pursuing her. Philip rescues her from this unsavory character, and on their wedding night, *he* breaks out in a rash. This time around, despite the best efforts of the stars, the ingredients fail to jell, and little of the agreeable humor of *Pillow Talk* or *Lover Come Back* can be found in the Stanley Shapiro–Nate Monaster screenplay.

In America, the sexual revolution was getting under way. On screen, while rebels were starting to challenge the old-fashioned concepts about love, sex, and marriage, Doris Day was holding back. As we are about to see, even in the emerging battlefield of married life, Doris still opted for the peace of home and hearth. It is hardly surprising that she was the most popular film star of her time.

That Touch of Mink *(Universal, 1962). Once again, Doris Day appears to be in a compromising position, this time with Cary Grant. Never fear—as usual, there was less than meets the eye, and Doris's honor remained secure.*

Chapter 16

Across the Parlor and into the Bedroom

Marital and Domestic Comedy in the Sixties

aving finally surrendered to Rock Hudson and Cary Grant, respectively, in her early sixties comedies, Doris Day turned to marriage and domesticity. At the start of the decade, she already had tasted the fruits (some sweet, some sour) of husband and children in Charles Walters's *Please Don't Eat the Daisies* (1960), loosely based on Jean Kerr's book about life with her drama critic husband, Walter Kerr, and their many children. In this instance, however, domesticity seemed to be something of a waking nightmare, replete with rambunctious children, an English sheepdog, and assorted daffy visitors. Confronted with one family dilemma after another, mother (Day) and father (David Niven) spend most of the film's running time in an overwrought state. Not for the first or last time, incessant shouting and frantic activity were mistaken for the ingredients of farce.

Several years later, Doris Day coped much more successfully with marriage and parenthood in one of her best sixties comedies, *The Thrill of It All* (1963). Here, in a deftly amusing screenplay by Carl Reiner (from a story by Reiner and Larry Gelbart), she was able to display her talent for light comedy as Beverly Boyer, wife of a successful obstetrician (James Garner) and mother of two. The story hinged on Beverly's sudden rise to national popularity as television spokeswoman for Happy Soap, and the devastating impact of her fame on her life and family.

The movie's targets were not exactly fresh: The inanity of television commercials and the monotonous sameness of much television drama had been spoofed

many times in the fifties. Yet, under Norman Jewison's skillful direction, the material seemed inventive and funny, and for once even the farcical interludes drew laughs rather than winces. Clever sight gags abound, with several of the best involving the Boyers' brand-new backyard pool: Unaware that the pool has been built in a day, Dr. Boyer drives his car into the water and sinks, with a bemused expression on his face; another time, in a fit of pique, he kicks boxes of Happy Soap detergent into the pool, creating mountains of suds that become a playground for the sanitation workers. (Like happy children, they dance and frolic with the bubbles.)

Costarred again later that year in another marital comedy, *Move Over, Darling* (1963), Doris Day and James Garner were unable to duplicate the buoyant humor of *The Thrill of It All.* Nor was there much fun to be had in Day's next comedy, *Send Me No Flowers* (1964), derived from the Broadway play. Reunited for the occasion with Rock Hudson, she was obliged to play the patient, long-suffering wife of a hypochondriac who feels continually threatened with serious illness. When he overhears the wrong diagnosis by his doctor, he assumes he is fatally ill, and, to his wife's bewilderment, goes about finding her a new husband. On this single joke, the movie builds a series of gags and slapstick situations, most of them hardly worth a chuckle despite the energetic playing of the cast and Norman Jewison's strenuous direction.

While wifely Doris Day was busily confronting her marital dilemmas, she seemed scarcely to notice that the rumblings of a sexual revolution could be heard all around her. In the same vein as the romantic comedies of the period, the marital comedies were also taking on a somewhat more candid approach to the sexual proclivities of husbands and wives. Of course everything turned out well in the end—this was, after all, a movie dream world—but along the way to the end of the decade, a new, leering emphasis revealed many straying husbands and cheating wives who were actively enjoying their infidelity.

Not that there was always fun to be had in extramarital activities. Bob Hope, who had spent the previous two decades playing the quipping lecher to a bevy of Paramount ladies, found infidelity a rocky road when he attempted to travel it with Lucille Ball in Melvin Frank's 1960 comedy, *The Facts of Life.* A marked improvement over most of his fifties films, the movie cast him against type as a somewhat paunchy, happily married suburbanite who enters into an unexpected affair with his neighbor's wife (Ball) and lives to regret it. The humor in the Norman Panama–Melvin Frank screenplay came from the couple's discovery that the logistics of extramarital romance can get comically—and even poignantly—complicated. Their blundering attempts at secret assignations, and the mishaps they endure when they set out on the "honeymoon" they never enjoyed with their spouses, had the ring of truth rather than the dull thud of gags manufactured by a team of writers.

Even the pretense of infidelity could provide the basis for a sixties marital comedy. David Swift's *Good Neighbor Sam* (1964) drew some laughs from the predicament of Jack Lemmon as Sam Bissel, a married advertising executive, comfortably ensconced in suburbia, whose life turns into chaos. When his beautiful next-door neighbor (Romy Schneider) must pretend to have a husband to inherit a huge legacy, Sam volunteers for the role. At the job, to remain in the good graces of his boss (Edward G. Robinson, of all people), he must demonstrate that he leads a moral life. Inevitably, home and work collide in all sorts of farcical ways. With Jack Lemmon leading the way in his manic, frazzled style, *Good Neighbor Sam* was lighthearted fun.

Given all these hapless husbands and wives who only appear to be working at extramarital activity, one would think that sixties comedy was not quite as bold and "liberated" as it claimed. Yet in the closing years of the decade, it was clear that the broad wink and lecherous smile were becoming characteristic of the movie husband. Curiously, the dominant figure was not a sleekly handsome Lothario but a rumpled, gangly, and homely actor with over a decade of film credits in both comic and villainous roles. Part of the joke, one assumes, lay in the wildly unromantic appearance of Walter Matthau.

Until Billy Wilder's *The Fortune Cookie* in 1966, Matthau could be found in substantial supporting roles in such films as *Charade* (1963), *Fail Safe* (1964), and *Mirage* (1965). *The Fortune Cookie* brought him stardom and an Academy Award—as Jack Lemmon's conniving brother-in-law Willie Gingrich, who lures him into an elaborate insurance swindle, Matthau was the ideal embodiment of the film's derisive view of humanity. His broadly drawn, wickedly funny Willie was only the principal figure in the gallery of vipers created by Wilder and his frequent coscenarist, I. A. L. Diamond.

Drawn into the marital wars of the late sixties, Matthau was first cast as a husband obsessed with the tempting possibilities of infidelity in Gene Kelly's *A Guide for the Married Man* (1967). In the film's central conceit, Matthau's desire to cheat on wife Inger Stevens leads him to his best friend, Robert Morse, who is not only willing but eager to instruct him in the ways that he himself has found successful. The instruction takes the form of a series of ribald and sometimes funny

A Guide for the Married Man *(Fox, 1967). Robert Morse continues his instruction to Walter Matthau on the techniques of infidelity. The film was typical of the leering, "aren't-we-devils" comedies of the sixties.*

sketches in which guest stars Lucille Ball, Jack Benny, Sid Caesar, and others appear to demonstrate Morse's theories. In its view of married men as secretly lusting, overgrown boys, *A Guide for the Married Man* was typical of the period, and a forerunner of the tone and attitude many marital comedies would take in the next decade. Amusingly, Matthau switched gears for *The Secret Life of an American Wife* (1968). Here, rather than being the husband entangled in the pitfalls of infidelity, he appeared as a nameless movie star who becomes the object of lustful attention by a fantasy-minded surburban housewife (Anne Jackson).

When husbands and wives of sixties marital comedies were not busily straying from home and hearth, they were often engaged in finding reasons to break up altogether. Whereas couples in earlier decades had separated on the basis of a single and often erroneously presumed indiscretion (a harmless kiss, a chance meeting), the more embattled couples of the sixties found deep-seated reasons for dissension. Particularly in the late sixties, and again reaching into the years beyond, there was a sense of malaise in the marital orbit that gave a darker, more sardonic cast to the comedies of the period. The more realistic view that husbands and wives could draw blood in the marital wars was becoming evident in such films as *Divorce, American Style* and *Two for the Road*.

From its opening moments of satirical fantasy, Bud Yorkin's *Divorce, American Style* (1967) proved to be a sly commentary on the comical—and not so comical—consequences of divorce. A middle-aged man, carrying an attaché case, walks to a hillside, dons the judicial robe he removes from the case, and begins to conduct the chorus of fury and vituperation emerging from the married couples in the houses below. We move into the well-appointed home of Richard and Barbara Harmon (Dick Van Dyke and Debbie Reynolds), where, in a cleverly staged pantomime scene, the couple reveals the anger and frustration that will lead them to divorce.

Until it runs aground with a frenetic climax in a nightclub, *Divorce, American Style* manages to carry off scenes that poke fun at some of the rituals of separation and divorce. The Harmons' encounter with a pompous psychologist (Martin Gabel)

Divorce, American Style *(Columbia, 1967). Richard and Barbara Harmon (Dick Van Dyke and Debbie Reynolds), on the road to Splitsville. The movie offered some amusing comments on the ramifications of divorce.*

provokes more hostility than enlightenment, while a meeting with their lawyers strips Richard of virtually everything he owns. (The lawyers, however, express their mutual admiration for each other.) In one of the film's funniest scenes, the confusion that can come with extended families is nicely spoofed when the children of various broken marriages are assembled in a single place. The delirium of trying to match children with parents and stepparents has seldom been captured as accurately, or as comically.

The trials and tribulations of a rocky marriage were also exposed in Stanley Donen's offbeat and sophisticated comedy *Two for the Road* (1967). Using a time-splintered framework in which events were not seen in chronological order but were shifted and rearranged arbitrarily, the movie concerned the sometimes happy, often troubled twelve-year marriage of Joanna and Mark (Audrey Hepburn and Albert Finney). As Joanna travels to be with her wealthy and arrogant husband, she recalls the events of their married life, but not in sequence. The flashbacks move from a tour of France with their young daughter to their honeymoon, then on to another trip, when they were forced to endure an insufferable family. All the while, as the viewer is transported from one time period to another, and from one lush European backdrop to another, Joanna and Mark quarrel bitterly and make up romantically to a Henry Mancini score. Behind the humor, Frederic Raphael's screenplay is clearly intended as a serious dissection of modern marriage, with all its scratchy, exasperating, and loving ramifications.

One film that commented obliquely on the pitfalls of marriage was Gene Saks's adaptation of Neil Simon's long-running play *The Odd Couple* (1968). It was not a marital comedy by any stretch of the imagination, and yet in a curious sense, it was intended to be just that: a rumination on what takes place when two divorced men of radically different temperaments are obliged to share an apartment, as if they *were* married. The result is abundantly clear: The same hang-ups, biases, and eccentricities that drove them away from their respective mates are still present in full force.

Replacing the stage's Art Carney as the fussy, hypochondriacal Felix Unger, Jack Lemmon gives a performance that edges too much in the direction of realism, making Felix rather more intolerable than comic. His despair over losing his wife seems uncomfortably genuine, without the touch of comic exaggeration that made Art Carney's stage interpretation so funny. Other elements of the original stage production of *The Odd Couple* are happily in place, and under Gene Saks's assured direction, Walter Matthau duplicates his memorable incarnation of Felix's

Two for the Road *(Fox, 1967). Using a framework in which events moved back and forth in time, this film revealed the many sides of the troubled marriage of Audrey Hepburn and Albert Finney, seen here on one of their many trips together.*

easygoing slob of a roommate, Oscar Madison. A perhaps too faithful version of the play, the movie is, in a sense, a marital comedy without marriage.

By the end of the sixties, after a decade in which marital comedies, for the most part, took a winking attitude toward what might be called a "naughty little boy" approach to normal everyday lust, it seemed time for a film that would look inward at marriage and examine relationships, sexual and otherwise, that confronted husbands and wives. The screen appeared to be ready for a movie that would offer "a guide for the married man" as he worked his way through the pitfalls of his own marriage rather than through his extracurricular activities, one

that would investigate "the secret life of an American wife" in her very own bedroom. The movie turned out to be Paul Mazursky's directorial debut, *Bob & Carol
& Ted & Alice* (1969).

Several decades after its release, this film is heavily dated; the sharp edges of
its satire of marital encounter groups and California lifestyles have become blunted with the years. In its time, however, it created a stir and some controversy with
its view of two couples who pretend to seek sexual freedom and honesty in their
marriages and then find themselves in situations for which they had never bargained. We first meet Bob (Robert Culp), a documentary filmmaker, and his wife,
Carol (Natalie Wood) at a meeting of an encounter group at the Institute, where
they are drawn hesitantly into releasing their deepest feelings. Along with the others, they pound pillows and scream, then end up sobbing in each other's arms.
Thrilled by the experience, Bob and Carol convince their good friends Ted and
Alice (Elliott Gould and Dyan Cannon) to join them in this exciting nirvana of marital truth.

The consequences are not unexpected but quite funny. To their eventual dismay, Bob and Carol discover that honesty is not always the best policy, and that
extramarital affairs, openly conducted, are not necessarily conducive to a blissful
relationship. The rudest shocks, however, are felt by Ted and Alice, who are clearly too timid for the sexual revolution. Ted must now deal in a new and open way
with his sexual feelings and with the walking bundle of hang-ups and neuroses
called Alice, while she must learn to let down the guard she has built around herself over a lifetime. Smoking pot with their friends, they start to unravel, with Ted
losing his inhibitions and Alice mortified by Bob's blithe confession of infidelity
and by Carol's serene acceptance of it ("So beautiful!") Later, in one of the film's
funniest scenes, an aroused Ted tries to have sex with Alice, only to be confronted
by her seething anger about Bob. (It also happens that she is out of pills.)

Although Robert Culp and Natalie Wood give competent performances, most
of the humor that still resides in *Bob & Carol & Ted & Alice* stems from Elliott
Gould and, especially, Dyan Cannon. As a man whose sexual fantasies are emerging like hidden demons to plague and tantalize him, Gould is exceptionally funny,
but it is Cannon who draws the most frequent laughs. In a tour-de-force scene
with her unflappable psychiatrist, played, incidentally, by a true analyst, Donald
F. Muhich, she fairly twitches with repressions and Freudian slips. Later, however, aroused by everyone's "openness" about sex, she is willing to join with the others in a game of "switching." "We'll have an orgy!" she exclaims in the film's cli-

A poster for **After the Thin Man** (MGM, 1936), the second in the comedy-mystery series. Note that a virtual newcomer named James Stewart receives first featured billing.

This poster for **Woman of the Year** (MGM, 1942) has Hepburn saying to Tracy, "I want you to kiss me—for luck." No such line appears in the movie.

A poster for **Animal Crackers** (Paramount, 1930), with the Marx Brothers.

Louis Calhern, flanked by Chico and Harpo, in a poster for **Duck Soup** (Paramount, 1933).

A poster for **Bombshell** *(MGM, 1933). In some areas, the film was billed as* Blonde Bombshell *to prevent its confusion with a war picture.*

A poster for Laurel and Hardy's **Going Bye-Bye** *(MGM, 1934).*

The Thrill of It All
(Universal, 1963). Beverly Boyer (Doris Day) and her doctor husband (James Garner) share a romantic moment. Later, the romance will curdle when Beverly becomes a television salesperson.

Carnal Knowledge (*Avco Embassy, 1971*). *Sandy (Art Garfunkel) gazes adoringly at Susan (Candice Bergen), whom he eventually will marry. Mike Nichols's film followed the sexual proclivities of two men from youth to middle age.*

Shampoo (*Columbia, 1975*). *George Roundy (Warren Beatty), part-time hairdresser and full-time stud, does the hair of former lover Jackie (Julie Christie). This racy comedy had some oblique but pungent comments on American life in the late sixties.*

Working Girl *(Fox, 1988). Tess (Melanie Griffith) enjoys a personal and business relationship with Jack Tanner (Harrison Ford). The movie offered an engaging view of a woman who is both smart and sexy.*

Moonstruck *(MGM/UA, 1987). Cher won a well-deserved Oscar for her performance as Loretta Castorini in Norman Jewison's hugely entertaining comedy. Here, a transformed Loretta attends the opera with her fiancé's oddball brother Ronny (Nicolas Cage).*

Roxanne *(Columbia, 1987). Roxanne (Darryl Hannah) realizes that C. D. Bales (Steve Martin) has been writing all the marvelous love letters she has been receiving. Martin excelled in this modern-day version of* Cyrano de Bergerac.

Home Alone (Fox, 1990). Resourceful little Macaulay Culkin reacts to the surprising tingle of after-shave lotion in this phenomenally popular comedy.

Parenthood *(Universal, l989). Gil Buckman (Steve Martin) discovers the pleasures and perils of parenthood in Ron Howard's observant family comedy.*

The Big Chill *(Columbia, 1983). The film's brilliant ensemble cast gathers for a portrait. Seated left to right: JoBeth Williams, Tom Berenger, William Hurt, Meg Tilly, Kevin Kline, Glenn Close. Standing: Jeff Goldblum and Mary Kay Place.*

Hannah and Her Sisters *(Orion, 1986). Nurturing, sensible Hannah (Mia Farrow) converses with her ex-husband, Mickey (Woody Allen). Allen's comedy-drama viewed the lives of neurotic New Yorkers with exceptional warmth and sympathy.*

Ghostbusters *(Columbia, 1984). The cosmic crusaders against New York City's vaporous villains go into action.*

Radio Days *(Orion, 1987). A family portrait from Woody Allen's recollection of a vanished era. Left to right: Dianne Wiest, Julie Kavner, Michael Tucker, Seth Green, and Renee Lippin. Standing: William Magerman and Josh Mostel.*

The Cheap Detective *(Columbia, 1978). Detective Peter Falk poses with ladies of the cast in Neil Simon's parody of "tough detective" movies like* The Maltese Falcon.

Tootsie *(Columbia, 1982). You guessed it—behind this glamorous lady is an ambitious actor named Michael Dorsey (Dustin Hoffman), who has disguised himself as a woman to win a role on a television soap opera. Hoffman's completely persuasive performance made his "Dorothy" endearing.*

mactic scene, when the four assemble in a Las Vegas hotel room. To nobody's surprise, least of all the two couples, they are unable to go through with it. Together in a single bed, they realize the absurdity of the situation. So much for sexual freedom as a prerequisite for a happy marriage.

At the end, *Bob & Carol & Ted & Alice* reveals the conventionality that lies at the heart of its "daring." Yet here at the end of the sixties, after years in which many movies dealt with marriage (and romance and sex) as topics for locker-room stories, Paul Mazursky's film, and his screenplay with Larry Tucker, served as a beacon for the seventies and the years beyond, or at least an indication that it was possible to deal frankly and humorously with sexual relations without resorting to winks and leers.

Bob & Carol & Ted & Alice *(Columbia, 1969). This foursome of the title (left to right: Elliott Gould, Natalie Wood, Robert Culp, Dyan Cannon) are amused—rather than titillated—at ending up in bed together.*

Chapter 17

Dark Laughter

Black Comedies and Rude Farces

I f romantic and marital comedies were becoming, on the whole, somewhat bolder and more explicit in the sixties, what then of satire? Where were the films that ridiculed or savaged their targets even as they made us laugh? In the fifties, movie satire had sharpened its teeth largely on the presumed enemy, otherwise known as television. Spoofs of that period enjoyed poking fun at the often dim-witted antics of the burgeoning new medium. However, in the new climate of the sixties, especially in the later years of the decade, everything, or just about everything, was fair game. There was still room for lighthearted spoofs of movie genres—*Cat Ballou* (1965) and *Support Your Local Sheriff* (1969) took aim at the conventions of the Western—but as large segments of the population began to look at life in America, and life in general, with mockery and disdain, many films took on the current scene rather than the past, darkening their hues while increasing their irreverence and their bite.

In a surprising number of comedies, laughter seemed to be echoing from the grave. If life was no longer sacrosanct, why not poke fun at death, as well? Many films found their humor in taking an impudent attitude toward the rituals and attitudes that surrounded the specter of death. In earlier decades, in such comedies as *Arsenic and Old Lace* and *Murder, He Says*, murder had been treated merely as a farcical device. Death had usually called for a certain amount of reverence and awe, however; movies such as *Death Takes a Holiday* and *On Borrowed Time* metamorphosed the Grim Reaper into a dignified and even regal personage. In the sixties, however, death became a central metaphor to be treated without mystery or delicacy, as the world's—or God's—last joke on a ridiculous humanity.

Death, for example, dominated J. Lee Thompson's elaborate black comedy *What a Way to Go!* (1964), in which Shirley MacLaine, a modest farm girl, acquired untold wealth by marrying a series of men who become millionaires and then

The Graduate *(Joseph E. Levine/Embassy, 1967). Mrs. Robinson (Anne Bancroft) and Benjamin Braddock (Dustin Hoffman) share one of their few reflective moments together. And why not? The lady is, after all, one of the "nicest" of his parents' friends.*

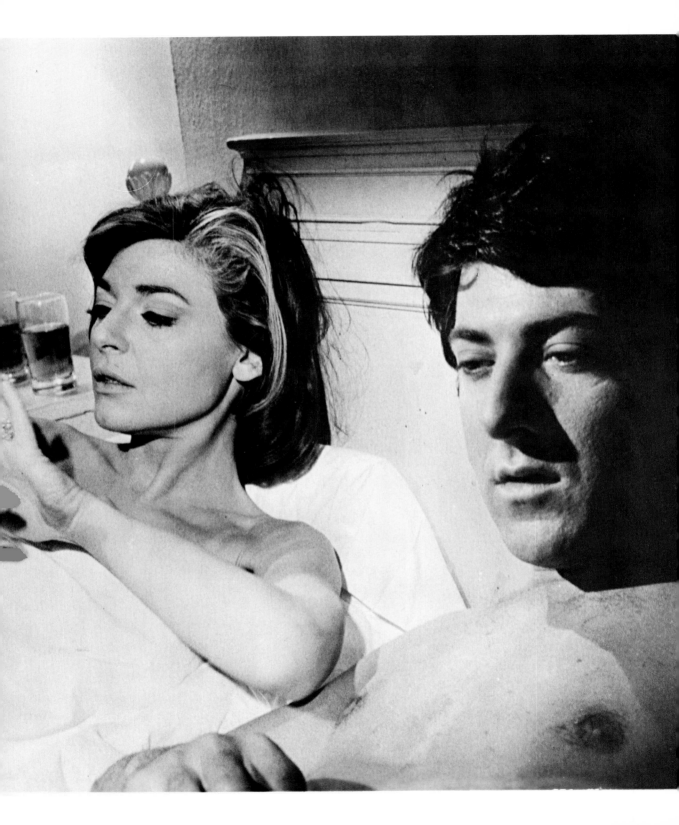

promptly die in some bizarre fashion, leaving her all their money. In Betty Comden and Adolph Green's chaotic screenplay, life with MacLaine's doomed husbands was depicted as a series of revue sketches, a few cleverly wrought, or at least mercifully brief, others clumsily handled; the husbands were played by Paul Newman, Gene Kelly, Robert Mitchum, Dean Martin, and other male stars of the period. The best of the sketches, or perhaps the least objectionable, had Paul Newman as a painter who, after acquiring unexpected success, is killed when his own invention—a lunatic machine that turns sound into oil paintings—goes berserk and strangles him. (So much for modern art.)

Other sixties comedies mocked the solemnity and mystique surrounding death by edging it toward the grotesque. Tony Richardson's *The Loved One* (1965), based on Evelyn Waugh's short satirical novel, went about as far in that direction as any film in memory. Deliberately outrageous and proudly tasteless, the Terry Southern–Christopher Isherwood screenplay (Southern reworked Isherwood's original script) had the American way of death as its principal target, but its barrage of satirical fire also blasted other of Los Angeles' (and by implication, America's) hang-ups, foibles, and rituals with malicious glee. By the time the film ended (somewhat later than it should have), one had the queasy feeling of having been a guest at an indigestible meal.

Advertised as "the movie to offend everyone," *The Loved One* worked hard to live up to its promise. Robert Morse starred as Dennis Barlow, a young British poet who comes to Los Angeles to visit his uncle (John Gielgud) and, following the uncle's suicide, becomes caught up in the activities at Whispering Glades, an extravagant and bizarre cemetery very much like Forest Lawn. Among the demented creatures he encounters are the Blessed Reverend (Jonathan Winters), the unctuous, greedy founder of Whispering Glades, who has secret plans to turn the cemetery into a senior citizen community; an oily casket salesman (Liberace— "Rayon chafes, you know"); and the effete chief embalmer, Mr. Joyboy (Rod Steiger), whose grotesquely fat mother (Ayliene Gibbons) reacts orgasmically to television commercials for food. Dennis also falls in love with Aimee (Anjanette Comer), the naïve and rather daft Whispering Glades cosmetician whose peculiar fate provides the film's finale.

With humor that has all the lightness of an anvil, *The Loved One* savages the ways in which Americans try to disguise the facts of death with elaborate cosmetics, massive statuary, and such euphemisms as "the loved one" and the Slumber Room. Some of this satire hits the target, but by the time the film also has aimed

its scattershot fire at the fatuousness of the military, the greed and sycophancy of
Hollywood people, and America's overreverence for its pets, the humor has become
clogged and heavy-handed.

Clearly, if films were now prepared to mock the usually somber trappings of
mortality in such films as *What a Way to Go!* and *The Loved One*, then the spoofs
and satires of the sixties could be counted on for added measures of irreverence;
they would be more willing to take risks with subjects that were usually handled
with discretion. And as the decade deepened, and America's expanding involvement in Southeast Asia provoked a generation of protest and rebellion, films with
satirical intent began to take on stronger colors than ever before.

At the same time, a dependable satirist such as Billy Wilder was ready to
return to a topic he had dealt with some years earlier in *A Foreign Affair*: the clash
of cultures in postwar Germany. In his nimble, frenetic comedy *One, Two, Three*
(1961), he again explored the consequences when Americans—here a Coca-Cola

executive played by James Cagney—are forced to deal with the perils of life in a divided, occupied Berlin. In the last acting he would do for two decades, Cagney raced through his role of C. R. McNamara, the wheeler-dealer head of Coca-Cola's operations in West Germany, who learns, to his dismay, that Pamela Tiffin, his boss's bubble-headed daughter, has married a young East German communist played by Horst Buchholz. To compound the trouble, his boss (Howard St. John) will soon be arriving for a visit. A frantic McNamara plunges into a scheme to convert the arrogant groom into a card-carrying capitalist, leading to farcical complications that take him beyond both sides of the Berlin wall.

Played at a machine-gun pace, with Cagney leading the way in his old pugnacious style, *One, Two, Three* takes us back into Wilder's sardonic world of liars, cheats, and fools. Nobody escapes unscathed, with the possible exception of McNamara's acerbic wife (Arlene Francis): The boss's daughter has the brain of a gnat; the Russians are bombastic, greedy, and overtly lustful; and McNamara himself, for all of Cagney's still-potent Irish charm, is an amoral rascal. Yet, as he had before, Wilder made it all explosively funny. With dialogue uttered as swiftly as a speeding bullet, his screenplay with I. A. L. Diamond (from a play by Ferenc Molnar) merrily skewers the absurdities behind the obvious dangers of the Cold War.

Part of the pleasure of *One, Two, Three* comes from watching the soldiers from both sides of the Berlin Wall (especially the Eastern sector) trying to deal with the hectic activities triggered by McNamara's scheming. Indeed, as in the fifties, the military life became a favorite subject for satirical farces of the sixties. Few of these films offered more than pleasant diversions, and their carefree attitude toward a destructive war might have rightfully troubled many of those who fought in it. Yet the notion of World War II as a giant romp for its participants drew laughs in such films as *The Wackiest Ship in the Army* (1960), *The Horizontal Lieutenant* (1962), and *What Did You Do in the War, Daddy?* (1966).

While these military comedies continued the long-standing tradition of depicting military service, even in wartime, as an opportunity for graft and chicanery by overage Rover Boys, one audacious and unsettling film took a point of view more attuned to the irreverent sixties. A savage cartoon of a movie, Stanley Kubrick's jet black comedy, *Dr. Strangelove or: How I Learned to Stop Worrying and Love the Bomb* (1964) spared nobody—neither military brass nor high-level politicians—in its view of a world rushing blindly toward oblivion.

The film's apocalyptic vision even begins with a lunatic: General Jack D. Ripper (Sterling Hayden), the demented head of Burpelson Air Force Base, becomes convinced that the Russians have launched a full-scale invasion of America. In his mind, they have already been sapping his "precious bodily fluids" through the fluoridation of drinking water. Going "toe to toe, with the Rooskies," he orders a squadron of B-52s to hit strategic Russian targets with atom bombs. Through the intricate system devised by well-meaning fools, the planes cannot be recalled, and General Ripper seals off his base from the rest of the world. But the worst is yet to come: the bombing of Russia will set off a "Doomsday" device that will destroy all life on earth for over a century.

A blistering parody of an impotent macho man gone berserk, General Ripper quickly involves others in his mad act: his sensible British aide Captain Mandrake (Peter Sellers); the belligerent, snarling General Turgidson (George C. Scott), and the well-meaning but ineffectual American President Muffley (Sellers again). While Mandrake tries frantically to learn the recall code from Ripper, and Turgidson challenges the "commies," President Muffley talks over the hot line with the drunken Soviet premier ("Dmitri, how do you think *I* feel about it?"). On the sidelines is the German scientist Dr. Strangelove (Sellers in a third role), who speaks with relish about the "nucleus of human specimens" remaining after an atomic holocaust. Unfortunately, he is unable to control the Nazi salute his mechanical arm insists on making.

In its brilliant screenplay by Stanley Kubrick, Terry Southern, and Peter George, based on George's novel *Red Alert*, *Dr. Strangelove* skewers the sort of primeval thinking that would lead to widespread protest and alienation in the late sixties and seventies. General "Buck" Turgidson, played with manic exuberance by George C. Scott, blithely suggests mass bombing of Russia and dismisses the American casualties resulting from retaliation as "no more than 10 to 20 million killed." Major "King" Kong (Slim Pickens), in charge of the one plane that manages to penetrate Russian defenses, treats the cataclysmic bombing as a lark and, in the end, rides the bomb himself with a Texan roar of pleasure. A dull-witted corporal named "Bat" Guano (Keenan Wynn)—the authors couldn't resist using scatological or sexual names for their characters—comes upon Captain Mandrake in General Ripper's bombed-out office and insists that he is a "deviated *pree*-vert" who is up to no good.

Dr. Strangelove himself is perhaps the film's most chilling creation. Arrogant in what he regards as his scientific superiority, he is as mechanical as his arm, a creature devoid of feeling whose dark past continually rises up to haunt him. His mouth locked in a mirthless smile that exposes the teeth of a predator, Peter Sellers, who is remarkable in all three of his roles, turns Strangelove into a terrifyingly logical monster. For all of its humor, *Dr. Strangelove* is a film made by iconoclasts who have little regard for—or faith in—our military, political, or social institutions.

By the mid-sixties, as America's involvement in Southeast Asia deepened, an urgent new theme joined military madness as a subject for film satire. As young people in increasing numbers began to question not only that involvement but also all the basic tenets that the country had held sacred over the years, a sense of alienation began to find its way into politics and culture. Inevitably, films in the mid- and late sixties took stock of this disaffection of the young and turned it into the stuff of satire.

Francis Ford Coppola's *You're a Big Boy Now* (1966) was an early example: a disjointed and irreverent comedy that examined the growing pains of seventeen-year-old Bernard Chanticleer (Peter Kastner) as he learns about life and love from an assortment of eccentric and crackpot New Yorkers, including his parents. Another (and more successful) film that took its young hero into the labyrinths of sex and family life was Larry Peerce's 1969 adaptation of Philip Roth's novella *Goodbye, Columbus*. A biting look at upwardly mobile Jewish suburban life as seen through the eyes of a young librarian named Neil (Richard Benjamin), the movie did not cast its satirical net over a wide area; instead, it concentrated on the wildly materialistic life of the prosperous Patimkin family and Brenda (Ali Mac-Graw), the popular Patimkin daughter Neil adores and longs to marry.

Drawing on Roth's novella but changing the locale from Short Hills to Westchester, Arnold Schulman's screenplay captures, with deadly accuracy, the lifestyle and prevailing attitudes of the Patimkins. The film shows them moving in an upwardly mobile world of overdecorated furniture, overstuffed freezers (fruit is a great favorite at their house), and overelaborate wedding receptions (a wince-inducing orgy of consumption). Neil himself, like many other young film heroes of the time, is aimless and undirected, ready to sail with the prevailing wind, while Brenda is a satirical and well-realized portrait of a pampered princess, aloof, self-absorbed, and unable to express genuine feelings.

Like *You're a Big Boy Now, Goodbye, Columbus* reflects the unease and dislocation that would grow increasingly strong as the decade waned. Both Bernard and Neil are uncertain of their place in the scheme of things. Yet no young hero of the period better expressed the prevailing mood than Benjamin Braddock in Mike Nichols's landmark 1967 comedy, *The Graduate*. Over the years, there have been few images more expressive of alienation than Benjamin, in the diving suit he has received as a graduation gift, marching into the gathering of his parents' friends, an outer-space monster in a privileged world.

Dapk Lauphtep

Adapted by Calder Willingham and Buck Henry from Charles Webb's novel, *The Graduate* sets its tone from the opening moments: To the music of Simon and Garfunkel's "Sounds of Silence," the "award-winning scholar" Benjamin Braddock (Dustin Hoffman) arrives in Los Angeles and rides the airport escalator; his face registers no feeling, and as the camera stays on him, he seems to be in a symbolic state of limbo. At the party in his honor, his parents and his parents' friends, beaming inanely about his accomplishments, pay no heed to his signals of distress. Only one person—the elegant, neurotic, alcoholic Mrs. Robinson (Anne Bancroft)—treats him as a person rather than an object, and she is trouble, headed for disaster.

Mrs. Robinson's seduction of Ben—the steps by which she lures him into an affair with unforeseen consequences—is depicted in scenes that by now have become part of movie folklore: their first encounter in her bedroom ("Mrs. Robinson, you're trying to seduce me"); their hilarious hotel tryst ("I find you the most attractive of all my parents' friends"); and their continued clandestine meetings that relieve his aimless existence at home. Until this time, Ben is not much different from the young man at the airport: affectless, isolated, and "just a little worried" about his future.

But then life intrudes, messily and unexpectedly: Reunited with Mrs. Robinson's daughter Elaine (Katharine Ross) after some time, he finds himself falling in love with her. Suddenly, he has discovered someone to care about in his wasted life, and all the feelings he has suppressed or refused to acknowledge overwhelm him. His love becomes an obsession, enraging Mrs. Robinson and causing Elaine to flee to college at Berkeley where he tells her about his involvement with her mother. He pursues her desperately, enfuriating and repulsing everyone, including Mr. Robinson (Murray Hamilton). Finally, he breaks into Elaine's wedding to a pipe-smoking, blond jock, taking her away while Mrs. Robinson rages in the background. The ending is ambiguous: In the bus carrying them off, Ben and Elaine (in her wedding gown) stare blankly into space, a faintly troubled, wondering look on their faces. Alienated by the empty, meaningless concerns of their time, these young people ultimately may become exactly like those they deplore. Alienation, the film suggests, is a sometime thing, especially when real life intervenes.

Aside from its acknowledged place as a key film of the late sixties, *The Graduate* made a star of Dustin Hoffman. At age thirty, Hoffman plays a twenty-one-year-old convincingly; his little squeals of dismay and discomfort, his nasal, constricted voice expressing a jittery state of mind, and his eyes gazing with mistrust at a world he couldn't fathom—all these characteristics help to turn a potentially unappealing character into an amusing one. As the sleek, glacial Mrs. Robinson, Anne Bancroft gives a splendid performance. Whether coolly blowing smoke from her cigarette just after Ben kisses her, or screaming with rage at the thought of his dating her daughter, she etches a memorable portrait of a hard-as-nails virago. Both she and Hoffman, as well as Katharine Ross, received Oscar nominations, but lost, respectively, to Katharine Hepburn, Rod Steiger, and Estelle Parsons. Mike Nichols, however, won the award as Best Director.

Although it contained no reference to the upheavals taking place outside its domain, *The Graduate* proved to be, in a sense, a beacon for the film decade that lay ahead. In only a year, the screen would be awash with comedies that mocked an established society that seldom related to—or cared about—the true and sometimes revolutionary needs of young people. There were other sixties films (*The Americanization of Emily, The Loved One*) that could claim a more direct link to the seventies than *The Graduate*, but no other comedy of the period seemed to speak so directly to an emerging generation that objected to "rules made by all the wrong people."

Amid the irreverent attacks on the military or the paeans to alienation, one sixties farce had no axes to grind, no point of view to advance, except, perhaps, that of the rampant greed pervading American society. Stanley Kramer's gargantuan film *It's a Mad Mad Mad Mad World* (1963) sought only to unite virtually every practicing comedian of the day in a 154-minute tribute to movie slapstick. Every conceivable physical gag, every collision, explosion, or chase that had ever turned up on the screen, from Mack Sennett to Abbott and Costello, was duplicated in ways that suggested animated cartoons on a grandiose scale. The film was not only "mad" but madly extravagant.

William and Tania Rose's screenplay even had a plot of sorts: As gangster Jimmy Durante lies dying in a car wreck, he tells the assembled onlookers about $350,000 buried in Rosita Beach State Park. Immediately, everyone is dashing off independently to find the money, including cronies Mickey Rooney and Buddy Hackett; married couple Sid Caesar and Edie Adams; Milton Berle, wife Dorothy Provine, and his monstrous mother-in-law, Ethel Merman; and the terrible-tempered Jonathan Winters. As they scramble into their own mishaps and adventures, they are joined by a host of others and hotly pursued by police captain Spencer Tracy (painfully miscast), who turns out to have a larcenous streak of his own.

By the time the film has reached its climax, and nearly the entire cast is swinging on an extension ladder high above the city, the premise—and the audi-

ence—have been exhausted. Although a few sequences generate laughs, what is left as the residue in this overextended film is its spirit of utter meanness. For all of its knockabout humor, there is a nasty spirit in the depiction of these frantic clowns. Greed and larceny are apt subject for comedy (W. C. Fields and the Marxes thrived on it), but when there is no balance of decency or even simple civility, the unrelenting avarice becomes wearying rather than funny. (Even W.C. had a daughter or a niece whom he cherished.) Long before the principals are grappling over the money (it is not difficult to guess who finally gets it), one ceases to care about the fate of these obnoxious people.

In the decade ahead, other comedies would play on our worst instincts as humans, but in the best of them, there would be leavening amounts of wit and inventiveness. There was precious little of either in this mad mad mad mad world.

It's a Mad Mad Mad Mad World *(United Artists, 1963). During their frantic search for a buried fortune, the cast of this outsize comedy pauses for a photo opportunity. The movie's nonstop slapstick grew wearisome after a while.*

Chapter 18
The Old Guard—Plus Woody and Mel

I
n the midst of the titillating sex comedies and the outrageous satires, the familiar comedy figures of past decades continued to work, if not to flourish. For a mainstay such as Bob Hope, the sixties proved to be the start of a precipitous descent. The formula that had worked especially well in the forties—Hope as the brash, quipping coward in hot water—began to seem strained. Yet by way of contrast, Jerry Lewis found his popularity largely unabated after leaving Dean Martin in 1956. Those who enjoyed his raucous slapstick and pantomime, and his characterization of a manic or unruly child in a man's body, continued to attend his films. Many felt that he was doing his best work in the sixties, finding inventive new ways to extend and refine his special comic persona. (Some French film critics, in fact, regarded him as a master of comedy, worthy of extended analysis.) Others, however, admitted to being hostile to the near-imbecility his characters projected, and to the lack of discipline and precision in his work.

Lewis's comedies in the sixties can be grouped loosely into two categories: those in which he played virtually a solo role as the center of the slapstick that spiraled out of his bumbling, childlike ineptitude, and those in which he mainly interacted with other players. In the former category, Lewis was usually given a job for which he was supremely unqualified and turned it into a comic shambles. *The Bellboy* (1960), which he wrote and directed (his first effort), cast him as a bellhop at Miami's opulent Fontainebleau Hotel, where he undergoes a series of slapstick misadventures in his efforts to carry out his duties. *The Errand Boy* (1961) turned him loose to wreak havoc on a movie studio, while *The Ladies' Man* (1961) cast him as a handyman at a girls' school run by former opera diva Helen Traubel. Again, Lewis directed both films.

One of Lewis's popular, although hardly better, films of the period, Frank Tashlin's *The Disorderly Orderly* (1964), focused on his destructive activities at a sanitarium. The setting allowed him to add a bit of Chaplinesque sentiment to his usual slapstick mix—adoring a bitter, suicidal young patient (Susan Oliver),

The Nutty Professor *(Paramount, 1963). The laboratory experiment of bizarre Julius Kelp (Jerry Lewis) is about to turn him into swinging Buddy Love. Neither character, however, inspires more than a few chuckles.*

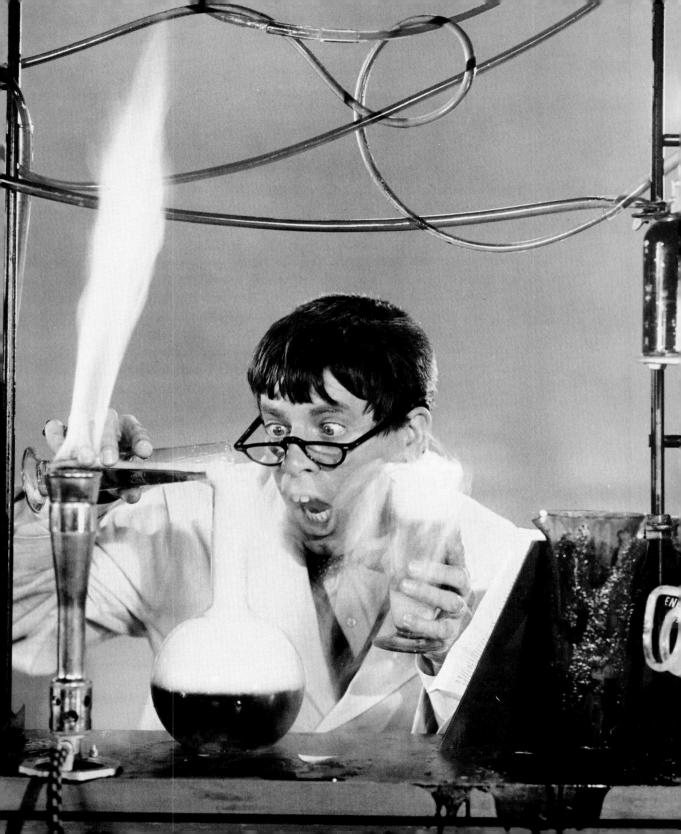

he turns her into an angel with his altruism—but most of the movie dealt with his disruption of procedures at the sanitarium. With his background as an animator and comic-strip artist, Frank Tashlin at least understood the nature of Lewis's knockabout humor, and when he directed a number of the comedian's plottier movies in the sixties, he managed to give them bursts of kinetic energy. However, he was unable to bring much variety to Lewis's spastic clowning in such films as *Cinderfella* (1960), *It's Only Money* (1962), and *Who's Minding the Store?* (1963).

When Lewis returned to directing his own vehicles, the resulting films were somewhat more ambitious, and in the case of *The Nutty Professor* (1963), brought him his first admiring reviews in years. Generally regarded as his best film, this venture into the comic aspects of a Jekyll and Hyde personality at least allowed Lewis to stretch his basic characterization of the ultimate nerd. In a screenplay coauthored with Bill Richmond, he played Julius Kelp, a grotesquely inept, accident-prone college professor who, under the influence of a potion concocted in his laboratory, turns into the suave, swinging, obnoxiously egocentric Buddy Love. Complications multiply as the two personalities interact, until the night of the senior prom, when Buddy Love reverts to Julius Kelp before everyone's eyes. Kelp, who has learned that it is better to be oneself, finally wins the girl (Stella Stevens) he has always loved.

Considering that *The Nutty Professor* is generally looked upon as Lewis's funniest film, it is rather astonishing to realize how meager the laughs actually are. Except for a few isolated moments, the movie is glum and dispirited, and both sides of the hero's split personality are off-putting. Julius Kelp is merely a gargoyle, neither a larger-than-life character nor a recognizable human being, and Buddy Love, who may well be Lewis's wicked parody of his ex-partner Dean Martin, is a bully and a braggart whose every appearance inspires loathing rather than laughter. Lewis's other self-directed films, which included, among others, *The Patsy* (1964), *The Family Jewels* (1965), and *Don't Raise the Bridge, Lower the River* (1968), grew increasingly monotonous and heavy-handed.

While Bob Hope and Jerry Lewis continued to ply their trade, new comedy performers were emerging in the sixties. However, except for Walter Matthau, slouching his way through a series of rumpled roles, there were few whose very appearance and manner denoted comedy; most were attractive performers such as Doris Day and Jack Lemmon, who could summon up the suitably light touch that comedy required. By the mid-sixties, one comedian was making a strong impression in American films with his remarkable gift for mimicry and his creation of a durable and popular character.

For some years, Peter Sellers had been a favorite in his native country of England, where he appeared in such adroit comedy films as *I'm All Right, Jack* (1959) and *Only Two Can Play* (1962). Following his expert performances as predatory cad Clare Quilty in Stanley Kubrick's *Lolita* (1962) and as multiple characters in Kubrick's *Dr. Strangelove* (1964), Sellers starred as a vain, womanizing pianist in George Roy Hill's diverting comedy *The World of Henry Orient* (1964). Lighthearted, yet with melancholy undertones, the movie actually belonged to Tippy Walker and Merrie Spaeth as two New York teenagers who idolize the conceited Sellers and turn his life into a shambles with their relentless pursuit. Frantically trying to keep his life from becoming unraveled by his unwelcome fans, Sellers's Henry Orient provided the movie's broadly comic base. It was a plum role for the actor, but he followed it with an even choicer role, that of the amazingly stupid, extraordinarily clumsy, and very funny Inspector Jacques Clouseau in Blake Edwards's *The Pink Panther* (1964). It proved to be the role with which he would be forever identified.

Highly scenic and intermittently amusing, *The Pink Panther* was not intended as a vehicle for launching the character of the inept inspector. It is actually an elaborate caper comedy, revolving about the suave Sir Charles Litton (David Niven), aka "The Phantom," Europe's leading jewel thief, and his intention to steal the priceless Pink Panther diamond from the princess (Claudia Cardinale) who owns it. The cream of the jest is that the Phantom's confederate and lover is the wife (Capucine) of Inspector Clouseau. Also involved is Sir Charles's nephew George (Robert Wagner), who is as crooked as his uncle. Much of the time, the film's humor derives not from the attempt to steal the diamond but from Clouseau's virtually nonstop clumsiness and from his blank ignorance of his wife's infidelities.

The box-office success of *The Pink Panther* suggested the immediate return of Inspector Clouseau, and within a few months he was back destroying everything in sight in a second Blake Edwards comedy, *A Shot in the Dark* (1964). Loosely derived from the stage play by Harry Kurnitz (and an original French version by Marcel Achard), the film offered a series of slapstick episodes that were better sustained than those in *The Pink Panther*. Here, to the increasing dismay and horror of his superior, Chief Inspector Dreyfus (Herbert Lom), the world's worst detective is summoned to investigate a murder at a château. He becomes romantically involved with the principal suspect, a saucy housemaid named Maria (Elke Sommer), and, in an attempt to prove her innocence, bumbles his way into deep trouble.

The Producers *(Joseph E. Levine/Embassy, 1968). A delirious moment from the movie's highpoint, the outrageous* Springtime for Hitler, *subtitled* A Gay Romp with Adolf and Eva at Berchtesgaden.

Soon, plot gives way to sight gags and slapstick sequences, mostly at the expense of Clouseau: He continually trips and falls, with disastrous results for objects and people; he plays a hilarious game of billiards with a curved cue; and he miraculously survives a number of attempts on his life. Clouseau's feelings for Maria lead him into the movie's funniest sequence: Finding himself at a nudist camp, he obligingly strips, clutching a guitar for modesty, then flees the camp in his car, with an also-nude Maria.

By the end of the sixties, after a decade of bawdy sex farces and outrageous black comedies, there was clearly an urgent need for new comedy voices for the years ahead. Since the days of Preston Sturges and Joseph Mankiewicz, there had been few writer-directors of their class, few filmmakers with a unique style and point of view. Before the decade ended, there were two such figures, both of whom could claim originality derived from their own special perspective. One, Mel Brooks, came from the world of television, where his writing had contributed notably to "Your Show of Shows," the wittiest, most memorable comedy-variety program of the fifties. The other, Woody Allen, was a television writer who had turned successfully to stand-up comedy, where his characterization of an intellectual loser constantly buffeted by life won a receptive audience. Later on, Brooks would perform in his own comedies, while Allen immediately cast himself in the leading roles. Like Jerry Lewis, but with greater success, they became triple threats, combining writing, acting, and directing in a single project.

Proudly and shamelessly outrageous, Mel Brooks had appeared on the scene as an extension of the bawdy, irreverent comedians who had worked the borscht belt circuit of hotels in the Catskill Mountains in the years before and after World War II. To their "naughty little boy" ribaldry and their barrage of Yiddish-flavored jokes, he added a broad sense of satire or, more specifically, burlesque, as well as a unique way of taking an idea to its ludicrous extreme. (Why shouldn't a two-thousand-year-old man talk like a cranky retired pants presser from Miami Beach?)

Ultimately, Brooks turned to filmmaking with his first full-length feature, *The Producers* (1968). Without an iota of subtlety, restraint, or good taste, he set about poking malicious fun at a number of targets. The harebrained excesses of the legitimate theater were fair game, but to those he added, with cheerful disregard for sensibilities, such groups as homosexuals, the elderly, and those who were not inclined to find much humor in Adolf Hitler and the Nazis. *The Producers* was by no means a polished film—like most of his later efforts, its helter-skelter style resulted in hits and misses—but audaciously, it both amused and offended viewers.

Brooks's chief weapon in his assault was the rotund comedian Zero Mostel. Mostel played Max Bialystock, a down-on-his-luck theatrical producer who raises money by romancing elderly ladies. When an hysterical accountant named Leo Bloom (Gene Wilder) suggests that Max could make a fortune by investing his backers' oversubscribed money in a flop play, Max is in business—with Leo as his partner. He produces the world's worst play—a zany musical called *Springtime for*

Hitler—but its very outrageousness turns it into a hit. Max and Leo end up in prison, where they plan to start all over again.

Some of *The Producers* is undeniably funny: Until his hysteria begins to wear thin, Leo Bloom draws laughs with his security blanket and his sudden desire for material goods—he has a wonderful moment at the Lincoln Center fountain, where he shouts, "I want everything I've seen in the movies!" Also, once a viewer can get past the idea of dancing gestapo men and a psychedelic Hitler (Dick Shawn), the excerpt from the production of *Springtime for Hitler* is, for at least part of the way, cleverly conceived.

Still, *The Producers* leaves much to be desired, and part of the fault lies with Zero Mostel. On stage, he is a funny man, but on screen, he becomes oppressive, pushing his face constantly into the camera like an uninvited party guest who can't wait to show you how outrageous he is. Brooks is also unable to maintain the suspension of disbelief that even the craziest comedy requires—we are never persuaded that the stupefied audience at *Springtime for Hitler* would suddenly find the play riotously funny and turn it into a resounding hit. Finally, it must be said that bad taste, though presented proudly and shamelessly, is still bad taste.

A year after *The Producers*, Woody Allen made his debut as a director, writer, and star with *Take the Money and Run* (1969). Until then, his screen work had been erratic: a highly uneven screenplay for *What's New, Pussycat?* (1965); a crudely funny feature-length film called *What's Up, Tiger Lily?* (1966), in which he dubbed a Japanese spy film with American voices and gags; and a role as Jimmy Bond, James Bond's nephew, in *Casino Royale* (1967). Although more parodic than his later work—basically, it is a spoof of prison and gangster movies—*Take the Money and Run* set the pattern for Allen's comedies in the upcoming decade. With jokes that combined New York sophistication and a kind of logical lunacy, and with a persona in Allen that was neither smart-alecky like Hope nor subnormal like Lewis, but rather like that of an intellectual nebbish, the film clearly heralded an original new comic voice on the movie scene.

In *Take the Money and Run*, Allen played Virgil Starkwell, a would-be robber of monumental ineptness whose luck is all bad. His pathetic attempts to rob banks only land him in prison, where his efforts to escape also come to disaster. In flight from the law between aborted robberies and prison sentences, Virgil meets a girl named Louise (Janet Margolin), who learns only later of his life of crime. Inevitably, he ends up serving an eight-hundred-year sentence. Superficially, the plot sounds like a slightly peculiar retread of an old James Cagney–Ann

Sheridan movie for Warners, but with Allen in control (in a screenplay written with Mickey Rose), the well-worn situations are sent spinning in a new direction. All the old prison clichés are given an Allenesque twist: Virgil fashions a gun from soap but it melts in the rain; he finds himself alone in a prison break ("Hey, where *is* everybody?"); and his road-gang punishment consists of one meal a day—"a bowl of steam"—or being "locked in a box with an insurance salesman." Virtually every bromide of the prison-and-gangster films is given a fresh new twist—a mean-looking road-gang guard snarls, "Any questions?" and Virgil asks coyly, "Do you think a girl should pet on her first date?" (Groucho Marx would approve.)

Take the Money and Run shows evidence that Allen had yet to find his style as a director; he tried to cover his lapses by using a grainy documentary approach, but some of the scenes are awkwardly staged and unconvincing. Also, many of the jokes have no relation to the characters; funny as they are, they seem to have been lifted intact from one of Allen's stand-up comedy routines. Yet for all of its flaws, *Take the Money and Run* shows a fresh new comic mind at work.

Take the Money and Run *(Cinerama Releasing Corporation, 1969). Bank robber Virgil Starkwell (Woody Allen), so inept that he must get his holdup note initialed by a vice president, finds himself in prison. Here he converses with girlfriend Louise (Janet Margolin).*

Part 5

DOWN WITH EVERYTHING

Movie Comedy in the Seventies

A decade of pride (America's bicentennial) and shame (Watergate) . . . and new challenges for the future . . .

The decade begins with continuing antiwar protests throughout the country, while President Nixon asks for the support of "the Great Silent Majority" of Americans. By January of 1973, the American combat role in Vietnam is terminated with a cease-fire agreement.

At home, President Nixon faces the most devastating controversy of his term in office. While 1972 marks his historic visit to Red China, it is also the year in which a break-in at Washington's Watergate complex causes growing concern within his government. The following year, an ongoing investigation reveals startling new allegations and cover-ups. Another blow is the resignation of Vice President Spiro T. Agnew following charges of income tax evasion. In 1974, faced with further charges and impeachment, Nixon resigns from office.

Yet the seventies are also a time of historic advances and landmarks. The twenty-sixth Amendment is passed in 1971, giving the vote to eighteen-year-olds. In 1973, in the *Roe v. Wade* decision, the Supreme Court overturns all state laws that restrict or deny a woman's right to obtain an abortion during the first trimester of pregnancy. And in 1976, America joyously celebrates its bicentennial year with pageantry and cultural events.

On the popular culture scene, the seventies also witness the arrival of such popular television series as "All in the Family," "M*A*S*H," and "Dallas," as well as the unprecedented mini-series "Roots," which is about seven generations of a black family. Disney World opens in Florida in 1971, and by mid-decade, videocassette recorders (VCRs) are moving into American homes. Top movies of the seventies include *Patton, The French Connection, The Godfather, Rocky,* and *Kramer vs. Kramer.*

Shampoo (*Columbia, 1975*). *Warren Beatty starred as womanizing hairdresser George Roundy in Hal Ashby's biting comedy about sex, politics, and lifestyles in the late sixties.*

Chapter 19

Offbeat Love

Romantic Comedy in the Seventies

On the whole, despite the pervasively wholesome presence of Doris Day, romantic comedy in the sixties had been marked by the screen's belated discovery of the more prurient aspects of s-e-x. In the changing climate of the late sixties and early seventies, when a new atmosphere of dissent and antiestablishment rebellion prevailed, another change in attitude took place. Although the old traditions of romantic involvement continued to linger, there was a new emphasis on unconventional romance. Romantic comedies surfaced in which the couples appeared to be wildly mismatched, with disparities in their ages, backgrounds, and attitudes. Like those in the real world who were marching to their own drummer, lovers in seventies romantic comedies, at least early in the decade, frequently carried out their affairs in unusual circumstances that defied convention.

The leading players in these comedies even looked and sounded unconventional. In place of the classic beauty of Irene Dunne, or the soft, breathy voice of Doris Day, viewers were exposed to the less than classical features and the New York–Jewish intonations of Barbra Streisand. Gifted with a remarkable singing voice, she had emerged from the Broadway stage, where she had reached stardom in *Funny Girl,* to repeat her performance in the 1968 film version. The moment she appeared on-screen as comedian-singer Fanny Brice her film-star potential was evident, and her offbeat looks became a virtue. It was also clear that she had an innate talent for comedy; she could elicit laughter with her odd line readings and brash, aggressive personality (too brash and too aggressive for some viewers). However, her next two films seemed almost to offset her newly won star status— she was blatantly miscast in Gene Kelly's overstuffed film version of the long-running stage musical *Hello, Dolly!* (1969), and she played a befuddled student with extrasensory perception in Vincente Minnelli's lavish, rather muddled adaptation

Harold and Maude *(Paramount, 1971). An unlikely romance blossoms between nearly eighty-year-old Maude (Ruth Gordon) and twenty-year-old Harold (Bud Cort). Over two decades, this dark, offbeat comedy has become a cult classic.*

of another stage musical, *On a Clear Day You Can See Forever* (1970). Nor did she have much success when she turned from the musical stage to romantic comedy with *The Owl and the Pussycat* (1970), adapted by Buck Henry from Bill Manhoff's long-running Broadway comedy. She was hardly endearing as an aggressive New York City prostitute who intimidates, cajoles, and finally wins the love of an intellectual bookstore clerk and aspiring writer, played by George Segal.

Streisand fared much better with her next film, Peter Bogdanovich's *What's Up, Doc?* (1972). The director's homage to the screwball comedies of the thirties, most particularly to *Bringing Up Baby*, the movie was more flat-out farce than romantic comedy, a nonstop barrage of pratfalls, noisy altercations, and chases. Happily, most of them were well executed and funny. Like Katharine Hepburn in *Bringing Up Baby*, Streisand played a blithe and dizzy young woman who wreaks havoc wherever she goes—a one-woman disaster area. She meets and immediately sets her cap for an absentminded young archaeologist (Ryan O'Neal), who has come to San Francisco for a musicologists convention with his bossy fiancée (Madeline Kahn). Before the ninety-four minutes have elapsed, Streisand has reduced his life to shreds ("You are the last straw that breaks my camel's back,"

What's Up, Doc?
*(Warner Bros., 1972).
In mad flight from
their pursuers, Barbra
Streisand and Ryan
O'Neal careen through
the streets of San
Francisco on a grocery
cart. This climactic
sequence trotted out
timeworn gags from
old chase comedies—
and made them all
work as if new.*

he tells her), and she has set in motion a brouhaha involving jewel thieves, government spies, and four identical overnight cases.

The screenplay by Buck Henry, David Newman, and Robert Benton makes no sense whatever (it isn't supposed to), but the slapstick sequences and sight gags flow freely and hilariously. Among the highlights are an all-out brawl at the reception for the musicologists, at which all the opposing forces converge with guns, and the inevitable but well-staged climactic chase scene through the streets of San Francisco. For this sequence, every hoary sight gag from the days of Mack Sennett is trotted out and polished as if new. At one point, fleeing from his pursuers on a delivery bicycle (with Streisand perched on the handlebars), O'Neal rides pell-mell into a Chinese New Year's parade, sending the participants scrambling for safety.

Another unconventional heroine of seventies romantic comedy emerged from the serious British theater of the sixties. Tall and striking-looking but far from conventionally pretty, with a husky voice and an assertive acting style that projected intelligence and a strong will, Glenda Jackson made a vivid impression in a 1969 adaptation of D. H. Lawrence's *Women in Love*, winning a Best Actress Oscar. She was equally impressive in *Sunday, Bloody Sunday* (1971), moving away to some degree from the neurotic roles she was usually given to play.

Judging from her acting credits, Jackson was not the likeliest candidate to play the heroine of a romantic comedy, yet she moved comfortably into that niche with her first American film, Melvin Frank's *A Touch of Class* (1973). She still retained the brittle style of her earlier roles, but, slanted in the direction of comedy, it gave a tart edge to her playing of a London divorcée, the mother of two, who enters into an affair with a married American insurance executive (George Segal). They go off together for a romantic week in Malaga, and not surprisingly, things go seriously wrong. They quarrel fiercely, make up passionately, and find that the logistics of an illicit romance can be exhausting and difficult. Ultimately, they come to a bittersweet parting.

For all of its "adult" trimmings, the Melvin Frank–Jack Rose screenplay for *A Touch of Class* is not substantially different from a score of other comedies about the pitfalls of romantic assignations. Also, the vituperative arguments that spring up early in their relationship start too quickly and go on far too long. Still, there are amusing moments, such as their total destruction of a hotel room, during a raging quarrel, with a hapless bellboy caught in the line of fire; or Segal's frantic attempts to juggle a visit to his mistress and a concert with his wife on the same evening. The stars work well together, her cool, slightly acerbic manner balanced

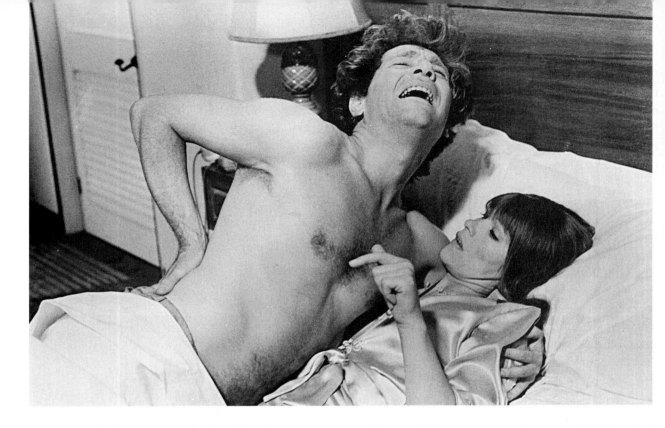

A Touch of Class
(Joseph E. Levine/ Avco Embassy, 1973). During what he hoped would be a romantic tryst with divorcée Glenda Jackson, married man George Segal wrenches his back. Segal had the pain—but Jackson won the Oscar as Best Actress.

against his boyish eagerness to please. Jackson was again awarded the Best Actress Oscar for her performance.

Later in the decade, Jackson found an even more compatible costar in Walter Matthau. Her crisp authority meshed nicely with his soft-centered grumpiness in Howard Zieff's dark screwball comedy, *House Calls* (1978). Jackson played a recently divorced woman who takes a job as administrator at a monumentally inefficient hospital, where she meets Matthau, a recently widowed doctor. Faithful for thirty years, middle-aged Matthau has decided to make up for lost time by becoming a top-ranking lecher. Instead, he finds himself falling in love with Jackson. Their bumpy romance takes place against a hospital background in which lunatics are in full control, many of them apparently posing as doctors and nurses. The Jackson-Matthau relationship, reminiscent of Hepburn and Tracy in its mixture of scratchiness and affection, was much the best thing in the screenplay.

Some heroines of seventies romantic comedies not only looked different from the sleekly beautiful actresses of earlier years, they also, on occasion, found romantic fulfillment with men much younger than they—a situation that would have called for shocked whispers or a tragic denouement in other times. Actresses who would not be expected to indulge in May-December relationships found themselves cast as mature women who dallied proudly with young men still wet behind the ears.

The ultimate example of what might be called an early April–late December romance turned up in 1971. Hal Ashby's determinedly offbeat and very dark comedy *Harold and Maude* brought together the decade's, or at least the year's, most unlikely couple: a distinctly odd twenty-year-old named Harold (Bud Cort), whose apparent hobby is attempting suicide by various means, and a wildly eccentric nearly eighty-year-old woman named Maude (Ruth Gordon). They meet at one of the "anonymous" funerals they both enjoy attending, fall in love, and carry out a number of pranks, such as stealing a suburban tree and replanting it in a forest. Emotionally committed to each other, they marry on the eve of Maude's eightieth birthday. Although their romance ends on a sadly ironic note, Maude's attitude has restored Harold to the real world of life-affirming possibilities.

Played by Ruth Gordon as the world's oldest flower child, Maude is also a bit of a fraud; like Colin Higgins's screenplay, her affirmation of life disguises an obsession with death (her love of funerals, her final solution for her own life). To justify her blithe disregard for the law, she also resorts to rationalizations that have a hollow ring. ("It's best not to be too moral. You cheat yourself out of too much life.") *Harold and Maude* actually works best in the fringe areas away from the central love story; the broad satire of the military, for example—Harold's uncle is a gung ho army officer who is determined to straighten him out—is much funnier than any of Harold and Maude's gambols.

If Barbra Streisand, Glenda Jackson, and, yes, Ruth Gordon could be considered as assertive and offbeat leading ladies for romantic comedy, it follows that the leading men would emerge as somewhat less aggressive and more vulnerable than the macho male stars of earlier times. As a reflection of the expanding feminist movement of the period, many actors turned up in roles that characterized them as weak, pliant, and easily intimidated by women. Unprepossessing heroes appeared throughout the decade, often in tandem with women who were usually more assured and self-possessed than they: Charles Grodin as the nerdlike young man who pursues a golden girl while on his honeymoon with somebody else, in Elaine May's *The Heartbreak Kid* (1972); Alan Arkin as a middle-aged restaurateur who fancies himself, erroneously, as the *Last of the Red Hot Lovers* (1972) in Gene Saks's wretched adaptation of the Neil Simon play; and Alan Alda, in Robert Mulligan's *Same Time, Next Year* (1978), as a married man who has a once-a-year assignation, for twenty years, with also-married Ellen Burstyn.

The Heartbreak Kid
(Palomar, 1972). Lenny (Charles Grodin, center) works hard to make an impression on Mr. Corcoran (Eddie Albert), the father of his golden dream girl (Cybill Shepherd). He is not succeeding.

Of those films, *The Heartbreak Kid* was the most successful, with a Neil Simon screenplay (adapted from a Bruce Jay Friedman story) that, while far from perfect, outclassed any previous adaptation of his plays. As Lenny Cantrow, a sporting goods salesman who abandons his new bride (Jeannie Berlin) to court the girl of his dreams, Charles Grodin etched a convincing portrait of an ambitious, essentially shallow young man who follows the path he is expected to take—marriage with a nice, drab, hopelessly dull girl—then finds he wants another path, after all. Obsessed with rich, spoiled Kelly Corcoran (Cybill Shepherd), he lies to his unsuspecting wife, Lila, alienates Kelly's bigoted, deeply skeptical father (Eddie Albert), and finally, after leaving Lila, gets to marry his dream girl. An ambiguous ending, resembling the one in *The Graduate,* leaves him seated alone at his second wedding, reflectively staring into space; Lenny has achieved his goal but has yet to resolve the basic emptiness of his life. Much of *The Heartbreak Kid* is funny and sharply observant, especially in the early scenes when Lenny and Lila carry out the rituals of middle-class newlyweds. Yet for all its merits, the film suffers from a sourness of tone that curdles the intended humor. Simon, without one-line jokes to sustain him, and perhaps encouraged by Friedman's harshly satirical story and the acerbic wit of Elaine May, permits a sardonic edge in his writing to emerge.

Another comedy of romantic—or at least sexual—obsession appeared near the end of the decade. In Blake Edwards's *"10"* (1979), diminutive British comedian Dudley Moore, playing his first leading role in an American film, starred as George Webber, a successful musical-comedy composer unhappy with the onset of middle age. Although involved in a long-standing romance with divorcée Samantha ("Sam") Taylor (Julie Andrews), his life spins out of control the moment he sees the ravishingly beautiful Jennie (Bo Derek), only recently married but, on a scale of one to ten, the perfect ten of his dreams. His preoccupation with Jennie leads him ever deeper into trouble, but circumstances finally bring him to a sexual liaison with his dream girl. When she turns out to be willful, amoral, and none too bright, George returns happily to Sam.

An unlikely romantic hero but a skillful comic actor, Moore tried to invest George's predicament with humor, but Edwards's screenplay defeated him. Too many of the intended laughs depend on the calamities George experiences during his search for Jennie: He crashes his automobile into a police car, undergoes extensive dental work, and suffers a bad bee sting, all to diminishing comic returns. Although he is ill matched with Julie Andrews (the only thing they seem to have in common is their place of birth), Dudley Moore registers amiably.

Among the romantic heroes and heroines of the seventies, there were some who fit into the long-standing pattern of couples who truly belong together but who fail to realize their compatibility until the last minutes of the film. Yet even here, in variations of the formula that had been a mainstay in comedy for decades, the romantically inclined men and women of the seventies were offbeat figures in a changing society. Films had come a considerable distance from the pert secretaries and square-shouldered boss ladies who fell for reporters and playboys. Now, a chubby, thirtyish would-be singer (Renée Taylor), who has been "a failure in everything," could meet an unhappy, thirtyish womanizer (Joseph Bologna) at a group therapy session and discover, despite their obvious unsuitability, that they are really *Made for Each Other* (1971). Now, in Billy Wilder's *Avanti!* (1972), a businessman (Jack Lemmon) could meet and fall in love unexpectedly with the daughter (Juliet Mills) of his late father's mistress. Even the clean-cut young hero could be cut from a different cloth: In *Butterflies Are Free* (1972), adapted from Leonard Gershe's stage comedy, Edward Albert played a sensitive, intelligent young blind man who falls in love with free-spirited Goldie Hawn and learns self-reliance from her.

Later in the seventies, couples were still vigorously denying their compatibility for most of the film, then embracing it passionately by the closing credits. After adapting many of his Broadway plays, as well as writing several original screenplays, all with limited success, Neil Simon finally scored a triumph with his warmly appealing screenplay for Herbert Ross's comedy, *The Goodbye Girl* (1977). For once, the laughter was laced with humanity and sentiment, and Simon's comically driven, fallible characters were not merely proficient joke machines but recognizable people in a real, and not a sitcom, world.

The protagonists of *The Goodbye Girl* seem, at first, to be ill equipped to handle themselves, let alone each other. Giving a charismatic performance that won him the Best Actor Oscar, Richard Dreyfuss played Elliott Garfield, an aspiring actor from Chicago who sublets a New York apartment now occupied by Paula McFadden (Marsha Mason), a thirtyish ex-dancer, and her young daughter, Quinn Cummings. Paula is a perennial victim, the "goodbye girl" who is usually deserted by her lovers. She and Elliott agree to share the apartment, and although their relationship begins and continues on a hostile note, they come to understand each other's needs and hang-ups. Eventually, their feelings blossom into true love.

Forgoing the usual one-liners, Simon created two endearing characters in Elliott and Paula, and Dreyfuss and Mason embodied them with élan. In the way he rushes from despair to elation, in the nonstop prattle with which he overwhelms Paula, even in the manner in which he flings his scarf around his neck, Elliott is a man for whom all life is a stage: Dreyfuss comes perilously close to being too puppy-dog "cute" in the role, but happily he invests the character with boundless charm. Mason's Paula is a fully rounded creation as well, likable despite her too-quick tears and transparent vulnerability.

Along with Barbra Streisand and Glenda Jackson, Marsha Mason represented the new style in romantic heroines, more recognizably human, less feature-perfect, than the glossy goddesses of other years. And so did Jill Clayburgh, a superb actress with New York theater credits, who, after appearing in several forgettable films, won acclaim and an Oscar nomination for her subtle performance as a newly divorced woman in Paul Mazursky's intelligent comedy-drama *An Unmarried Woman* (1978). The following year, she revealed her facility with romantic comedy by costarring with Burt Reynolds in yet another film about the ramifications of divorce. In Alan J. Pakula's *Starting Over* (1979), she played Marilyn, a nursery-school teacher who meets Phil (Reynolds), a man reeling from the trauma of a sudden divorce from wife Jessie (Candice Bergen), who fancies herself as a liberated woman with a career as a songwriter. After some false starts, Marilyn and Phil are deeply attracted, but the alluring presence of Jessie continues to come between them. Eventually, despite Marilyn's fierce resistance, Phil's love for her prevails.

Although the plot line of *Starting Over* is hardly exceptional, James L.

Brooks's often perceptive screenplay etches characters who are all too recognizable in their frailties and hang-ups. As Jessie's ex-wife, Bergen draws a comical and surprisingly sympathetic portrait of a woman seeking to find herself. Clayburgh is also fine as a woman wary of commitment, but it is Reynolds's performance that gives *Starting Over* its strength and substance. Playing a self-effacing, vulnerable man, as opposed to his usual macho type, he remains firmly in control, whether reacting to the overeager women he now dates, or—in a memorably funny scene—having an anxiety attack in the middle of Bloomingdale's.

In the sixties, romantic comedy, like the marital comedy, had leaned heavily on teasing titillation. Free of the novelty of "naughtiness," the seventies comedies took male and female sexuality in its stride, concentrating more on adult relationships and less on adolescent winks and leers. Also, the leading players, while not lacking in charisma, resembled ordinary people rather than the movie stars of old. Whatever the loss in glitter and glamour, the romantic comedy was entering the grown-up world.

The Goodbye Girl
(Warner Bros., 1977). Paula McFadden (Marsha Mason) and Elliott Garfield (Richard Dreyfuss) move from antagonists to lovers during the course of the film. Dreyfuss's skillful, exuberant performance won him an Academy Award as Best Actor.

245

Chapter 20

Don't Send Flowers

Marital Comedy in the Seventies

B y the start of the seventies, the leering, "bad little boy" approach to extramarital activities had abated, and although the landmark 1969 film *Bob & Carol & Ted & Alice* dealt with straying partners, it was infidelity by the cheerful mutual consent of husband and wife who were not *really* giving their consent at all, of course. (The film ended with the two couples in bed together, chortling at the absurdity of switching partners.) In the early seventies, a number of marital comedies turned from concentrating on sexual concerns to investigating many other facets of married relationships. The tone became sharper and more sardonic, betraying an edge of bitterness and melancholy over lost chances and lost hopes.

In contrast with marital comedies of the sixties, some films were willing to probe more deeply beneath the surface of modern marriage. The problems of a dissatisfied husband, for example, were treated astutely in Irvin Kershner's sharp-edged comedy-drama *Loving* (1970). A film that examined aspects of the married state without equivocation or soft-pedaling, it starred George Segal (in one of his best performances) as Brooks Wilson, a commercial artist and family man who lives the good suburban (New York–Westport) life but finds himself suddenly overwhelmed by the sheer complexity of getting through each day and week. Drowning in his basic mediocrity, he must cope not only with meeting the demands of a new house, a wife, and children, and his all-important clients but also with satisfying his own libido. The film climaxes at an elaborate cocktail party in which closed-circuit television exposes Segal in an on-camera sexual betrayal with a neighbor's wife, leaving his future an open-ended question.

Don Devlin's screenplay for *Loving*, from a novel by J. M. Ryan, is unusually scrupulous in its treatment of the troubled central character. Watching him interact with his unhappy wife and bratty children, or coping with his angry or

Loving (Columbia, 1970). Portrait of an unhappy marriage: harried George Segal and disgruntled wife Eva Marie Saint. This rueful comedy-drama presented some clear-eyed observations on the married state.

246

Plaza Suite *(Paramount, 1971). An increasingly frantic couple (Lee Grant and Walter Matthau) try to lure their about-to-be-married daughter out of the bathroom, where she has locked herself. This third segment of Neil Simon's three-part screenplay contained some good farcical moments.*

amorous neighbors and high-pressure business colleagues, we come to understand his feeling of being trapped. Yet despite Segal's likability as an actor, his Brooks Wilson is ultimately a less than admirable figure, a man who lies and cheats with impunity. Segal's expert performance is well matched by Eva Marie Saint, who subtly conveys the mixed emotions of a woman who knows her husband only too well and who is fully aware of her humiliating position.

Other discontented husbands, searching for intangible moments of romance or meaning in their lives, continued to turn up in films of the early seventies. In the first segment of Neil Simon's adaptation of his three-part Broadway comedy *Plaza Suite* (1971), Walter Matthau played Sam Nash, the straying middle-aged husband of Karen (Maureen Stapleton). Sharing a room—and little else—in a suite at New York's Plaza Hotel, the two confront the widening gap in their twenty-four (or is it twenty-three?) years of marriage. As in other Simon plays, there is an undercurrent of anger and melancholy beneath the laughter. For Sam, his infidelity is a furious reaction to advancing age ("I don't accept getting older"); for Karen, covering her pain with wisecracks, there is the awareness of irrevocable loss as she discovers his cheating ("Everyone cheats with his secretary. I expected something better from you than that!"). Perceptively written, this segment of *Plaza Suite* was the best of the three. Matthau also starred in the other two, first as a famous movie director who attempts to seduce old schoolmate Barbara Harris, and then as a desperate father whose daughter has locked herself in the bathroom on her wedding day. The latter episode, with Lee Grant as the equally frantic mother, hid its basically sour tone under several layers of farce.

Matthau played another unhappy husband, but of an entirely different stripe and inclination, in Elaine May's dark comedy *A New Leaf* (1971). Here, he was Henry Graham, a carefree millionaire who spends his way into insolvency and then must marry a rich woman in order to continue his self-indulgent lifestyle. He chooses Henrietta Lowell (May), a clumsy, myopic heiress to a fortune. After disposing of her cheating servants and lawyer, he plans to murder her and inherit her money. He nearly succeeds, until his guilt overwhelms him, and he rescues her from a watery grave, only to realize that he has placed himself in her hands forever.

Although *A New Leaf* brings a number of sly touches to Henry's plight, the film as released cannot be said to reflect Elaine May's work. Author of the screenplay, as well as the film's director and costar, May asked to have her name removed from the credits when the studio cut nearly eighty minutes from her original version. We can only guess at the material that was excised, but what's left is frequently diverting in a haphazard and off-the-wall fashion. Until Henry turns to murder as a solution to his problems, the film resembles a thirties screwball comedy with its high-living playboy, an all-knowing butler (George Rose), a much-hated uncle (James Coco), and an exasperated lawyer (William Redfield). Once Henrietta, played to a fare-thee-well by May, enters the scene, the movie takes on a new comic dimension; she resembles every unmarriageable daughter that hapless screwball-comedy heroes shunned until the attractive heroine came along. Whatever may have been the desecration of May's work, her Henrietta is a unique creation, a graceless and pathetic nonentity.

Among the discontented husbands and troubled wives of the seventies, there were a number of couples whose problems stemmed not from their own psyches but from a hostile world that impinged on their daily lives. As a number of films amply demonstrated, there was no better representative of the harried modern husband than Jack Lemmon. With the passing of the years, the genial actor who had been an ideal foil for Judy Holliday began to take on the worn, desperate look of the perennial victim; he might be a victim by his own hand, as in *Days of Wine and Roses* (1962) or *Save the Tiger* (1973), but the world was not a friendly place for this actor.

In several instances conceived by Neil Simon, life for Lemmon and his wife turned positively harrowing. Ostensibly, since Simon was a prominent writer of comedy, their dilemmas would be funny as well as nerve-racking, but in truth there was not much to laugh at in either his original screenplay for *The Out-of-Towners* (1970), or his adaptation of his Broadway comedy *The Prisoner of Second Avenue* (1975). In both, Lemmon and his wife were subject to a series of indignities that would send even hardier people to a padded cell. The former film, an oppressive farce directed by Arthur Hiller, trapped the incredibly naïve George and Gwen Kellerman (Lemmon and Sandy Dennis) in a nocturnal urban nightmare in New York City. Subject to every horror the city can devise, the hapless couple end up broke and broken. Any vague humor that may have existed in their plight was dissipated by Lemmon's angry ranting and Dennis's endless whining.

Lemmon's plight in *The Prisoner of Second Avenue* was also dire but somewhat less harrowing, and also funnier. Here, he played Mel, a once-happy city dweller suddenly down on his luck and badgered at every turn by neighbors, relatives, and the daily trauma of urban life in the mid-seventies. He nearly loses his mind, but helped by his sensible wife Edna (Anne Bancroft), he prevails to fight on. Feisty even to the point of collapse, Mel keeps a reserve of tenacity and strength that makes him a more appealing beleaguered hero than the overwrought George Kellerman of *The Out-of-Towners*. Lemmon also has a much more compatible costar in Anne Bancroft, whose wry performance is the film's best feature.

Neil Simon's married folk surfaced again in *California Suite*, the 1978 film version of his Broadway play. A multipart comedy like *Plaza Suite*, it intermingled the stories of a number of married couples (plus one ex-couple) who come to stay at the posh Beverly Hills Hotel in Los Angeles. Despite the stellar cast that included Jane Fonda and Walter Matthau, and competent direction by Herbert Ross, only one of the four episodes held any real interest. In a sharply written screenplay, Maggie Smith played Diana Barrie, a prominent British actress who has come to Los Angeles with her husband Sidney (Michael Caine) for the Oscar ceremonies. (She has been nominated as Best Actress.) The dialogue exposed Diana's desperate fear of losing her bisexual husband, which she conceals under a steady flow of brittle banter. In a case of life imitating art, Maggie Smith won an Oscar for Best Supporting Actress for her assured performance.

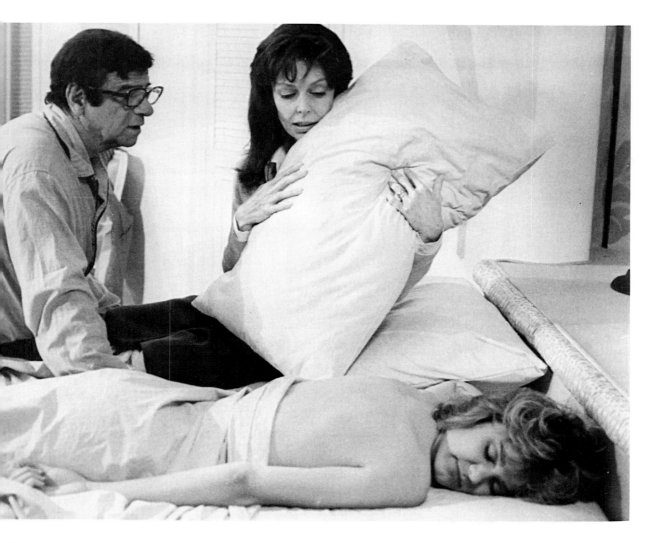

ike the romantic comedy, marital comedy of the seventies had turned away from the salacious point of view in order to deal, in comedy terms, with more mature themes. In the process, it had come upon the worm in the apple, finding a sour discontent, a lingering malaise, at the heart of many marriages.

Still, laughter was hardly extinct, and we could continue to enjoy the sight of a confounded Walter Matthau or a harried Jack Lemmon finding more blisters than bliss in the game of marriage.

California Suite *(Columbia, 1978). Elaine May (center) confronts the evidence of husband Walter Matthau's apparent indiscretion.*

Chapter 21
Nose-Thumbing for Fun and Profit
Blacker Comedies and Ruder Farces

Many comedies of the sixties had taken pleasure in mocking American traditions—social, political, and military—and in turning accepted tenets of civilized behavior on their ear. With the seventies, the mockery grew deeper and blacker. In the early years of the decade, film after film chose to focus on a disordered world in which nothing was what it appeared to be, and nobody was safe from crackpots and predators. It was a world in which government officials were devious crooks, doctors could be killers in white, and cities were hotbeds of depravity and murder.

As in the sixties, death was an integral part of many comedies, its blackness and finality bringing a mordant tone to the humor. But now the locales in which death took its toll—the battlefields, the hospitals, the inner cities—became metaphors for a civilization in disarray. The "down with the establishment," "end the Vietnam War" attitudes that inspired marches and rallies seeped into many films, often obliquely or symbolically—these were, after all, Hollywood films, where audacity could go only just so far.

So a film such as Robert Altman's *M*A*S*H* (1970) used the Korean "police action" of the fifties, rather than the Vietnam War of the late sixties and seventies, to assault the futility, foolishness, and brutality of all wars. Alternating scenes of bloody carnage with brashly farcical sequences, Altman's film plunged the viewer into the midst of a M*A*S*H (Mobile Army Surgical Hospital) unit in Korea. The comedy centered on Captains "Hawkeye" Pierce (Donald Sutherland) and "Trapper John" McIntyre (Elliott Gould), two brilliant surgeons who, when they are not

patching up the broken, bleeding bodies of wounded soldiers, enjoy carrying on in the style of ribald teenagers. To mask their rage and sorrow, they take pleasure in chasing and often catching the nurses, and especially in humiliating anyone they look upon as a pompous fool.

A rare sort of film—a farce with deadly serious intentions—*M*A*S*H* succeeds, for the most part, in keeping its mixture of bloodshed and slapstick under control. There are many audaciously funny scenes in Ring Lardner, Jr.'s screenplay (adapted from Richard Hooker's novel), most memorably a climactic football game that the MASH unit wins by injecting the rival team's star player with a paralyzing drug. In other scenes, the comedy turns unduly harsh and cruel, especially in the treatment of Major Margaret "Hot Lips" Houlihan (Sally Kellerman) and her priggish, Bible-spouting lover, Major Frank Burns (Robert Duvall). The film's treatment of women, in general, is rather insulting—the nurses seem to serve as either prey or therapy. Still, Altman's improvisational style, with its overlapping dialogue, often works to point up the grim reality behind the laughter.

War as both charnel house and loony bin was also the central concern of Mike Nichols's adaptation of Joseph Heller's novel *Catch-22* (1970). A scathing, mordantly funny comment on the irrationality, blatant stupidity, and numbing brutality of war, the film extended the attitudes of such sixties movies as *The Americanization of Emily* into the area of surrealism. Buck Henry's screenplay combined comic devices such as exaggeration and reverse logic with grimly realistic details to make a deadly serious point about war. The result irritated many critics and baffled many viewers, especially those who had never read the novel, but *Catch-22*, for all its clutter and overlength, could boast a number of stunningly effective sequences.

The film's central character is Yossarian (Alan Arkin), a bombardier stationed on a small Mediterranean island during World War II, who is convinced that, in the crazy wartime world, everyone is determined to see him dead. Lying seriously wounded after being stabbed by a German prisoner of war, Yossarian reflects on his experiences, his memory ranging across the many demented characters he has encountered. These include Colonel Cathcart (Martin Balsam), who keeps raising the number of bombing missions, and whose main goal is to be written up in *The Saturday Evening Post*; Major Major (Bob Newhart), a reluctant officer who vacates his office by the window whenever anyone wants to see him; Milo Minderbinder (Jon Voight), for whom the war is merely a giant business-making opportunity; and General Dreedle (Orson Welles), who likes to say "Take him out and shoot him!" whenever anyone incurs his displeasure. The relatively sane few, such as Art Garfunkel's naïve Captain Nately, are far outnumbered by the crackpots.

In a fragmented series of sequences—some outrageously funny, others harrowing—*Catch-22* captures the mounting madness that finally prompts Yossarian to desert. For example, when Yossarian refuses to obliterate an Italian town that has no strategic value and drops his bombs into the water, General Dreedle insists on awarding him a medal anyhow, only casually noting that Yossarian is stark naked. ("Unless I miss my guess, you're out of uniform.") In this demented wartime environment, a dead pilot is buried at a funeral where nobody knows or remembers him, and Yossarian is arrested for being AWOL, while a colleague (Charles Grodin) who has just murdered an Italian whore is casually ignored. Amid all this perversity, the specters of death and destruction in battle shroud every waking moment.

Away from the battlefields, there were other film characters of the period who tried desperately to hold on to their reason and their humanity in the midst of chaos. In Arthur Hiller's *The Hospital* (1971), Dr. Herbert Bock, played intensely by George C. Scott, can find no solace nor even temporary peace; an emotionally drained man, he is driven by both the demons in his own mind and the demons of ineptness, indifference, and hopelessness that lurk in the halls of the hospital he administers. Paddy Chayefsky's screenplay for *The Hospital* is frequently dazzling in its verbal dexterity as it traces the steps by which Dr. Bock is reclaimed to life.

Indecently overcrowded and monumentally inefficient, the hospital becomes a metaphor for the national malaise, and Dr. Bock's anger and impotence reflect a national mood that was coalescing at the time. As he tries to cope with a vociferous local action group, an ill-trained, overworked staff, and—as a capper—a homicidal maniac stalking the hospital corridors, Dr. Bock sinks even further into drink and despair, until Diana Rigg, the attractive daughter of a patient, draws him into a brief but passionate affair. Once again, the movies' view of the healing power of sex has been demonstrated, and Dr. Bock now has the strength of purpose to take charge of the besieged hospital and say, "Somebody has to be responsible." Despite its lapses in logic and its overstated points, *The Hospital* is a pungent example of the period's jet black comedies.

An even blacker film came from the acid-tipped pen of Jules Feiffer. Following an erratic history on and off Broadway (and also in England) in the late sixties, his play *Little Murders* finally reached the screen in 1971 under the direction of actor Alan Arkin. A grim absurdist farce, it offered a nightmarish vision of an urban world gone insane, where sudden death can occur at random, and where armed, besieged families fight for their lives like soldiers in a war zone. In its day, the play had been called surrealistic; now the film version seemed sadly prophetic.

Elliott Gould starred as Alfred Chamberlain, a photographer whose view of the world is reflected in his choice of subject—he specializes in pictures of excrement. Alfred meets Patsy Newquist (Marcia Rodd), an incurably optimistic young woman with an excitable father (Vincent Gardenia), a light-headed mother (Elizabeth Wilson), and a strange brother (Jon Korkes). Alfred and Patsy fall in love and marry in a bizarre ceremony conducted by a hippie minister played by Donald Sutherland, but not long afterward, Patsy is killed by a stray bullet fired into their apartment. By the film's end, Alfred and Patsy's family are holed up in the apartment, firing at pedestrians. After they have killed their first victim, these cheerful assassins settle down for a happy family dinner.

With savage humor, *Little Murders* depicts the last gasp of urban civilization. In a New York City that bears an uncomfortable resemblance to the city of the 1990s, snipers, who may be your next-door neighbors, fire at random, muggers are everywhere, and pedestrians have the ashen look of the walking dead. What makes *Little Murders* funny as well as chilling is the way in which the characters respond to the mayhem in their midst, either accepting disasters large and small with blankly smiling equanimity or giving way to rampant hysteria at inappropriate times.

Some of the absurdist comedies of the period invited laughter by deliberately and perversely taking their humor to the further reaches of outrageousness. Carl Reiner's 1970 farce, *Where's Poppa?*—adapted by Robert Klane from his novel— hoped to startle viewers into rethinking such modern-day topics as filial responsibility, the judicial system, and (yet again) urban living. George Segal starred as a thirty-five-year-old lawyer burdened with a senile mother (Ruth Gordon) who is not only ruining his life and career but also destroying his chances with the woman (Trish Van Devere) he loves. His desperate efforts to deal with Momma—he harbors thoughts of matricide—also involve his married brother (Ron Leibman), who is repeatedly mugged in the park and who, under duress, rapes an undercover cop (the cop enjoys it and sends flowers.) Casting aside logic and reason, and building one absurdity upon another, *Where's Poppa?* succeeded in generating nasty laughter in some quarters, and revulsion in others.

While films such as *Where's Poppa?* were using outrageous absurdist humor to comment on the continuing malaise in American society at the start of the seventies, other comedies were investigating the widening schism between generations. The theme of conservative-minded parents at odds with their antiestablishment children provided the mainspring for *Taking Off* (1971), the first American film by noted Czechoslovakian director Milos Forman. Taking a freshly satirical look at the topic of disaffected, runaway teenagers that was being widely discussed and argued in the media, the film concerned a typical suburban couple (Buck Henry and Lynn Carlin) whose young and impressionable daughter (Linnea Heacock) suddenly vanishes into the dropout rock-music culture of New York City's East Village. In their search for her, the couple come upon eye-opening new situations that release their own inhibitions. They smoke pot at a black-tie banquet of the Society for Parents of Fugitive Children, and they play strip poker with newly acquired friends; ultimately, they sit down to dinner with their daughter and her hirsute boyfriend, who earns a huge income from his music.

Within this slender narrative, *Taking Off* constructs a series of comic sketches, written by playwright John Guare and others, and artfully edited in a jagged, improvisational style so that they comment on each other. Scenes of fresh-faced youngsters sweetly singing or sharing their dreams at a rock audition alternate with scenes of bewildered parents shedding their hang-ups. At the Society banquet, as the pot takes effect, nervous coughing gives way to giggling euphoria and then singing, ironically linking these uptight adults to their free-spirited children. It is the film's funniest, most observant sequence, questioning whether the children or their foolish, bewildered parents are the true fugitives.

America's changing attitude toward sexuality, implicit in *Taking Off*, became the central theme in several seventies films. Mike Nichols's blistering comedy *Carnal Knowledge* (1971) underscored the point that men who viewed women as castrating creatures, to be used and discarded like so many Kleenex tissues, continue to persist in society, despite the presumed changes in male-female relationships. Jules Feiffer's screenplay, following the blunt, unadorned style of his comic strips, concentrated on the sexual hang-ups of two men from their youthful college days in the 1940s to middle age some years later: sex-obsessed, irresponsible Jonathan (Jack Nicholson) and his more romantic and sensitive (but, in the long run, equally shallow) friend Sandy (Art Garfunkel). The women in their lives include the lovely Susan (Candice Bergen), whom Jonathan beds and Sandy marries, and Bobbie (Ann-Margret), the voluptuous good-time girl who becomes Jonathan's unhappy mistress.

Using frequent close-ups so that the characters' faces often resemble talking cartoon heads in a Feiffer strip, Nichols draws a bead on the callow and insensitive attitudes of Jonathan and Sandy toward women in general and their own women in particular. The young Jonathan of college days who thinks only of making out with the girls becomes the perpetually adolescent older man who treats Bobbie shabbily and falls into a rage at her desire for domesticity and marriage. Sandy himself proves to be as adolescent as Jonathan, trapped in an empty marriage with Susan and still admiring of Jonathan's sexual prowess. *Carnal Knowledge* may present an unflattering view of man as sexual predator and would-be sexual champion. Yet, like Jules Feiffer's cartoon strips, it exposes a few unpleasant truths with a jaundiced eye and sardonic wit.

At first glance, Hal Ashby's film *Shampoo* (1975) also appeared to be primarily a commentary on America's sexual mores. Set in Beverly Hills on the eve of Richard Nixon's election in 1968, the movie presents a sexual roundelay in which the pivotal figure is George Roundy (Warren Beatty), a popular hairdresser who is used by his women clients as a sounding board, confessor, and readily accessible stud. While currently involved with Jill (Goldie Hawn), George is also having an affair with Felicia (Lee Grant, in a stunning Oscar-winning performance), an older woman married to wealthy Lester (Jack Warden). Lester's mistress is Jackie (Julie Christie), a former lover of George's, who is still attracted to him. During the course of the film, relationships are changed or shattered, and George, essentially a hollow, uncommitted man unable to feel or express any genuine emotion, is deserted by everyone.

While the Robert Towne–Warren Beatty screenplay for *Shampoo* contains more sexual manipulations than a French farce, it soon becomes clear that the film has other things on its mind. At a party that turns into a victory celebration for Nixon, these people pay little heed to the high-minded, ironic speeches emanating from the television set ("The President can end the permissive attitudes . . ."). At the start of one of the most chaotic, duplicitous periods in American history, the guests, and the principal characters in the film, are living in a moral and emotional vacuum that may have begun on that momentous evening. George likes to pretend that he is at the "epitome" of his life, and he may find his fulfillment in sex— "It makes me feel like I'm going to live forever"—but in reality, he is baffled and frightened, unable to deal with any crisis or dilemma. (Jill tells him, "You never stop moving! You never go anywhere!") The other characters are no less lost or insecure as they discover that wealth, power, and sex cannot buy happiness. *Shampoo* offers an acrid satirical portrait of a glittering society beginning to rot, and the shallow people heedlessly perched on the edge of a turbulent era. As a film, it is sometimes unfocused and overbaked; as social commentary, it is fascinating.

In 1979, Hal Ashby directed *Being There*, another film that commented ironically on American society, this time the nation's obsession with the media, and its tendency to take any pronouncement in print on or television as the gospel truth. In his penultimate role, Peter Sellers starred as Chance, a retarded gardener who knows only gardening and what he sees on television, which he mimics. Cast into the world of Washington, D.C., by the death of his employer, he finds himself living in the palatial home of Eve Rand (Shirley MacLaine), the wife of Benjamin Rand, an influential but dying financier (Melvyn Douglas in his last—and Oscar-winning—performance). Soon, every one of Chance's meaningless remarks, exclusively about television or gardening, is regarded as profoundly wise, and he becomes a media celebrity in great demand, as well as a sounding board for policymakers. Even the President (Jack Warden) is impressed, and Eve, who is attracted to Chance, regards him as a chance for sexual fulfillment. At the end, after Benjaain Rand's funeral, Chance is viewed as a potential presidential candidate. Once the point has been made that America's media madness can turn a fool into a prophet, *Being There* has little place to go, and the single joke eventually wears thin despite some amusing scenes.

In the deflating tone of the period, other films cast a satirical eye on familiar American rituals, and in the process pointed out how self-deluded, self-serving, and thick-skinned poor mortals could be. Michael Ritchie's diverting, underrated *Smile* (1975) concentrated on the events and the antics surrounding a real beauty pageant staged in Santa Rosa, California. Jerry Belson's screenplay brought together a number of people intensely involved in the pageant, including the mobile home dealer (Bruce Dern), who is the contest's chief judge, and the prudish head of the proceedings (Barbara Feldon), who is having marital problems. Without being unduly harsh, *Smile* captured all the foolishness and frenzy of the pageant: the dashed or threadbare hopes, the fierce ambitions, and all the silly, endearing displays of "talent" by participating contestants. (One girl demonstrates how to pack a valise.)

As a mosaic of American life, with multiple characters and points of view, *Smile* resembled Robert Altman's masterly *Nashville*, released that same year. Altman himself clearly found satisfaction in this approach, using it for two much less successful films that appeared later in the decade and were subject to delayed or limited release. Using his familiar pattern of interlocking stories and overlapping dialogue, *A Wedding* (1978) depicted the utter chaos surrounding a lavish wedding. An unusually strong cast that included Carol Burnett, Mia Farrow, Vittorio Gassman, and Lillian Gish shouted and hurtled their way through a series of intrigues, mishaps, and sexual encounters that became increasingly incoherent as the film progressed. Altman's 1979 film, *H.E.A.L.T.H.*, more closely resembled *Nashville* in its attempt to use a single major event—here a health-foods convention—as a metaphor for the nation as a whole. The squabbling between Lauren Bacall (claiming to be an eighty-three-year-old virgin) and Glenda Jackson as bitter rivals for the presidency of a national health organization was obviously a not so oblique commentary on U.S. presidential politics.

Not all the broadly farcical comedies of the seventies were necessarily satirical or metaphorical. A number of movies were merely inclined to take advantage of relaxed industry standards by pressing the limits of rude or even obscene behavior and cheerfully "letting it all hang out." Raucous farces such as *Car Wash* (1976), *Up in Smoke* (1978), and *National Lampoon's Animal House* (1978) worked strenuously for their laughs by trading in gross and raunchy jokes, or, as in the case of the all-black *Uptown Saturday Night* (1974) and its two sequels, by offering freewheeling slapstick. Matching their style and intention to the targeted audience, they occasionally succeeded.

John Landis's *Animal House*, in fact, was hugely popular; a nonstop assault on convention and propriety, it concerned the residents (or, more accurately, inmates) of Delta House, a reviled fraternity at Faber College in 1962, and their besting of the college's uptight dean and the vicious, snobbish rival fraternity, Omega House. John Belushi starred as Bluto, Delta's grossest resident, who smashes beer cans on his forehead, instigates food fights, and spies on the undressing sorority girls from a strategically placed ladder. The fact that the Delta boys cheat, lie, and steal to exact their revenge on the "enemy" would probably only occur to viewers who have reached the age of reason. In keeping with the film's intended audience, adults are depicted as mean-spirited, corrupt, stupid, and sexually frustrated. Still, the movie earns some laughs, as when Bluto, at a toga party, listens to a guest's rendition of a folk song and proceeds to calmly demolish his guitar.

While comedies were getting ruder and blacker, the seventies also witnessed an influx of the movie parody. Over the years, an occasional film such as *Destry Rides Again* would spoof the conventions of its genre while making certain to keep some of them intact. On the whole, however, the movie send-up was confined to television and such programs as "Your Show of Shows," where parodies of popular genres were often executed in brilliantly conceived sketches. (Stanley Donen's 1978 film, *Movie Movie*, expanded this idea into a feature film.) Believing that movie audiences would now respond to feature-length versions of such sketches, filmmakers began offering them fairly regularly throughout the decade.

Inevitably, many of these spoofs came from Neil Simon and Mel Brooks, both of whom had worked on Sid Caesar's 1950s comedy and variety program, "Your Show of Shows" (Simon occasionally, Brooks as one of the regular contributors). Both writers had the qualifications to carry off such parodies: a sense of the absurd, a taste for the outrageous gag (Brooks more than Simon), and a tacit fondness for the genres being spoofed. Simon's *Murder by Death* (1976) mocked the conventional murder mystery in which a group of people are summoned to appear at a mysterious and sinister locale (*The Cat and the Canary, And Then There Were None*) and confront murder and mayhem. In this preposterous send-up, the world's greatest detectives (broadly drawn takeoffs of Nick and Nora Charles, Hercule Poirot, Sam Spade, and others) come to the remote mansion of eccentric Norman Twain (author Truman Capote), where they are challenged by their host to solve a murder that has not yet taken place. A stellar cast headed by David Niven, Peter Falk, Peter Sellers, and Maggie Smith struck some funny, and some heavy-handed, blows at the "haunted house" mysteries. Simon followed *Murder by Death* and *The Goodbye Girl* with *The Cheap Detective* (1978), a spoof of the hard-boiled detective story, which mixed stale gags with on-target allusions to old movies.

Although Mel Brooks took a similar approach when he turned to parodying genres in the seventies, his films, on the whole, were more successful than Simon's. (They were also cruder, and more tasteless, which probably made them more popular.) Unlike that of Simon, Brooks's humor was influenced less by the sophistication and discipline of "Your Show of Shows," which tended toward pure parody, than by the outrageous, scatological humor he had cultivated in his earlier days. Free from the constrictions of television, Brooks was able to play the wicked boy who writes dirty words on the blackboard, the class cutup who shocks his teachers into dismay and his fellow students into laughter. In the seventies, when his popularity peaked, he found the movie audience that considered this sort of material uproariously funny. The bad taste that permeated his films was irrelevant—one either laughed at amorous old ladies and wind-breaking cowboys or did not; what was relevant was that, for a time, Brooks had struck a vein of anarchic, burlesque humor that had not surfaced since the days of the Marx Brothers.

Following his debut feature film, *The Producers*, and *The Twelve Chairs* (1970), a mildly diverting farce set in old Russia, Brooks did not create another film until 1974, but when he did, it proved to be one of his most popular efforts. A freewheeling burlesque of the Western, *Blazing Saddles* is also a compendium of Brooksian humor: the scatological jokes; the blatant anachronisms (Count Basie's band appears out of nowhere to play "April in Paris"); the startling reversal of stereotypes (homespun townsfolk using four-letter words); and the cheerful disregard of time and place (asked to sing "a good old nigger work song," the black chain gang breaks into a chorus of "I Get a Kick Out of You"). The screenplay by Brooks, Richard Pryor, Andrew Bergman, and Norman Steinberg takes the familiar Western characters—the stalwart cowboy, the rowdy saloon queen, the grizzled gunslinger, and others—and sends them spinning impudently into Brooks's own comedy orbit.

Merely a peg on which to hang the gags, the plot of *Blazing Saddles* involves Bart (Cleavon Little), a black drifter who becomes sheriff of the beleaguered Western town of Rock Ridge—the citizens are not too thrilled to see him—and vows to clean out the corruption. Opposing him are Harvey Korman's Hedley Lamarr—"*Hedley! Not Hedy!*"—the attorney general who covets the land; his featherbrained henchman, Slim Pickens, and the state's governor (Brooks), a certified idiot more concerned with his "secretary"'s cleavage than with running the government. On Bart's side, helping him rout the villains, is the Waco

Blazing Saddles (*Warner Bros., 1974*). *Lili Von Shtupp (Madeline Kahn) trots out a tune for the saloon regulars. With her Germanic style, insinuating wisecracks, and pronounced lisp, Lili was clearly a takeoff on Marlene Dietrich's Frenchy in* Destry Rides Again.

Kid, played by Gene Wilder. A once-famous alcoholic gunslinger down on his luck, Waco sees things clearly: To him, the folks of Rock Ridge are "simple farmers, people of the land, the common clay of the new West—you know, morons." Also taking part in the melee is Lili Von Shtupp (Madeline Kahn), a seductive, lisping Dietrich-like singer. ("A wed wose! How womantic!")

With little regard for rationality or taste, the sight gags and jokes in *Blazing*

Saddles fly thick and fast, and many of them can startle an uncritical viewer into laughter. Bart's chic cowboy costume, complete with Gucci bag, is a visual joke in itself, and Lily's saloon rendition of "I'm Tired!" parodies Dietrich's world-weariness and toneless singing with sidesplitting accuracy. Western conventions are turned on their ear. For example, Brooks wickedly sends up the obligatory town meeting, at which an old codger, clearly a graduate of the "Gabby" Hayes School of Western Diction, speaks in "authentic pioneer gibberish."

Young Frankenstein *(Fox, 1974). Accompanied by assistants Inga (Teri Garr) and Igor (Marty Feldman), young Dr. Frankenstein (Gene Wilder) tries to recapture the Monster (Peter Boyle). A later film highlight was the Wilder-Boyle duet of "Puttin' on the Ritz."*

Brooks's next film, *Young Frankenstein* (1974), is a much more disciplined effort, although once again he cannot always resist the prurient or obvious joke. A clever parody of the horror film, particularly the *Frankenstein* cycle, it captures accurately the visual style and familiar conventions of the genre and then tilts them giddily in the direction of parody. All our memories of the old Saturday afternoon thrillers—the surrealistic sets, the bizarre characters, the sudden jolts of fright—are reawakened, only to be sent up by Brooks's screenplay with Gene Wilder. Wilder himself plays the title role, a teacher and grandson of the original overweening scientist, who returns to Transylvania to recreate the old Monster and unleash the same nightmare as before.

Surrounding Frankenstein are the familiar figures of past years and countless movies, now ripe for spoofing: Igor (Marty Feldman), the leering humpbacked gargoyle who assists in the experiments (his hump keeps shifting from side to side); Frau Blucher (Cloris Leachman), the sinister housekeeper, whose very name causes horses to whinny in terror; Elizabeth (Madeline Kahn), Frankenstein's untouchable fiancée who secretly harbors (as we always suspected) a streak of nymphomania; and the Teutonic inspector (Kenneth Mars), who cannot control his false arm (no doubt he is a distant relative of Dr. Strangelove). Finally, there is the Monster himself (Peter Boyle), the usual mixture of horrific and pathetic, who turns out to have hidden talents as an entertainer and a lover.

Although it occasionally lapses into coarseness or gratuitous cruelty, *Young Frankenstein* contains many moments

of inspired lunacy. The key scene, in which the Monster is animated in the laboratory, reproduces the sense of awe and terror—the thunderbolts, the crackling equipment, Frankenstein's cry of "Give my creation life!"—while simultaneously mocking the absurdity of it all. When the escaped Monster finds his way to the blind old man (an unbilled Gene Hackman), we remember the original touching sequence from *Bride of Frankenstein*, but here Brooks reverses the expected by

High Anxiety *(Fox, 1977). One might say that Dr. Thorndyke (Mel Brooks) suffers from an advanced case of acrophobia. Brooks's broad take-off of Hitchcock thrillers, especially* Vertigo, *occasionally hits the mark.*

making the Monster the victim of the blind man's kindness—he has scalding pea soup poured into his lap, and his thumb is set on fire instead of his cigar. The film's highlight occurs when the Monster, transformed into a fair approximation of a human being, joins Frankenstein in performing a song and dance to "Puttin' on the Ritz" before an invited audience of scientists and journalists.

Following *Silent Movie* (1976), an intermittently amusing farce without spoken dialogue but with lots of old-style knockabout slapstick, Brooks returned to parody with his next movie. Ostensibly a tribute to Alfred Hitchcock—the film is dedicated to him and borrows liberally from his work—*High Anxiety* (1977) aimed at the sort of psychological melodrama (disordered minds in sinister settings) at which the master director excelled. The film centers on Dr. Richard Thorndyke (Brooks), a psychiatrist who comes to take over the top position at the mysterious Institute for the Very, Very Nervous, where murder and kinkiness appear to be the norm. Involved in the tangled plot are the institute's scheming director (Harvey Korman), his grim head nurse (Cloris Leachman), whose breasts could penetrate steel, and patients in advanced stages of madness induced by the management. Thorndyke also comes to the rescue of Victoria Brisbane (Madeline Kahn), whose father is a patient under the delusion that he is a dog. In true Hitchcockian fashion, the good doctor, who happens to suffer from a fear of heights, soon becomes a murder suspect, pursued by the police and targeted by the villains.

As in his other parody films, Brooks is less concerned with shaping a coherent narrative than with spoofing the familiar conventions of old movies. Here, however, Brooks runs into an obstacle that damages his humor severely. Whereas the Western and the horror film were timeworn genres, Hitchcock's films were unique creations of one vastly gifted (if rather peculiar) filmmaker. It is neither homage nor satire merely to seize upon the shower scene in *Psycho*, or the attack of the winged creatures in *The Birds*, or James Stewart's acrophobic ascent to the tower in *Vertigo*, and give them an outrageous comic spin.

In a decade of movies that began with the blood-splattered humor of *M*A*S*H*, continued to skewer our sexual and political mores in *Shampoo*, and then ended with a bitterly ironic toast to our *H.E.A.L.T.H.*, the operative color for many comedies was clearly jet black. Complementing the films about offbeat romances and unhappy marriages were movies that took a sour view of institutions we had formerly revered: Hospitals were havens for incompetents and killers; colleges were hotbeds of rebellion and disaffection. Why continue to honor parents when they were hopelessly confused (*Taking Off*), bothersome and senile (*Where's Poppa?*), or just plain silly (any number of films)?

If there was little joy in seventies comedy, there were those who could still laugh at the absurdities of life in what Preston Sturges called our "cockeyed caravan." And one owlish writer-actor-director rejected the mocking, iconoclastic tone of his colleagues and forged his own path through the byways of comedy.

Chapter 22
Woody Allen in the Seventies

oody Allen's first film of the seventies, and his first after *Take the Money and Run,* proved conclusively that he was a major comedy talent who could write, direct, and even act in his own movies without showing the strain of wearing three hats. An uneven but often sidesplitting film, *Bananas* (1971) succeeded in bringing together and also improving on the elements that had made his first work so original; it created a unique comedy world in which ordinary events turn into ludicrously funny surprises (the hero talks to his middle-class Jewish parents while they perform surgery on a patient who joins in the conversation) and activities never seen by the camera eye somehow become media events (the movie begins with a televised assassination and ends with a televised wedding-night consummation).

Bananas also went one step further in crystallizing the Allen persona that appeared through most of the seventies and finally deepened with *Annie Hall:* the consummate nebbish at large in a lunatic society, who, with no justification whatever, fancies himself as a confident statesman and stud. When he learns the bitter truth, as he always does, he survives through his wit and his intellect. Finally, *Bananas* synthesized Allen's early style: the jokes about the hero's inadequacies (his girlfriend tells him that he has something "emotionally, sexually, and intellectually missing"); the comic twist on a dramatic situation (a man is tortured by being forced to listen to the score of *Naughty Marietta*); the slapstick derived from the great silent comedians (the inept hero's training as a revolutionary evokes memories of Chaplin and Keaton).

Allen plays Fielding Mellish, a products tester (shades of Chaplin in *Modern Times*) who meets and falls in love with Nancy (Louise Lasser), an activist currently opposing the dictatorship in San Marcos, a tiny South American country. When Nancy rejects him, a dejected Fielding flies off to San Marcos, where he becomes involved with its revolution. When he is kidnapped by the rebels, he somehow evolves into their leader, and when the current regime is overthrown, he is declared

Annie Hall (United Artists, 1977). Woody Allen's Oscar-winning comedy traced the on-again, off-again romance of Annie (Diane Keaton) and Alvy Singer (Allen). Keaton's oddball clothing for the movie started a fashion trend.

the country's president. Back in America, wearing a Castro-like red beard, Fielding is brought to trial and found guilty of various crimes. His sentence is suspended, however, and he is reunited with Nancy, who now claims to love him.

Without a shred of reason or common sense, Allen's screenplay for *Bananas*, written with Mickey Rose, uses the wildly improbable situations as a springboard for a steady stream of sight gags, slapstick, verbal byplay, and send-ups of movie conventions. In some instances, the jokes, grafted arbitarily onto a situation, fall flat, but much of the material evokes laughter. The funniest sequences occur after Fielding is captured by the rebels and forced to learn about guerrilla warfare and survival. He nearly blows himself up with a grenade; at a lunch counter, he orders (among other things) one thousand grilled cheese sandwiches and seven hundred cups of regular coffee; and, during a raid against the enemy, he manages to inject his fellow rebels with sodium pentothal. There are also some jibes at America's continual interference in the political and cultural life of its neighbors to the south.

Although they also had moments of inspired comedy, Allen's 1972 films were not among his most memorable. In *Play It Again, Sam,* adapted by Allen from his Broadway play, he appeared as Alan Felix, a writer whose life is shaped by the movies. Devastated by his recent divorce, he turns periodically to the ghost of Humphrey Bogart (Jerry Lacy, from the Broadway cast), who materializes to offer advice on women ("I never met one who didn't understand a slap in the mouth or a slug from a .45.") Encouraged by his married friends Dick and Linda (Tony Roberts and Diane Keaton, also from the Broadway cast), Alan stumbles from one disastrous date to another, until he finds unexpected romance with neglected Linda. Their affair ends with the couple reprising the famous airport scene between Rick and Ilsa at the end of Casablanca, a scene Alan has waited all his life to perform. Despite the relative absence of Allenesque one-liners, and a predictable screenplay that seldom ventures beyond its basic gimmick, the film is never less than amusing.

Allen's second 1972 film was, on the whole, a misfire. Suggested by, rather than adapted from, Dr. David Reuben's best-selling book, *Everything You Always Wanted to Know About Sex, But Were Afraid to Ask* brought together seven sketches on that ever-popular subject. Some of the sketches were extended single jokes—in "Do Aphrodisiacs Work?" court jester Allen is unable to open the chastity belt of the Queen (Lynn Redgrave) after giving her an aphrodisiac; others worked for laughs by placing an ordinary-looking man in a bizarre sexual predicament: In "What Is Sodomy?" Gene Wilder falls in love with an Armenian sheep named

Daisy. The most imaginative of the sketches, "What Happens During Ejaculation?" had an apprehensive Allen as a sperm cell who is sent out from a giant mission-control center (a wittily executed set) by operator Tony Randall, only to come up against a four-hundred-foot diaphragm. The entire film takes some wicked swipes at America's preoccupation with sex, but on the whole, the material is more heavy-handed than amusing.

Allen's next film proved to be one of his best of the decade. Mixing science fiction and satire, *Sleeper* (1973) presented his most sustained comic vision to date, a flight of fancy that offered surprises at every twist and turn of the story. Allen played Miles Monroe, part owner of a New York health-food restaurant, who goes into the hospital in 1973 for a minor operation and, after being frozen by his cousin when complications develop, wakes up two hundred years later in a totalitarian futuristic society where everything is changed. Now considered a dangerous alien, Miles flees into the camp of the rebels, taking with him Luna (Diane Keaton), a girl who was once his reluctant prisoner. Determined to overthrow the government in power, Miles and Luna attempt a most unusual coup: posing as doctors, they run off with the nose of the nation's mysterious leader—all that is left after an accident—before it can be cloned into a facsimile of the same tyrant. Now in love, the two have triumphed for the rebels.

Around all this inspired silliness, the screenplay by Allen and Marshall Brickman constructs a network of sight gags (many of the sets are splendid visual jokes), Allenesque one-liners ("I believe there's intelligence in the universe, except in certain parts of New Jersey"), and bursts of slapstick that, once again, emulate the great silent comedians. Allen is especially fond of using the futuristic setting to comment humorously on personalities of the mid-seventies. Asked to identify figures from his own time, Miles reports that Bela Lugosi was mayor of New York and Billy Graham "knew God personally. . . . they went on double dates together."

Although the film is studded with contemporary Allen jokes ("What does it feel like to be dead for two hundred years?"/"It's like spending a weekend in Beverly Hills"), *Sleeper* comes closest to matching a timeless Buster Keaton comedy in its style and content. Like Keaton, Allen is the badgered little man, trying to hold on to his life and his composure in a hostile world where even objects are threatening. (A major difference is that Keaton knows no fear, while Allen is a self-professed coward.) Also like Keaton, Allen is often handicapped in his adventure by a girl who is not overly bright. Luna, who majored in cosmetic sexual technique and poetry in college, can barely remember anything she is told. She entangles Miles in a mechanical lift by pressing every wrong button, and nearly gets them arrested on more than one occasion with her dithering.

Allen followed *Sleeper* with *Love and Death* (1975), one of his most fascinating and least accessible films. His previous movies had demonstrated a clear intellectual bent—the screenplays are studded with literary references—but now he chose to devote most of the film to a spoof of classic Russian novels, adding, for extra measure, homages to Chaplin and to great foreign filmmakers from Eisenstein to Bergman. It was not a venture calculated to please a wide audience, but in a handsome production set to the stirring music of Prokofiev, *Love and Death* generated abundant laughter.

Not all the elements were brand-new. Once again, Allen played the consummate nerd, a cowardly, sexually frustrated, and bookish young Russian named Boris Grushenko who lives through the Napoleonic Wars only to be executed for killing Napoleon himself. (Well, not really, but the charge remains.) Narrating the story from his prison cell, Boris describes his experiences on the battlefield, his unrequited love for his beautiful cousin Sonia (Diane Keaton), and his collusion with Sonia in the plan to assassinate Napoleon. As in many a long Russian novel, the plot fairly teems with other characters, including Boris's dim-bulb father (Zvee Scooler), who owns a plot of land a few inches wide and hopes to build on it someday, and Father Nikolai (C. A. R. Smith), a priest who dresses entirely in black. (Boris: "For years I thought he was an Italian widow.")

As in his earlier films, Allen delights in outrageous anachronisms that send familiar situations spinning into a kind of delirium. During his experiences as Russia's worst soldier, Boris is badgered by a black drill sergeant who seems to have wandered out of a modern-day war film, watches the army's primitive idea of a hygiene play warning soldiers on furlough, and takes part reluctantly in a battle in which blinis are sold by hawkers. At the same time, Sonia keeps reappearing in Boris's life. Out of unrequited love for Boris's burly brother Ivan, she marries a merchant whose sole interest in life is herring, and apparently she takes as her lovers the entire male population of Saint Petersburg. Eventually, she marries Boris, but only when there seems to be nobody left.

After playing the leading role in *The Front* (1976), Martin Ritt's weakly conceived and overly pat comedy-drama about blacklisting in the fifties, Allen returned to "triple threat" filmmaking as the star, director, and coauthor (with Marshall Brickman) of *Annie Hall* (1977), his most successful film to that point. For the first time, Allen decided to move beyond the familiar ingredients: the put-downs of his appearance and personality; the string of jokes that play surprising, funny variations on such sober topics as death and anti-Semitism; the fears and obsessions that are transformed into farce. These ingredients are all present in *Annie Hall*, but Allen also creates two believable, fully rounded leading characters whose romance clashes with their neuroses. In Alvy Singer and Annie Hall, Allen offers his first portraits of the bright, intense, angst-ridden New Yorkers who would populate many of his later films.

Clearly, *Annie Hall* has some autobiographical elements. Like Allen himself, Alvy Singer is a well-known comedian, married and divorced several times, and, if not true to Allen, at least a personification of the inept, put-upon character he created in his stand-up comedy routines. Currently in the throes of a devastating breakup with equally insecure Annie (Diane Keaton), Alvy ranges across his life, remembering his childhood, his ex-wives and girlfriends, and mostly his scratchy, exasperating, and exhilarating romance with Annie.

Annie Hall has the requisite Allen quips about sex ("That was the most fun I've had without laughing") and the usual skewed memories of the past (Alvy recalls living underneath a roller coaster in New York's Coney Island). The film is also a veritable anthology of Allen's concerns and attitudes, mouthed by the neuroses-ridden Alvy: the perils of being a celebrity (later a major theme in *Stardust Memories*); his deeply rooted pessimism (life is either miserable or horrible); his obsession with anti-Semitism (a number of jokes turn on his Jewishness and the hostility he believes it evokes in many people); and his dislike of intellectual cant. Favorite targets, such as the fatuousness of Hollywood types who "take meetings" and the strange eating habits in California, come in for some sharp ribbing. (At a restaurant, he orders alfalfa sprouts and a plate of mashed yeast.)

However, what sets *Annie Hall* apart from Allen's previous efforts and marks it as an advance is the loose, freewheeling way he uses film itself to tell his story of Alvy and Annie's checkered romance. Allen veers from fantasy to reality as he moves into Alvy's cluttered mind. When Alvy recalls his school days, he imagines children in the class telling the audience what they will become. (Inevitably, the mousiest girl is "into leather.") To refute the overheard remark of a pompous film scholar who quotes Marshall McLuhan, Alvy fantasizes bringing out McLuhan in person to burst the man's bubble.

Much of *Annie Hall*'s success can be attributed to Diane Keaton's Oscar-winning performance as Annie. (The film itself, Allen's direction, and the screenplay also received Academy Awards.) Whether one responds with irritation or delight to

the character's eccentricities or dithering manner, it is clearly a star-making role that Keaton invests with unique charm. In a sense, the film is Allen's tribute to Keaton; it ends with Alvy recalling moments from their past, as images of lovely, mixed-up Annie waft onto the screen. Unlike the screwball comedies of the thirties, where characters reacted to a world turned irrational, Alvy and Annie are the untidy products of their own internal irrationality, the end products of an introspective generation.

With his next film, a dark-hued comedy entitled *Manhattan* (1979), Allen delved deeper into that generation, exposing its neuroses and hang-ups with a subtlety and perceptiveness that surpassed even *Annie Hall*. This time, he concentrated on inhabitants of the fabled island of the title, examining their essentially selfish lives against Gordon Willis's stunningly photographed black and white

Manhattan (United Artists, 1979). Isaac Davis (Woody Allen) serenades girlfriend Tracy (Mariel Hemingway) with his harmonica. Allen's bittersweet comedy captured the tangled lives of a group of neurotic New Yorkers.

mosaic of the city. (Willis also photographed *Annie Hall.*) Allen played Isaac Davis, a successful comedy writer who is plagued by his ex-wife, Jill (Meryl Streep), at the same time that he is having a troubling affair with seventeen-year-old Tracy (Mariel Hemingway)—"I'm dating a girl who does homework." A third woman enters his life when he drifts into a love affair with Mary Wilke (Diane Keaton), the intensely neurotic mistress of his married friend Yale (Michael Murphy), who can never seem to get her life in order. Obsessed with his own feelings and unable to develop durable relationships, Isaac ends up virtually alone, baffled, regretful, and dissatisfied with his life.

Although *Manhattan* has sober and reflective overtones, it still contains the requisite number of laughs for a Woody Allen comedy. As usual, there are lines that reflect his cerebral bent—his relationships with women, he admits, should win him "the August Strindberg Award"—or comments that surprise us into laughter, as when Yale observes, "You think you're God," and Isaac replies, "I've got to model myself after someone." Even in the romantic scenes, Allen adds a refreshingly comic note. Riding in a taxi with Mary, he remarks, "You're so beautiful, I can't keep my eye on the meter." Still, a melancholy pervades the film; these are people who, for all their wit and sophistication, live with continual regret and a vaguely defined dissatisfaction. Scenes of rejection cause hurt and bewilderment. When Isaac tells Tracy that he loves someone else, her pain is very real, and at the film's end, when the reverse occurs, and Tracy leaves Isaac, his face reflects sorrow, confusion, and a fragment of hope. (This last shot is clearly modeled after the ending of Chaplin's *City Lights*.) Alvy Singer of *Annie Hall* agonized over his parting from Annie, but we know that he will paper over his pain with quips; Isaac Davis is a more deeply felt, more fully realized character, a would-be tiger who is really a timid tomcat lost in the city jungle.

There were even greater triumphs ahead for Woody Allen in the eighties. In the films in which he closed out the seventies, however, he revealed how far film comedy had come from earlier years. The familiar cut-and-dried distinctions between subgenres—romantic comedy, marital comedy, satirical farce—were becoming blurred and, in some cases, virtually invisible. Movies such as *Annie Hall* and *Manhattan* mixed romance with social commentary, slapstick with satire, stirring in a variety of cinematic techniques borrowed from the great masters. It was a heady mixture that resulted in human comedy rather than a specific subgenre, and many comedy films in the eighties, without necessarily being directly influenced by Allen, would also choose humanity for their canvas.

Part 6

THE HUMAN SIDE
Movie Comedy in the Eighties

A decade of crises and tensions abroad . . . and landmarks and scandals at home . . .

The decade begins with a disastrous attempt to free the fifty-two American hostages held by Iran, but early in 1981, on the day that Ronald Reagan becomes president, the hostages are freed after 444 days of captivity. There are other international crises throughout the eighties: in 1982, a force of American marines and rangers invade the tiny island of Granada to protect American citizens from "leftist thugs," and in 1983 Lebanon is the tragic scene of two violent incidents, six months apart. The decade is also marked by intense controversy over the selling of arms to Iran. Still, the eighties bring events of remembrance and pride: the Vietnam Veterans Memorial is dedicated in Washington in 1982, and in 1986, America celebrates the one hundredth birthday of the Statue of Liberty.

There are many notable "firsts" throughout the eighties, many involving women: Sandra Day O'Connor is named the first woman justice on the Supreme Court; Representative Geraldine Ferraro of New York becomes the first woman in American history to be nominated for vice president, and the aptly named Sally Ride becomes the first woman to ride in space. The following year, Dr. Kathryn Sullivan is the first American woman to walk in space.

The eighties have their share of both natural and man-made disasters. In 1980, a volcanic eruption at Mount St. Helens in Washington State registers 4.1 on the Richter scale. And in 1985, the Indian government files suit against the Union Carbide Corporation for damages arising from a gas leak at the company's plant in Bhopal, which killed 1,700 people. Late in the decade, scandal rocks America when popular evangelists fall from grace over their various indiscretions, and scandals on Wall Street involve the buying and selling of stocks based on illegal information.

During the eighties, Walt Disney World's EPCOT Center opens in Florida. . . . All America watches the stirring Olympic Games in Los Angeles in 1984. . . . And Johnny Carson celebrates the twenty-fifth anniversary of "The Tonight Show." Popular films of the decade include: *Raiders of the Lost Ark, Chariots of Fire, ET: The Extraterrestrial, Out of Africa,* and *Batman.*

The Four Seasons *(Universal, 1981). Alan Alda's winning, perceptive comedy starred (left to right) Jack Weston, Bess Armstrong, and Alan Alda as friends who share their seasonal vacations.*

Chapter 23

Love Isn't All

Romantic and Marital Comedy in the Eighties

I f romantic comedy in the sixties replaced a smile with a leer, while romantic comedy in the seventies turned eccentric and quirky, the eighties brought new rules to the perennial game of love. Whereas in previous decades the focus had remained on the lovers as they moved from ardent to argumentative, then back to ardent again, romantic comedy in the eighties had many other things on its mind. In former years, the heroine's job, whether as strident boss lady or coy interior decorator, had merely served as a springboard to the story's romantic complications. Her job actually had little true relation to her feelings—the climactic scenes usually took place in the living room, the bedroom, or the courtroom rather than in her workplace. With the arrival of the eighties, and the growing assertiveness of women, comedy films began taking note of the fact that a career could be as important, if not more important, than romance. There were other kinds of love, as well—love for family, friends, and especially oneself. A warm and involving romance was crucial, even indispensable; but there were other concerns, other relationships, that entered into the complex scheme of things.

From the very start of the eighties, some comedy films focused on heroines who strove to find a balance between their lives as women, career persons, and sometimes members of a family. Claudia Weill's *It's My Turn* (1980), for example, concerned a teacher (Jill Clayburgh) who discovers that she must reevaluate her priorities when she falls in love unexpectedly with the son (Michael Douglas) of her new stepmother. Other women learned to compete with their lovers in the corporate world—in Sidney Lumet's *Just Tell Me What You Want* (1980), Ali MacGraw, mistress to business conglomerate Alan King, wheels and deals for power with as much ruthlessness as he. Even Goldie Hawn shed her "blond airhead" image to

Tootsie *(Columbia, 1982). "Dorothy Michaels," alias Michael Dorsey (Dustin Hoffman), looks on as director Ron Carlyle (Dabney Coleman) makes a point with soap opera actor John Van Horn (George Gaynes). Sydney Pollack's comedy scored a few points itself on sexual roles in society.*

Broadcast News *(Fox, 1987). In this romantic comedy, Albert Brooks, Holly Hunter, and William Hurt played coworkers whose lives intertwine both on and off their jobs at a television station.*

play sharp professional women in Jay Sandrich's *Seems Like Old Times* (1980) and Norman Jewison's *Best Friends* (1982).

Curiously, the most successful striving woman of the period turned out to be not a woman at all but an intensely dedicated actor who disguises himself as a woman. In Sydney Pollack's hugely popular comedy *Tootsie* (1982), Dustin Hoffman played Michael Dorsey, a gadfly among actors, who defies his agent's edict that he is unemployable by winning a key role on a soap opera as "Dorothy Michaels."

Entering with a born actor's enthusiasm into the impersonation, Michael manages to turn his feisty character into a media celebrity. Major complications occur when he falls in love with Julie (Jessica Lange), a beautiful cast member, and also finds himself being courted by Julie's widowed father (Charles Durning). Ultimately, unable to sustain his deception any longer, he reveals his true identity during a live television performance, causing dismay and consternation all around. At the end, there is a suggestion that Julie will forgive his deception.

With a brightly written screenplay by Larry Gelbart and Murray Schisgal, which falters only in an unconvincing climax, *Tootsie* aims a few well-directed satirical arrows at the overwrought condition of many actors and the frenzied worlds of television and theater in which they thrive. Embodied by Dustin Hoffman, Michael Dorsey is a vastly amusing combination of talent and chutzpah. Whether defending his acting ability ("Nobody does vegetables like me") or entering enthusiastically into his female impersonation (fluttering fingers at his throat, a voice blending honey and steel), Michael carries self-absorption to a level far beyond mere vanity. As he falls ever deeper under Julie's spell (Jessica Lange's Oscar-winning performance gives this vulnerable character a radiant glow), he conveys a tangle of conflicting emotions, which Hoffman expresses beautifully.

Clearly, *Tootsie* has more on its mind than its comedy gambit of the female impersonator. As Michael Dorsey immerses himself in his role of Dorothy Michaels, he begins to inhabit her mind, to understand Dorothy's feelings as a woman. Apart from the obvious irony of his adding feminist sentiments to the role he plays on the soap opera, Michael learns a great deal by seeing the world through a woman's eyes. In the end, he can affirm that "Dorothy [was] the best of my manhood, the best part of myself." He was obliged to pretend to become a woman in order to become a better man. "I miss Dorothy," Julie tells Michael, sans disguise, and he replies, "You don't have to. She's right here."

Later in the decade, romantic comedies in which career considerations were at least as important as sex (and in some cases, even more important) continued to surface. James L. Brooks's *Broadcast News* (1987) set its story amid the hurlyburly of a television station in Washington, D.C., where producers, writers, staff, and on-camera anchorpeople engage in a fierce, high-pressure battle for ratings while trying to contend with each other's disparate personalities, as well as the magnet of sexual attraction. Brooks's crackling screenplay centered on three people: Jane Craig (Holly Hunter), a take-charge, driven young woman whose coiled springs tend to lose their tension when she is alone; Tom Grunick (William Hurt), the station's handsome, superficial, and not overly bright news anchor; and Aaron Altman (Albert Brooks), an erudite, acerbic, but uncharismatic news writer. Their lives and careers touch and intermingle in many ways. Jane and Tom finally have a sexual assignation, but ultimately they part forever. Interestingly, whereas in other decades hero and heroine would separate out of jealousy or some foolish misunderstanding, in this romantic comedy of the late eighties, the two break up when Jane learns that Tom has committed an unforgivable breach of ethics in one of the news stories they prepared together. There is no sudden capitulation for Jane—integrity in one's career supersedes any other consideration.

The following year, Mike Nichols's *Working Girl* (1988) also mingled business and sexual matters, featuring a heroine who apparently excels in both. ("I have a mind for business and a bod for sin!") In a role that would have either baffled or mortified the working girls of the thirties and forties, Melanie Griffith starred as Tess, a deceptively smart, ambitious secretary at a stock brokerage. When Katharine Parker (Sigourney Weaver), her manipulative, power-hungry boss, breaks her leg in a skiing accident, Tess rises in the ranks by taking over Katharine's job, wardrobe, and even her current lover, Jack Tanner (Harrison Ford). With a combination of nerve and savvy, Tess succeeds in impressing the higher-ups and entrancing Jack. Even after Katharine returns in a blaze of fury to point an accusing finger (actually an accusing crutch), Tess manages to triumph.

More of a fable with romantic trimmings than an accurate view of upward mobility in the business world, *Working Girl* amuses, largely due to Kevin Wade's lighthearted screenplay and Griffith's performance as Tess. Echoing Judy Holliday in her "dumb as a fox" routine, she invites trust with her innocent stare and a manner that is simultaneously naïve and sexy. Yet her mind is working overtime to achieve her goals. To get to an important figure involved in a major business deal, she crashes the wedding reception of his daughter, cagily manipulating her way into his presence and conning him into listening to her ideas.

Working Girl makes a fascinating contrast with the working-girl romantic comedies of the thirties and forties. Although it is set realistically in the offices of a high-powered brokerage in New York City, Nichols's film is no less a Cinderella story than those in which Jean Arthur or Claudette Colbert labored a half century earlier. Like her sisters-in-business, Tess enjoys a fanciful victory—we leave her with a topflight job, a loving fiancé, and the knowledge that she has triumphed over those who would do her in. The strong difference, however, lies in goals and intentions: Tess, a child of the late eighties, wants the position that comes with superior know-how and brain power; Jack Tanner is merely a pleasant "extra." On the other hand, the heroines of earlier decades, while no less smart (and certainly sharper-tongued than Tess), long for the men who will take them away from the drudgery of work.

If Tess represented a marked contrast with the working-girl characters of previous decades, what were we to make of a popular Cinderella heroine of 1990 who worked on the opposite end of the employment spectrum as a Hollywood hooker? In other years, prostitutes may have had proverbial hearts of gold, but their tawdry lives usually ended in humiliation or death. Vivian, however, played by Julia Roberts in Garry Marshall's enormously successful *Pretty Woman*, is a charmer, a wistful beauty with a sad past who dreams of being the central figure in a romantic fantasy. During the course of the film, she entrances a wealthy young businessman, who transforms her, Galatea-style, into a stylish, ravishing young woman. In turn, she teaches him humanity and generosity. Clearly, *Pretty Woman* is intended as yet another version of the Cinderella tale. (The movie even follows the tale closely: The hotel personnel who help her turn from prostitute to princess include variations of the fairy godmother and her cohorts.) What astonishes is that audiences in a realistic age could still readily accept as its Cinderella a good-hearted hooker who has had bad breaks. Apparently, like Vivian herself, who tells her benefactor, "I want the fairy tale!" the public's longing for fable and fantasy has never abated.

Having noted the movie's curious choice for a heroine, it should be added that *Pretty Woman* works moderately well as a romantic comedy. Once the improbable premise is accepted—New York wheeler-dealer Edward Lewis (Richard Gere), in Hollywood for a business deal, hires Vivian as his escort for a week—the film moves breezily to its preordained conclusion. Vivian's sorties into the posh, snobbish world of Beverly Hills are amusing, and the humanizing of Edward, though predictable, is nicely managed. The movie's greatest strength, however, lies in Julia Roberts's star-making performance as Vivian. With her infectious grin and unforced charm, she overrides her shortcomings as an actress and turns a potentially irritating character into an enchanting heroine.

Several comedies of the late 1980s touched lightly on the perennial movie concept that people are sometimes unable to recognize when they belong together and must work their way through a thicket of misunderstandings before they can reach commitment. Joan Micklin Silver's deft little comedy *Crossing Delancey* (1988) starred Amy Irving as Isabelle ("Izzy") Grossman, thirty-three years old and

entirely content with her single lot. Through a neighborhood matchmaker (Sylvia Miles) hired by her feisty grandmother (Reizl Bozyk), Izzy meets Sam Posner (Peter Riegert), a pickle vendor and "nice guy," who finally impresses her with the warmth and sensitivity beneath his down-to-earth exterior. Seasoned with New York ambience and bolstered by Amy Irving's perfectly tuned, appealing performance as Izzy, *Crossing Delancey* is a small film with charm to spare.

A romance that takes an entire decade to gestate emerges fully grown at the conclusion of the 1989 comedy *When Harry Met Sally . . ..* Rob Reiner's film traces the over-the-years relationship of Harry Burns (Billy Crystal) and Sally Albright (Meg Ryan). Focusing on the question of whether men and women can ever be friends without "the sex thing" getting in the way, Nora Ephron's screenplay takes Harry and Sally from overt hostility in 1977, to a polite but scratchy acquaintanceship in l982, and finally to passionate lovers in 1987, when they are both at their most vulnerable. (His wife has left him, and she has ended a long-standing affair.) For a time, the change from good friends to sexual partners disrupts their relationship, but in the end, they realize that they belong together.

Clearly using Woody Allen's films as a model (the lushly romantic musical score, the evocative New York photography, Meg Ryan's slightly dithering, Diane Keaton–like performance), *When Harry Met Sally . . .* fails to match Allen in either wit or humor. There are scattered laughs in Nora Ephron's screenplay, but the movie is essentially hollow and uninhabited—as played by Billy Crystal, Harry is rather boorish and smart-alecky, and Meg Ryan's Sally ranges from pertly appealing to oppressively "cute." With characters who elicit so little sympathy, and a story line so frail, the film must resort to gimmickry, such as having middle-aged and elderly couples addressing the camera periodically to describe their first meetings. Whereas Woody Allen uses such a device to point up and comment on the events, here it seems like an intrusion into a none too strong narrative.

In romantic comedy of the eighties, another theme that emerged regularly was that of obsessive love: the man who finds himself hopelessly in love with an unattainable woman. (In other decades, the idea could turn melodramatic—*The Phantom of the Opera, The Collector,* and so forth—but eighties filmmakers found it more amusing than aberrational.) The comedy often stemmed from the meek, unprepossessing nature of the man contrasted with the lush, almost unreal sexuality of the woman. (Almost inevitably, all the screenwriters were male.) Blake Edwards had advanced this concept in his 1979 comedy *"10,"* which featured Dudley Moore in reckless pursuit of the ravishing Bo Derek.

Crossing Delancey
(Warner Bros., 1988). In Joan Micklin Silver's pleasing romantic comedy, "Izzy" Grossman (Amy Irving, center) is annoyed with the matchmaking attempts of her grandmother (Reizl Bozyk, left), while the matchmaker herself (Sylvia Miles) looks on.

With a style that suggested hidden reserves of mischief and wickedness, Moore was apparently viewed as ideal for portraying secretly obsessed romantics, or eccentrics in search of love. In Steve Gordon's *Arthur* (1981), as an alcoholic, infantile young millionaire who falls in love with a waitress (Liza Minnelli), he was every top-hatted playboy of thirties screwball comedy brought to a logical extreme.

As Arthur's haughty, impudent, and wonderfully acerbic butler Hobson, John Gielgud also appeared to have wandered in from another era. (Arthur: "I'm going to take a bath." Hobson: "I'll alert the media.") Crisply and even touchingly played by Gielgud in an Oscar-winning performance, Hobson is the film's most amusing creation. None of Dudley Moore's subsequent comedies approached *Arthur* in popularity, but his characters' obsession with unattainable or out-of-bounds women continued largely unabated in *Lovesick* (1983) and *Micki & Maude* (1984).

One of the most diverting comedies on the theme of obsessive love, Fred Schepisi's *Roxanne* (1987) gave a new spin to an old tale. In a clever updating of Edmond Rostand's *Cyrano de Bergerac*, Steve Martin played C. D. (Charlie) Bales, fire chief in a picturesque Washington State ski town called Nelson (actually British Columbia). Burdened with a grotesquely long nose, Charlie submerges his melancholy in generous amounts of wit and charm. He falls hopelessly in love with Darryl Hannah's Roxanne, a beautiful astronomy student, only to find her attracted to Chris (Rick Rossovich), a handsome but dull-witted member of his fire team. Serving as romantic surrogate for Chris, Charlie sends Roxanne seductive letters in his rival's name, so that she finally surrenders to Chris. Eventually, Roxanne realizes that she has been responding to Charlie's poetic soul.

Arthur *(Warner Bros./ Orion, 1981). Childlike, hard-drinking, and very wealthy Arthur (Dudley Moore) shares a newspaper with his sharp-tongued but deeply caring butler, Hobson (John Gielgud). In many ways, the movie recalled the well-remembered screwball comedies of the thirties.*

An exceptionally sweet-natured and likable movie, *Roxanne* succeeds in blending romantic feeling with comedy that stems from character. There are also ample amounts of well-executed slapstick—Charlie's firemen are bumbling reincarnations of the Keystone Kops. But what makes the film work best is Steve Martin's stunning performance as Charlie. In his best role to date, Martin gives the character a physical grace and dexterity reminiscent of the great silent comedians. Whether demolishing town bullies with his tennis racket, or confounding with a display of verbal pyrotechnics an oaf who comments on his nose, Martin uses his body in ways that make Charlie both touching and funny.

The seventies had seen their share of men in thrall to a blond dream (*The Heartbreak Kid* comes quickly to mind), but at no time were these yearning romantics as prevalent as in the eighties. From Hoffman's Michael Dorsey gazing with rapt adoration at Julie, to Martin's Charlie Bales leaping fences and scaling buildings to be with Roxanne, the movie decade had been replete with men who sought, and occasionally even found, the Perfect Woman. On the other hand, romantic comedies in the eighties also included a number of women who considered their careers as vital, if not more vital, than their men. These were not the broad-shouldered boss ladies of the forties, ready to give up their jobs for a man; these women were hardworking professionals. Juxtaposing the fantasies of the men with the realities of the women, one might surmise that a clash of the sexes was in the offing. However, this would underestimate the power of movie lore. In romantic comedies of the eighties, men who went in search of Snow White never ended up with the Witch instead. And career women seldom, if ever, lost sight of their Prince Charming.

At the same time that romance in the eighties was taking on a new coloration by adding career considerations to the sexual mix, movie marriages were getting short shrift from the filmmakers. During the decade, relatively few films dealt with the rewards and tribulations of marriage; those that did, however, handled the subject in an extraordinarily vitriolic and even nasty fashion, suggesting that marriage was a disease that could be cured only by divorce. (Family life, as we shall see, was quite another matter.) Gone were the amiably befuddled husbands depicted by Walter Matthau or Jack Lemmon, to be replaced by satyrs in the throes of male menopause.

A cluster of marital comedies appeared at the start of the decade, touching on either dissatisfied couples seeking to regain their vanishing youth or couples whose marriages were being wrecked on the shoals of infidelity. Moving beyond the playful, winking attitude of *A Guide for the Married Man*, or the relative "sophistication" of *Bob & Carol & Ted & Alice*, such films as Richard Lang's *A Change of Seasons*, Jack Smight's *Loving Couples*, and Gilbert Cates's *The Last Married Couple in America* (all released in 1980) display a coarse, "let it all hang out" attitude devoid of either wit or style.

One film, *The War of the Roses* (1989), seemed to crystallize the decade's poisonous attitude toward marriage and divorce. Adapted by Michael Leeson from a novel by Warren Adler, actor-director Danny DeVito's jet black comedy carries to an horrific extreme the sadomasochistic possibilities inherent in a crumbling marriage and a nasty divorce. Narrated as a cautionary tale by divorce lawyer Gavin D'Amato (an improbable Danny DeVito), the story centers on affluent corporation lawyer Oliver Rose (Michael Douglas) and his wife, Barbara (Kathleen Turner), whose relatively happy marriage crashes in flames. Consumed by a vindictive hatred for each other, and an insatiable thirst for revenge, the Roses refuse to capitulate in the divorce war that follows, leading to a mounting series of outrageous and repellent episodes. Their ferocious conflict ends in total disaster.

From the moment that Oliver and Barbara insist on remaining together in their well-appointed home, *The War of the Roses* spirals over the top into an area beyond mere tastelessness and far beyond the audacious shock effects expected in any black comedy. As their fury increases, the Roses' appalling actions—he urinates on the food at her fancy dinner party; she serves up his pet dog as pâté—generate disgust rather than laughter. It is certainly no offense to strain the limits of permissibility in a film, but when the strain is unaccompanied by any saving wit or humor, and the characters, as here, are so intensely unlikable, the result becomes hugely offensive. *The War of the Roses* marked a sad end for comedy, marital or otherwise, in the eighties.

Chapter 24
People Are Funny
Human Comedy in the Eighties

Confronted with changing attitudes in society, especially the long-overdue assertiveness of women in the boardroom and the bedroom, filmmakers in the eighties felt the need to reassure the paying audience that the old verities of home and hearth and the long-standing ties of enduring friendships still applied in the fiercely competitive, success-oriented decade. After years in which family comedies—staples of the thirties and forties—were merely simmering on the back burner, the studios began to turn out a number of films in which relationships among family members and friends were closely scrutinized. Intertwined lives that clashed or collided, and then finally merged in blissful contentment or at least settled into a temporary truce, became the principal concern of many an eighties film.

Some of the films, such as *Kramer vs. Kramer* (1979) and *Ordinary People* (1980), took the dramatic route, examining the trauma of divorce and death that can tear a family asunder. Many others dealt with family problems in ways that blended comedy and tragedy, confirming that most families wear both masks during the course of a lifetime. The success of James L. Brooks's *Terms of Endearment* (1983), in which the largely comic over-the-years contention of a mother and daughter ends with the daughter's untimely demise, triggered other comedy-dramas, such as Sidney Lumet's *Garbo Talks* (1984), Garry Marshall's *Nothing in Common* (1986), and Blake Edwards's *That's Life!* (1986), in which death, or the specter of death, plays an important role. In the latter film, Jack Lemmon, taking on another of his many angst-ridden roles, is a successful architect in the throes of a total breakdown as he reaches the age of sixty. Events both comic and poignant swirl about his birthday weekend.

By the end of the decade, it was clear that Hollywood's filmmakers could expect to strike box-office gold by touting the virtues, the strengths, and, of

Trading Places *(Paramount, 1983). Through a nefarious scheme, well-to-do commodities broker Dan Aykroyd and street-smart hustler Eddie Murphy change places, with surprising results.*

course, the comic interactions of the American family. One comedy of the late eighties that makes this point with exceptional warmth and humor is Norman Jewison's popular *Moonstruck* (1987). Perceptively and affectionately written by John Patrick Shanley, this delightful comedy revolves about the proudly Italian Castorinis, a middle-class Brooklyn family consisting of Papa Cosmo (Vincent Gardenia), a plumber whose fear of growing old and dying (even sleep is "too much like death") leads him to taking a mistress; wise and plain-speaking Mama Rose (Olympia Dukakis); confused Grandpa (Feodor Chaliapin) and his dogs; and, most particularly, daughter Loretta (Cher), a sensible thirty-seven-year-old widow. During the course of the film, Loretta becomes engaged to decent but dim Johnny Cammareri (Danny Aiello), then proceeds to meet and fall in love with Johnny's oddball younger brother, Ronny (Nicolas Cage). Everything is resolved happily, and the film ends with a toast *a la famiglia* as the camera pans across a shelf of family photographs.

Around this simple story, *Moonstruck* weaves a tapestry of pungent humor that surprises while it pleases. Without overstating the color and flavor of Italian Americans, the movie creates an atmosphere in which the characters can indulge their eccentricities or their flamboyant, romantic inclinations. Affected mysteriously by the full moon (Grandpa insists that "the moon brings the woman to the man"), these endearing people finally come to terms with their ordinary lives: Cosmo agrees to give up his mistress; Rose confirms her love for him in an affecting moment; and Loretta, under the spell of an unexpected romance, is transformed into a ravishing woman. Even Ronny, burdened for years by bitter resentment of his brother—he blames Johnny for causing him to lose his hand in a bakery accident—finally forgives him and returns to life under the bracing influence of his love for Loretta.

Moonstruck abounds in fine performances: Olympia Dukakis, an Oscar winner as Best Supporting Actress, brings touches of tartness and melancholy to her commonsensical Rose, and Vincent Gardenia makes Cosmo a rounded portrait of the nagging dissatisfactions of aging. Usually an irritating actor, Nicolas Cage succeeds in combining looniness and gallantry in equal proportions. Yet Cher dominates the movie with her Academy Award–winning performance. Her transformation is entirely convincing: from someone who can accept a marriage of convenience to an immature drone, she becomes a woman who exudes confidence.

Late in the decade and into the next, the screen's reflections on the strength of *la famiglia* were joined by a new interest in the problems and rewards of being a

parent. Filmmakers decided that there was box-office clout in a smiling, gurgling infant, and infinite comic possibilities in coping with this tiny, mysterious creature. A batch of movies in the late eighties featured anonymous cuddly infants whose sole purpose was to disrupt and ultimately change the lives of their sophisticated, free-living elders.

One movie heroine whose life is changed inexorably by an infant was played with great aplomb by Diane Keaton in Charles Shyer's 1987 comedy, *Baby Boom*. An ambitious, high-powered business executive, Keaton's J. C. Wiatt is bequeathed the baby of her deceased cousins and suddenly finds herself overwhelmed by the duties of being an unexpected mother. Her work suffers and her boyfriend leaves her, while her devotion to the baby grows deeper. The movie, however, is a Hollywood fable rather than a treatise on single motherhood. J.C.

Look Who's Talking *(Tri-Star, 1989). John Travolta lends a helping hand to baby, played by no less than four infants. This time, the jokes all fall to the infant, who wisecracks in the swaggering style and voice of Bruce Willis.*

Big *(Fox, 1988). In one of this amiable movie's brightest moments, Josh Baskin (Tom Hanks), who's really a twelve-year-old magically turned into an adult, dances atop a giant department-store piano with his boss, Mac (Robert Loggia).*

leaves the corporate world, settles on a farm in Vermont, and eventually finds a sturdy new boyfriend (Sam Shepard), a thriving business (in baby applesauce), and total contentment with Baby Elizabeth.

Most of the films about parenting that appeared in the last years of the eighties were not concerned with women like J. C. Wiatt but with men who were discovering that their manhood no longer disqualified them from the pleasures and perils of being parents. With women more active in the workplace, with many articles about the sensitive, "feminine" side of the male sex, men were being required to take on the nurturing qualities that had usually been expected of women. Their macho attitudes would not be threatened if they learned how to feed, diaper, bathe, or otherwise tend to an infant.

More than one comedy of the late eighties included the obligatory scene in which the virile male star becomes unglued when he holds an infant in his arms. Joel Coen's eccentric and often funny farce, *Raising Arizona* (1987), concerns "Hi" McDonnough (Nicolas Cage), a petty thief and ex-convict who kidnaps a baby (one of quintuplets) from a furniture tycoon at the behest of his childless wife (Holly Hunter). In the comic chaos that follows, Hi learns something about the responsibilities of being a parent—and a man. John Travolta also found new direction for his life in Amy Heckerling's hugely successful *Look Who's Talking* (1989), in which he played a likable taxi driver who latches on to unmarried Kirstie Alley and her baby. Here, the gimmick was having the baby talk in the voice of Bruce Willis, using the same macho, wise-cracking manner that had made him popular on television's "Moonlighting." (Confronted with breasts, the baby yells "Lunch!") The gimmick wears thin by midpoint, but the movie's good-natured tone and amiable performances guaranteed it a wide audience, as well as the inevitable sequel, *Look Who's Talking, Too* (1990).

Perhaps the most representative of the cluster of "male parenting" comedies is Leonard Nimoy's huge box-office success, *Three Men and a Baby* (1987). Audiences responded enthusiastically to this tale, adapted from Coline Serreau's 1985 French comedy, *Three Men and a Cradle*, concerning three affluent, swinging bachelors (Tom Selleck, Ted Danson, and Steve Guttenberg) who suddenly find themselves saddled with a baby fathered by one of them (Danson). Added to the comic uproar caused by handling an infant—the three seem amazingly inept about even such simple matters as diapering and feeding—are some improbable complications concerning the confusion of the baby with a package of heroin, followed by the arrival of true mother Nancy Travis, who wants to reclaim her baby. Although extremely popular—it prompted a 1990 sequel called *Three Men and a Little Lady*—the film smacks of easy contrivance.

Surrogate parents aside, one film of the late eighties, more than any other, succeeded in conveying the thorny pathway leading to true parenthood. By scrutinizing the lives of one large family, Ron Howard's bluntly titled *Parenthood* (1989) captures the joys, heartaches, and hang-ups of being a mother or father. Blending humor and "heart" in the fashion of the day, the screenplay by Lowell Ganz and Babaloo Mandel, from a story by Ganz, Mandel, and Ron Howard, focuses largely on Gil Buckman (Steve Martin) and his family, especially his wife, Karen (Mary Steenburgen), and their troubled oldest child, Kevin (Jasen Fisher). Interacting with the Buckmans, each with his or her own all-too-human problems, are Gil's parents, as well as Gil and Karen's siblings and their families. Within this framework, *Parenthood* manages to offer some home truths, not only about the problems of raising small children but also about the scratchy relationships that develop in later years between older parents and their grown offspring. Many of these truths are expressed in scenes that are both perceptive and funny, such as one in which Gil, given to fantasizing, imagines his son as a college commencement speaker, effusively bestowing credit on his beaming father.

Many other family comedies surfaced in the eighties, and even into the nineties, some adding new elements into the familiar mix. Penny Marshall's widely praised 1988 comedy-fantasy *Big* concerned a twelve-year-old who wishes for adulthood and magically finds himself in the body of thirty-year-old Tom Hanks, baffling his family, friends, coworkers, and especially himself. Another exceptionally popular movie, Chris Columbus's *Home Alone* (1990), intrigued audiences with the advertising slogan "A family comedy without the family," and indeed it revolved about Macaulay Culkin, a ten-year-old boy who is inadvertently left behind by his parents on their trip to Paris. His resourceful behavior in dealing with two comically inept thieves apparently delighted viewers of all ages, especially with the addition of some cleverly executed slapstick.

While these family comedies were dispensing homilies about parents and children, other comedies sought to investigate the strong, often troublesome relationships that existed between friends. Since these relationships could be as problematic or as complex as those between husband and wife, or parent and child, the films offered a new source for combining humor and sentiment. In previous decades, friendship had largely been a dramatic device; friends were the listening posts against which the hero or heroine could bounce his or her ideas and feelings. Now friends became the central concern of films that examined the reasons they remained together over the years, as well as the influences that could separate them.

Occasionally, a comedy would use friendship merely as a means of setting the plot in motion. In Colin Higgins's hectic, intermittently clever *9 to 5* (1980), Jane Fonda, Lily Tomlin, and Dolly Parton (in an agreeable film debut) played office workers with nothing in common who rebel against their obnoxiously sexist boss, Dabney Coleman. More often, however, friendship was the film's core and raison d'être, as in Alan Alda's *The Four Seasons* (1981). The film concerns three married couples who have been devoted friends for years, sharing each other's joys and sorrows and taking vacations together with every change of season. A traumatic break in their usual pattern occurs when one of their number divorces his wife and marries a much younger woman.

An insightful view of the shifting winds of friendship, Alan Alda's screenplay for *The Four Seasons* (he also starred as a member of the group) succeeds in conveying the many facets of these couples' durable relationships: the not so casual competitiveness among the men; the wives' clear-eyed and dryly humorous acceptance of their husbands' foibles; and especially the couples' ungracious reaction to their friend's young bride. (They especially resent the newlyweds' sexual prowess.) While keeping the tone appropriately light and humorous, the film also touches on such serious themes as the tests that even the strongest friendships must undergo in order to survive, and the fear of growing old and dying that lurks at the edges of the men's vanity and boisterous behavior. As the embodiment of the latter theme, Jack Weston gives the film's best performance as a hypochondriacal dentist; a chubby mass of perpetual apprehension, he tells his friends, "You think I don't hurt because I'm quirky, but I'm quirky because I hurt."

Lawrence Kasdan's *The Big Chill*, a film that cuts much closer to the bone in its depiction of friendships, appeared in 1983. Adroitly written by Kasdan and Barbara Benedek, this serious comedy brings together a group of friends of the sixties—all former students at the University of Michigan—for the funeral of their mutual friend Alex, a suicide. Now two decades past their bright years of hope and rebellion, most of these people are either vaguely or emphatically discontent with their present lives. Only Harold (Kevin Kline) and his wife, Sarah (Glenn Close), at whose home the friends assemble, have come to comfortable terms with themselves, although Sarah's mourning for Alex is deeper than Harold surmises—Alex was a former lover. Sam (Tom Berenger), a television star, is uneasy with his fame. Karen (JoBeth Williams), mired in a loveless marriage, retains her secret yearning for Sam. Nick (William Hurt) is a bitter, rootless remnant of the sixties. Acerbic Michael (Jeff Goldblum), who wanted to be a novelist, writes, apologetically, for *People* magazine. And corporation lawyer Meg (Mary Kay Place), after too many failed love affairs, longs to have a baby, with one of her friends as the father. During the course of a weekend, these characters reflect on the past and the present, rekindle old relationships, and then part company, possibly forever.

For all of its dark undertones, *The Big Chill* remains essentially a film whose characters have all the delusions and anxieties we have come to recognize in comedy. Despite their soul-searching, the friends are often seen satirically. With his air of self-denigration, Sam mocks every "instant" celebrity who has come to success too soon. Michael's penchant for excusing the work he does for the magazine is accompanied by his foolish pipe dream of owning his own nightclub. Karen may profess boredom with her marriage, but she opts for returning to her husband after her liaison with Sam. And Nick's antisocietal attitude comes off as more of a pointless anachronism than the threat it might have been two decades earlier. *The Big Chill* looks at its characters with affection but also with an amused candor.

Barry Levinson's *Diner* (1982), marking his debut as a director, offers another wry, incisive view of friendship, but one quite different from the disaffected veterans of the sixties in *The Big Chill.* In fact, the film takes place shortly before the turbulence of that decade changed American life forever. Set in Baltimore at Christmastime in 1959, Levinson's autobiographical screenplay revolves about a group of close friends who have just graduated from high school and are perched at the edge of maturity. They spend most of their nights at the Fells Point diner, chatting, arguing, munching french fries with gravy, and contemplating an uncertain future. Among them are Eddie (Steve Guttenberg), about to be married but only if his fiancée can pass a football quiz; Boogie (Mickey Rourke), a soft-spoken and knowing womanizer who has shady dealings with gamblers; Fenwick (Kevin Bacon), a wealthy dropout whose private despair causes him to behave erratically, and the uneasily married Shrevie (Daniel Stern). Relationships shift and change as these young men move from easy jocularity to the serious concerns of adulthood.

An affectionate portrait of a generation, *Diner* is rich in sharply observed details that illuminate not only the daily existence of these close-knit friends but also their insecurities and their aspirations. Beyond their amusing, accurately recorded diner conversations—the arguments over the relative merits of Frank Sinatra and Johnny Mathis, the bravado chatter about girls—these characters are in uneasy transition, about to face terrifying new challenges. Each of them seeks a way to avoid the future, from Eddie's devising the football quiz for his bride-to-be to Shrevie's fierce attachment to his record collection, the center of his emotional life. The diner has been a certain source of comfort and continuity, but now time and experience are eroding that certainty. Ultimately, all the scattered pieces of *Diner* come together to form a funny and touching mosaic of the shaky bridge between adolescence and maturity.

The strong bonds of friendship, made even stronger by a shared feeling for the freedom and bounty of America, are also apparent in Paul Mazursky's sweet-natured, rambling 1984 comedy, *Moscow on the Hudson*. Blending quirky humor and flag-waving patriotism, the film concerns Vladimir Ivanoff (Robin Williams), a Russian musician who defects during his trip to America with the Moscow Circus. On his way to American citizenship, he meets a number of helpful people, including black security guard Cleavant Derricks and his family, Cuban lawyer Alejandro Rey, and pretty Italian immigrant Maria Conchita Alonso, with whom he falls in love. The film strains credulity by giving Vladimir a cluster of warmhearted friends who are too patly ethnic—one from each nationality—and Mazursky's soft-centered humanism and patriotic sentiment overpower the ripe satirical possibilities. Yet Williams's ingratiating performance, conveying a true sense of the immigrant experience, made the movie worth watching.

When not concerned with families and friends, many of of the "human" comedies of the eighties concentrated their stories on two opposing, wildly disparate characters who interact with others, or with each other, in some sort of fierce contention. In previous decades, these "one-on-one" films often involved two "buddies" who battled over the same woman, or sought to outsmart or outmaneuver each other, but who remained loyal and steadfast in a crisis: James Cagney and Pat O'Brien, squabbling in the navy or on a rubber plantation; Bing Crosby and Bob Hope on the road to everywhere; Paul Newman and Robert Redford confronting the Bolivian army or outwitting a kingpin gambler. In the eighties, a number of comedies revolved about two men of vastly different backgrounds and persuasions who were obliged to deal with each other, or, as the oddest of odd couples, to join forces against a common enemy. The broad implication of these films was that in the volatile eighties, people with opposing beliefs and lifestyles were required to live together or perish.

Occasionally, a film merely used two dissimilar characters as a catalyst for setting the story in motion. Jonathan Demme's winning and original comedy *Melvin and Howard* (1980), for example, begins with an encounter between two men in the Nevada desert. Driving his truck through the desert, Melvin Dummar (Paul LeMat), a genial but none too bright, irresponsible man, comes upon a scruffy, drunk, and incoherent codger (Jason Robards) who claims to be billionaire Howard Hughes. They sing together; Melvin gives him a quarter, and sends him on his way. After Hughes dies, a mysterious will turns up bequeathing $156 million dollars to Melvin. The will is contested, and Melvin never receives a penny.

Based on a true incident (the so-called "Mormon" will that gave money to Dummar was thrown out of court in June 1978), *Melvin and Howard* constructs its

story around Melvin, a perennial loser and haphazard dreamer, and his wife Lynda (Mary Steenburgen in a lovely Oscar-winning performance). A dissatisfied woman with dreams of her own, Lynda wins a large sum of money tap-dancing on a television quiz show and leaves Melvin. Their lives converge briefly again after Melvin becomes a "celebrity" over the Hughes will and must fight to establish its validity. In the end, these dreamers come to reasonable terms with reality: Melvin, remarried and running an insolvent gas station, remarks, "Howard Hughes sang Melvin Dummar a song. That's what happened."

Suggesting an unmalicious Preston Sturges in its feeling for offbeat dialogue, Bo Goldman's Oscar-winning screenplay views its characters with affection and without condescension. Their hopes and dreams are never belittled: Whether he earns his living as a factory worker, a milkman, or a gas-station owner, Melvin sees himself as a potential winner who has only had bad breaks; even as she performs as a go-go dancer at a sleazy bar, Lynda also holds fast to her aspirations. Jonathan Demme directed these futilely striving characters with a perceptive eye for the telling detail—when they remarry, an unctuous justice of the peace performs the ceremony while an organist plays the "Hawaiian War Chant" and two blank-faced witnesses sit nearby.

In a variation on the theme of two dissimilar characters who are required to interact, John Landis's popular comedy *Trading Places* (1983) builds its premise on a decent if overly familiar idea. In a wager to test the effects of environment over heredity, two wealthy old brothers (Don Ameche and Ralph Bellamy) scheme to have snobbish commodities broker Louis Winthorpe III (Dan Aykroyd), who manages their company, change places with streetwise Billy Ray Valentine (Eddie

Murphy, in his second movie). Not surprisingly, Winthorpe collapses into a desperate, pitiable wreck, while hustler Billy Ray's business savvy and his quick adjustment to high living confound the bigwigs. Angered when he learns about the brothers' callous duplicity, Billy Ray takes Winthorpe into his former home, and the two join in a plan to avenge themselves on the brothers. John Landis's well-paced direction and a lively screenplay by Timothy Harris and Herschel Weingrod made the frayed material seem almost newly woven.

Buoyed by a brash, cocky personality that mocked the white establishment, Eddie Murphy soared to popularity in the eighties, either joining burly Nick Nolte in several "odd couple" teamings (*48 Hrs.*, 1982; *Another 48 Hrs.*, 1990) or striking out on his own in the hugely successful *Beverly Hills Cop* (1984) and its 1987 sequel. An earlier—and much superior—black comedian, Richard Pryor, also carved a niche in films with a sly, knowing persona that maliciously poked fun at white society's perception of blacks. Starting with *Silver Streak*, a 1976 comedy-melodrama, Pryor teamed with Gene Wilder in occasional "odd couple" farces—*Stir Crazy* (1980); *See No Evil, Hear No Evil* (1989); and *Another You* (1991)—that followed a similar pattern: street-smart, resourceful Pryor and overwrought Wilder must extricate themselves from deep trouble, usually with the law or the underworld. Although his concert films displayed his profane, acerbic wit to good advantage, Pryor's attempts to strike out on his own, in such films as *Critical Condition* (1987) and *Moving* (1988), were not very successful. When he teamed with Eddie Murphy for *Harlem Nights* in 1989, the results were negligible.

Other black actors with the ability to write and direct as well as perform turned up in the eighties. Spike Lee made his feature-film debut in all three capacities with *She's Gotta Have It* (1986), an often sharply funny sex comedy set among young black people in Brooklyn. His story centers on a seductive, proudly promiscuous commercial artist (Tracy Camilla Johns), who can't make up her mind between three very different men. Lee, who also played one of the men, followed *She's Gotta Have It* with *School Daze* (1988), a raucous comedy about life on a black college campus in the South. His subsequent films, *Do the Right Thing* (1989) and *Mo' Better Blues* (1990) continued to reveal an original talent. Another black actor-writer-director named Robert Townsend attracted attention with his comedy *Hollywood Shuffle* (1987). Townsend coauthored (with Keenen Ivory Wayans) and starred in a loosely structured satirical story about a black actor in Hollywood who runs into stereotyping at every turn. The character's daydreams take the form of a series of wickedly funny sketches spoofing Hollywood's concept of blacks. The best is "Sneakin' in the Movies," a send-up of movie-review television shows.

Another actor who fared well in eighties comedies, often as half of a mismatched or oddball duo, was actor (and occasional director) Danny DeVito. A diminutive fireball of manic energy, DeVito had earlier won a devoted following in the television show "Taxi." In such films as *Wise Guys* (1986) and *Throw Momma from the Train* (1987), his ferocious performances, for all their excess, earned laughs, but few directors attempted to channel his trademarked persona in another direction. Barry Levinson came closest with his film *Tin Men* (1987), in which he added a becoming note of poignancy to the usual mix of rage and hostility. In this perceptive comedy, which Levinson also wrote, DeVito played Ernest Tilley, a coarse and hard-nosed salesman of aluminum siding in Baltimore of 1963. Following the pattern of one-on-one confrontation, the movie has Tilley clashing violently with another hustling aluminum-siding salesman named Bill (BB) Babowsky (Richard Dreyfuss).

In *Diner,* Levinson had returned to his hometown roots to offer an engaging portrait of young men on the brink of maturity in 1959. With *Tin Men,* nostalgia largely gives way to a funny yet also melancholy view of men becoming obsolete: the aluminum-siding salesmen whose outrageous scams to secure customers were being declared unlawful. The movie's plot line centers on Tilley's mounting feud with BB, after their cars collide at the film's start. Their mutual thirst for revenge increases until BB succeeds in seducing Tilley's unhappy wife, Nora, played by Barbara Hershey. Unexpectedly, and to his mortification, BB falls in love with Nora, while Tilley loses not only his wife but his car and his job as well. At the end, the two men are on the way to reconciliation.

Once again, as in *Diner*, Levinson's ear is perfectly attuned to the niggling day-to-day concerns, the attitudes, and even the speech patterns of his characters; sitting together in the ubiquitous diner, comparing scams (some of them amusingly shown on-screen), or fretting about the threat of the government's Home Improvement Commission, these siding salesmen are comic-pathetic dinosaurs facing extinction. As they play out their games of revenge, Tilley and BB are also anachronisms—their boorish, insensitive attitude toward Nora, for example, will soon collide head-on with feminism—but Levinson allows them to change by the film's close: After leaving Nora, BB finds that he needs and misses her, and Tilley, left with nothing, can subdue his belligerence and tell BB, "Take care of her." Despite this rather unconvincing ending, *Tin Men* is a pungent comedy that offers a few harsh realities behind the laughter.

Perhaps the ultimate one-on-one relationship between characters appeared in Carl Reiner's 1984 comedy-fantasy, *All of Me*. The film is based on a fanciful idea: a dying heiress and lifelong invalid named Edwina Cutwater (Lily Tomlin) arranges with a guru (Richard Libertini) to exchange souls after her death with Terry (Victoria Tennant), her stableman's scheming daughter. The girl's soul will become "one with the universe," and Edwina, in a healthy young body, will enjoy everything she has missed previously. Instead, by accident, Edwina enters the body of Roger Cobb (Steve Martin), a lawyer who would rather be a jazz musician. With both Roger and Edwina inhabiting the same body, chaos and confusion reign (Roger loses his job, his fiancée, and nearly his mind), but in the end, it all works out to everyone's satisfaction. Unfortunately, a promising idea goes seriously awry as scene after scene (Roger-Edwina in the men's room, or in bed with Terry) induces embarrassment rather than amusement. As the story line becomes increasingly chaotic and muddled, not even the talented leading players can save the day. Steve Martin's dazzling skill with physical comedy surfaces when, first inhabited by Edwina, he tries to walk normally and his legs move in different directions. But *All of Me* lacks the finesse and coherence of good film comedy.

In the midst of the celebration of family and friendship in comedies of the eighties, there had been dark strains intimating that mortals could be self-deluding, willful, contentious, and destructive. Considering the record of human history, this was hardly a revelation, but its sobering truth undercut the comedy. Yet we all laughed, and continue to laugh, at mankind's irrepressible and unfazable folly.

Chapter 25

A Crazy World

Knockabout Farces and Satires

W hile the eighties proliferated with romantic and "human" comedies that took a more mature and complex attitude toward relationships among people, one large segment of the movie audience was being attracted with an entirely different kind of movie. Film companies soon perceived that at the same time that the number of older viewers was declining, teenagers were storming the theaters in record numbers. Spurred by increasingly relaxed standards of what was permissible in films, and also by the feeling, prevalent since the late sixties, that the powers in charge were not to be trusted, this burgeoning audience of the eighties wanted comedies that thumbed their noses at every kind of authority. And the filmmakers obliged with a barrage of low-level farces that were ruder, and infinitely more vulgar, than any in previous decades.

The formula was soon established: Take a group of impudent, irreverent, barely functioning people, often at odds with society's strictures, and expose them to any institutions in which order and discipline are essential. At first scorned and humiliated by the establishment, these fun-loving misfits, or rebels, ultimately seize the initiative and show up the authority figures for the mean-spirited, self-serving fools they truly are. In other years, movies had mocked these authority figures with impunity: the truculent top sergeants who abused Lou Costello, the overbearing bosses who made life miserable for the hero. Now, however, the familiar twitting of the establishment turned into a gleeful assault designed to please teenage moviegoers. It was as if they had all been set free to scribble dirty words on the blackboard.

Clearly influenced by the hugely popular *National Lampoon's Animal House*, released in 1978, a number of eighties comedies (*Up the Academy*, 1980; *Up the Creek*, 1984; *Revenge of the Nerds*, 1984) featured irreverent young buffoons in noisy

Caddyshack *(Orion, 1980). Assembling at a country club (left to right): Chevy Chase as a rich member and champion golfer, Ted Knight as the club's president, and Rodney Dangerfield as an obnoxious tycoon.*

contention with stiff-necked, arrogant men in charge. By far the most popular of these raucous antiestablishment farces (it spawned a number of sequels throughout the decade) was Hugh Wilson's lively *Police Academy* (1984). Here, the setting is a police academy where the usual group of society's losers assembles to learn police procedures. Inevitably, these tangle-footed clowns are soon locked in battle with their archenemy, the ferocious Lieutenant Harris (G. W. Bailey). If the material is familiar, the execution occasionally has an energetic, free-wheeling lunacy that provokes laughter.

Few of these films created any starring performers—they were usually group efforts—but one actor succeeded in personifying the mischievous misfit who rallied his forces against the existing powers. An alumnus of television's ground-breaking "Saturday Night Live"—John Belushi and Eddie Murphy were others—Bill Murray instantly projected the manner of an unruly, insolent con man and opportunist for whom every sacred cow is fair game. Wearing a perpetual smirk, and forever ready with a wisecrack or a put-down, he starred in comedies that cast him as the scruffy champion of the world's losers and placed him in open warfare against the establishment. In Ivan Reitman's popular *Stripes* (1981), for example, he was a hapless taxi driver who joins the army and reduces strong-willed military men to quivering wrecks. Only some strong language and leering sexual activity separate the film from the innocent days of *Buck Privates* and *See Here, Private Hargrove.* Several years later, Murray reunited with Reitman (and also with another graduate of "Saturday Night Live," Dan Aykroyd) in the elaborate horror-comedy *Ghostbusters* (1984), in which he and his enterprising cohorts joined together to exorcise evil spirits plaguing New York City.

Murray also appeared with another "Saturday Night Live" veteran, Chevy Chase, in Harold Ramis's rowdy 1980 farce, *Caddyshack.* Here, he was cast in the relatively supporting role of Carl, the unkempt, horny, and probably

demented greenskeeper and gopher-chaser at a posh golf club where the snobbish old-line members are constantly at odds with the vulgar upstarts. Chase was featured as a wealthy, eccentric member who takes part in the movie's nonstop barrage of tasteless jokes and heavy-handed slapstick, all designed to amuse its targeted audience, and offend everyone else.

Chase would fare better in later eighties films, and for a while it seemed as if he would have a durable career as a likable leading man in such movies as *Seems Like Old Times* (1980) and *Fletch* (1985). Like Bill Murray, however, his smugly self-absorbed acting style—his lines seem directed at the viewing audience rather than at his fellow actors—wore thin by the end of the decade. (Both performers appear to be putting on the entire world.) Despite the one string to his bow, Chase managed to achieve popularity in a series of sophomoric slapstick comedies sponsored by the satirical magazine *National Lampoon;* in *Vacation* (1983), *European Vacation* (1985), and *Christmas Vacation* (1989), he played Clark Griswold, the monumentally inept father of a hapless family whose travels are rife with disaster.

Few movies aimed at the burgeoning teenage market attempted to deal with the way this group actually felt or behaved. One director did take a passing stab at getting inside the teenagers' heads to express their fears and longings, as well their proclivities for sex and high jinx. In the mid-eighties, writer John Hughes turned director with a series of teenage comedies that added some realistic and thoughtful touches to the usual raucous mix. Movies such as *Sixteen Candles* (1984) and *Pretty in Pink* (1986, written by Hughes but directed by Howard Deutch) at least suggested that teenagers could be as lonely, troubled, and confused as adults, while Hughes's *Ferris Bueller's Day Off* (1986) proved, perhaps inadvertently, that they also could be as overbearing. *Pretty in Pink* came off best, lacing its old hat plot (scorned poor girl Molly Ringwald loves and finally wins rich boy) with some glancing observations on the need to "belong" and the strength of family ties.

In addition to the profusion of rude and vulgar farces aimed at young audiences, the eighties witnessed a notable increase in parody films, a subgenre that had never enjoyed wide popularity. In the seventies, Mel Brooks had attracted viewers with his scattershot spoofs of the Western (*Blazing Saddles*), the horror film (*Young Frankenstein*), and the Hitchcockian thriller (*High Anxiety*). Now, filmmakers seemed to believe there was a market for movies that burlesqued other venerable genres and film styles. Brooks himself continued in the mode, failing miserably with the dreadful *History of the World—Part I* (1981), an episodic takeoff on periods of history from the Stone Age to the French Revolution, then redeeming himself in part later in the decade with the sporadically amusing science fiction spoof *Spaceballs* (1987). Brooks's influence was also evident in such parody films as *Wholly Moses* (1980), Gary Weis's takeoff of Biblical epics, and Amy Heckerling's *Johnny Dangerously* (1984), a send-up of the thirties gangster movie.

One parody, arriving at the start of the decade, won, and to some extent deserved, an unprecedented popularity for this sort of film. Written and directed by Jim Abrahams and Jerry and David Zucker, *Airplane!* (1980) aimed its satirical guns (actually more burlesque than satire) at the disaster films that had proliferated in the seventies, wherein a group of people are subjected to a terrifying and near-fatal experience. (*Airport*, released in 1970, was probably the progenitor.) Taking its plot most directly from a 1957 movie entitled *Zero Hour*, *Airplane!* revolved about a perilous flight in which most of the plane's crew and many of the passengers become violently ill from food poisoning. Robert Hays, a former war pilot with a troubled past, must land the crippled plane with the help of stewardess Julie Hagerty, who happens to be his ex-girlfriend.

Firing a continual volley of running jokes, puns, sight gags, and parody, *Airplane!* sends up every moth-eaten cliché of the subgenre. Even the passenger list includes all too familiar characters from the past, given a comic twist: the solemn—and here, utterly dense—doctor (Leslie Nielsen); the brave little sick girl (Jill Whelan) whose life-support system is knocked loose by the swing of a cheerful nun's guitar; the stalwart middle-aged lady (Barbara Billingsley), who turns out to have a surprising ability to talk "black jive." Wittily, the plane's crew and the ground personnel were cast with actors who parodied their sober, stalwart roles in earlier films, including Robert Stack as a hotshot pilot whose pair of dark glasses conceals a second pair of dark glasses, and Lloyd Bridges as the harried air traffic chief who, under pressure, surrenders to all his old bad habits. ("I guess I picked the wrong week to stop smoking/drinking/sniffing glue.") Thoroughly silly and unsubtle, *Airplane!* managed to generate a surprising number of laughs, nonetheless.

In addition to the rude teenage romps and scattershot parodies that turned up throughout the eighties, there were several more ambitious films that hoped to reach a wider audience by combining the trappings of traditional farce with the more permissive climate of the decade, which tolerated even the most excessive vulgarity, prurience, or scatology. The extent to which attitudes had changed can

Airplane! *(Paramount, 1980). In this spoof of disaster movies, Lloyd Bridges and Robert Stack won laughs as, respectively, the air-traffic chief who overindulges his vices and a truly dense hotshot pilot.*

be measured by the fact that two of the most popular of these raunchy farces of the mid-eighties were released by Touchstone Films, a division of the usually squeaky-clean Disney Studio.

Paul Mazursky's *Down and Out in Beverly Hills* (1986), based on Jean Renoir's 1932 French film, *Boudou Saved from Drowning*, related how the life of the rich, self-indulgent Whiteman family is altered drastically when Jerry (Nick Nolte), a scruffy bum of mysterious background, tries to drown himself in their swimming pool. Rescued by Dave Whiteman (Richard Dreyfuss), Jerry becomes the catalyst who releases everyone's inhibitions, sexual and otherwise. A hectic, intermittently funny farce that sputters to an unconvincing ending, the film benefited from Mazursky's usual humanistic touches (he wrote the screenplay with Leon Capetanos), and from Bette Midler's outrageous performance as Dave's repressed wife, Barbara. Bustling about her overdecorated Beverly Hills home, her fingers fluttering as if she was continually drying her nails, Midler turned her character into an authentic comic creation.

Her voice a nasal bray that could penetrate steel, Midler was also a driving force in *Ruthless People* (1986), a raucous black farce directed by the three-man team of *Airplane!*—Jim Abrahams and David and Jerry Zucker. Here, she played yet another Barbara, a shrill, monstrous, and overweight virago married to Sam Stone (Danny DeVito), a ferociously angry little man who would like to see her dead. His plot to murder her, however, is thwarted when she is kidnapped by the Kesslers, a good-natured couple (Judge Reinhold and Helen Slater) driven to seek revenge on Sam for his stealing some of Sandy Kessler's fashion designs. Under the couple's benign captivity, Barbara becomes a thinner and better person, while she and her former captors now conspire in their own revenge scheme against Sam. Other characters and complications keep the pot boiling. Written by Dale Launer and played in the broadest comic-book style, *Ruthless People* resembled the sort of vitriolic assault on human greed, corruption, and duplicity that sometimes came from the poisoned pen of Billy Wilder, but without Wilder's wit, discipline, or cinematic know-how.

Amid the many bumptious farces released in the eighties, there was little room for the impudent and slashing wit of satire. Yet there were topics that remained ripe for occasional mockery by the satirist's jaundiced eye. One was Hollywood, where sycophants, liars, fools, and opportunists thrived in every decade. Whereas a number of older films (*Once in a Lifetime, Boy Meets Girl, Dreamboat*) had slashed at the film capital's peculiar ways, very few of them had drawn blood.

With the new and blunter approach of the eighties, a film such as Blake Edwards's *S.O.B.* (1981) was clearly intended to inflict wounds on its target of the Hollywood establishment. Written and directed by Edwards in what was apparently a spirit of vindictiveness—Edwards felt that he had been treated badly in the early seventies—this pitch-black comedy lashed out mercilessly at the film industry's greedy, mendacious, and easily corrupted people. A seasoned cast headed by Julie Andrews (Edwards's wife), William Holden, and Robert Preston struggled to make something mordantly funny out of the uproar surrounding a megaflop movie, but the film's relentlessly shrill, abrasive tone becomes wearying even before midpoint. The result is a mean-spirited diatribe.

Another spoof of the entertainment world, Richard Benjamin's *My Favorite Year* (1982), took on television in the 1950s. Actually too affectionate to be considered truly satirical, the movie concerns the mishaps surrounding the production of a television variety program very much like the classic "Your Show of Shows" of the early fifties. Joseph Bologna played the show's burly, Sid Caesar–like star comedian, and Mark Linn-Baker was the fledgling writer required to chaperone the week's guest, a dissipated, lascivious film star (Peter O'Toole in a superb performance). Instead, O'Toole leads Linn-Baker in a wild night of revelry, ending in a free-for-all at the program's live performance. The movie captures the frenzied and haphazard style of early television, which, on rare occasions, resulted in a program as imaginative and ground-breaking as "Your Show of Shows."

Of the few satirical comedies of the eighties, one of the funniest was an offbeat surprise. Rob Reiner's exceptionally clever *This Is Spinal Tap* (1984) purported to be a documentary film concerning a British rock band called Spinal Tap and their whirlwind tour of America. The band is, in fact, not only fictional but also terrible, and the movie, a wickedly accurate parody of the documentary form, reveals their precipitous descent to near-oblivion. A documentary filmmaker named Martin DiBergi (Reiner himself) uses the camera's eye to record their dwindling audiences, their bickering among themselves, and their inane lyrics ("The looser the waistband, the deeper the quicksand"). The band's manager, Ian Faith (Tony Hendra), tries in vain to justify the frequent cancellations ("Their appeal is becoming more selective"), and their attempt to change the act ends in disaster. All the familiar documentary techniques—the one-on-one interviews, the roving camera, the overheard conversations—are used to reveal Spinal Tap's fatuousness and lack of talent. A modestly made but thoroughly original film, *This Is Spinal Tap* found an audience that responded to its deadpan satire.

The eighties had seen a slew of coarse and raunchy farces that appeared to please the growing teenage audience. While adult viewers watched the "relationships" that developed among lovers, families, and friends, young viewers were content to mock the status quo and the authority figures determined to preserve it. It was if Andy Hardy and the Dead End Kids had been freed from the shackles of convention and allowed to pursue the anarchy and the sexuality that could never even have been suggested in earlier years. Adults may not have been pleased, and the art of film was certainly not served, but for the younger set of moviegoers, it was a kind of release.

Chapter 26
Woody Allen in the Eighties

n the last years of the seventies, Woody Allen achieved his greatest recognition to date, winning three Oscars (including Best Picture and Best Director), as well as audience approval, with *Annie Hall* in 1977. His 1979 ode to Manhattan (*Manhattan*) added some darker hues to his canvas in its bittersweet story of urban neurotics. The Allen one-liners were still abundant, startling us into laughter with their lopsided truths, but a more serious tone, a suggestion that we were all fools playing out a hopeless game under the baleful eye of some nameless deity, undercut the humor.

As he entered the eighties, Allen's comedies became more "special," more inaccessible; private expressions of his complex psyche, they seemed almost calculated to put off the filmgoers who had loved *Annie Hall*. His first film of the decade, *Stardust Memories* (1980), was also one of his most eccentric. His most overtly autobiographical effort, it revolves around Sandy Bates (Allen), a lionized filmmaker who agrees to attend a festival of his films at a resort hotel at the New Jersey shore. A quivering bundle of neuroses, Sandy is assaulted on all sides by fanatically adoring fans, pompous movie freaks and academics reading deep meaning into his films, and people soliciting his time or his money. While the past and present interact in his troubled mind, he must also cope with tax problems, relative problems, and troubles with his new film—his first serious effort—which his producer is condemning as shallow, pretentious, and morbid. "I don't want to make funny movies anymore," he insists. "I don't *feel* funny." Yet Sandy is trapped by his fame.

Clearly a public expression of Allen's private feelings about his work and his celebrity, *Stardust Memories* angered many critics with its poisonous attitude toward his fans and admirers, and indeed the film turns them into inane, even dangerous grotesques. Yet Allen is actually as hard on himself as he is on his followers—he mocks the unshakable angst that always seeps into his movies, the feeling that he cannot escape "the terrible truths of existence." Playfully, he acknowledges, and simultaneously spoofs, the influence of other filmmakers on his work—scenes emulating Ingmar Bergman or Federico Fellini (mostly *8 1/2*), or echoing Preston Sturges (especially *Sullivan's Travels)* recur constantly. He also pokes fun at such recurring autobiographical themes in his films as his tangled relationships with women, or his memories of childhood. Although the screenplay contains scattered Allenesque one-liners, Allen is more concerned with excoriating his fans and, to some extent, himself. Loathing and self-denigration are not exactly popular subjects for comedy, and most critics and audiences were not amused. (Groucho Marx and W. C. Fields largely got away with it by concealing their misanthropy in quips and outlandish attire.)

Allen's continued fascination with the films of Ingmar Bergman surfaced again with his next effort, *A Midsummer Night's Sex Comedy* (1982). Obviously inspired by Bergman's *Smiles of a Summer Night*, this new movie attempted to capture the insouciance and exuberance of the Swedish film. Set at the turn of the century at the country retreat of Andrew Hobbs (Allen) and his wife, Adrian (Mary Steenburgen), it brought together a group of people for a weekend of sexual intrigue. Partners change as assignations take place or go comically awry, and there are a few magical moments in the midsummer night. Despite the sudden death of one guest while making love, matters are resolved happily. Exquisitely photographed by Gordon Willis in a lovely setting, *A Midsummer Night's Sex Comedy* at least has the look of a classic period comedy. Yet it is too slight, too uninvolving to be anything more than a charming bauble. Few of its characters are interesting or vital enough to make us care about their sexual peccadilloes.

If this film failed to excite the general moviegoing public, Allen's next effort, *Zelig* (1983), was even more calculated to win only a select group of admirers, while puzzling or irritating everyone else. Unlike any of his previous films, *Zelig* purported to be a documentary concerning one Leonard Zelig (Allen), a curious phenomenon and minor celebrity of the Depression years, whose ability to transform himself into other people astounded the world for a while. He was called a "human chameleon" who adopted the personality and appearance of whatever person or group he happened to encounter every day. The pseudodocumentary relates his meeting with Dr. Eudora Fletcher (Mia Farrow), a psychiatrist whose life becomes linked with Zelig's as his fortune changes over the years. (They share one of Woody Allen's few nonneurotic love affairs.)

A movie that works on several levels, *Zelig* is, for one thing, a quite remarkable technical achievement. Drawing on old Fox Movietone newsreels, Allen insinuated Zelig into the company of such historic personages as Calvin Coolidge,

Josephine Baker, and F. Scott Fitzgerald, or with clever camera trickery, he transformed his "human chameleon" into other people, ranging from an old Chinese man to a black jazz musician. *Zelig* also spoofs the documentary film with deadpan accuracy, duplicating the genre's penchant for grainy footage, lofty narration, and pompous interviews with "experts" on the subject at hand.

Most specifically, *Zelig* addresses a theme not unfamiliar in movies: America's mania for worshiping the celebrity of the moment. The phenomenon of Zelig prompts a barrage of exploitation, as people dance to "the Chameleon," buy Zelig dolls, or sing tunes about him ("You May Be Six People But I Love You"). Allen, however, takes the theme beyond the brash satire of a film such as *Nothing Sacred*—Zelig becomes the helpless victim of his peculiar celebrity, buffeted by the changing winds of favor. One minute, he is lionized; in the next, he becomes a sideshow freak. Allen is telling us that celebrity, even a fleeting celebrity such as Zelig's, can steal not only your identity but also your soul. Yet so many, desperately wanting to be loved and admired, willingly accept the risk.

With his next film, *Broadway Danny Rose* (1984), Allen turned from the rarefied atmosphere of *A Midsummer Night's Sex Comedy* and *Zelig* to the down-to-earth world of show business. This, however, is not the show business of *Stardust Memories*, with its lionized celebrities but, rather, the grubby underside, where odd and minimally talented "entertainers" eke out a meager living. Allen played Danny Rose, a small-time agent whose clients include a blind xylophonist, a stammering ventriloquist, and a couple who twist balloons into various shapes. An eternally hopeful loser, Danny has one promising client, a hefty Italian singer named Lou Canova (Nick Apollo Forte). Unfortunately, Lou has a mistress named Tina (a funny and nearly unrecognizable Mia Farrow), a brassy blonde with strong ties to the Mafia, especially a volatile mob chieftain named Johnny Rispoli (Edwin Bordo). Trouble ensues when Danny is mistakenly identified as Tina's current boyfriend, and he and Tina are hotly pursued across New York and New Jersey by Johnny's vengeful brothers. By the film's end, the two appear to be headed for a romantic relationship, although pathetic Danny loses Lou as a client.

In this modestly made but enormously likable movie, Allen played his usual jittery, put-upon, and guilt-ridden nebbish (at one point, he says, "I'm guilty—and I never *did* anything"). This time, however, instead of the character whose one-liners conceal a deep mistrust of—and hostility toward—society, he is someone who is sweetly hopeful, even about his bottom-of-the-barrel clients. As he suffers one indignity after another, Danny remains resilient, accepting his wretched fate as a fact of life. ("It's important to have some laughs, but you have to suffer a little, too.") Related in flashback by a group of comedians seated at a table in New York's Carnegie Delicatessen, Danny's story becomes a comic-poignant fable of endurance against impossible odds.

The astringency that marked many of Allen's comedies of the early eighties was also largely absent from his next movie, *The Purple Rose of Cairo* (1985). A slender and sometimes affecting period piece, it revolves about a single conceit: In the bleak Depression years, a young housewife named Cecilia (Mia Farrow), burdened with a boorish husband (Danny Aiello) and a wretched job as a waitress, lives her fantasies at the movies. On one night at the local Bijou, dashing screen hero Tom Baxter, played by movie idol Gil Shepard (Jeff Daniels), descends from the screen to proclaim his love and admiration for an astonished Cecilia. The resulting brouhaha brings Gil Shepard from Hollywood, and soon Cecilia is being courted by the fictional Tom, whose only knowledge of life comes from the movies, and a very real, and very vain, Gil, enchanted mostly by his notices. At the end, Cecilia is left only with her dreams, to be pursued once again in the darkness of the theater. Around this intriguing idea, Allen fashioned a comedy that, for all its slightness, offers a few reflections on the need for dreams, romance, and laughter in a cold and threatening world, and the ability of film's flickering images to fulfill that need.

Until this time, Allen's films of the eighties had used a narrow canvas, largely confining their scope to particular areas of his psyche. With his next film, *Hannah and Her Sisters* (1986), he expanded his canvas to include the entire human condition, and the result was his most mature, most complex, and most fully realized film until then. A Chekhovian mixture of comedy and drama (the title itself suggests Chekhov), this movie focuses once again on Allen's band of neurotic New Yorkers and their hopes and anxieties as they are buffeted by life. This time, however, their cross-purposes and self-deceptions are accompanied by a surprising—and welcome—generosity and affection, which gives *Hannah and Her Sisters* a glow missing from most of his earlier films. For once, Allen seemed to be concentrating on what was good and genuine in life, rather than its sour disappointments. His technical virtuosity (he used the vocabulary of film—voice-overs, flashbacks, narration, printed titles—to make a point, not to show off), as well as the stunning cinematography of Carlo Di Palma, contributed to the film's great success.

Framed by two Thanksgiving dinners, two years apart, the story centers on a family that has known both grief and happiness: father Evan (Lloyd Nolan) and mother Norma (Maureen O'Sullivan), old-time show-business figures of the second rank, have squabbled bitterly for years; Norma, grasping at her long-vanished youth, flirts too often and drinks too much. Their three daughters have their own problems: Lee (Barbara Hershey), a reformed alcoholic, is growing weary of living with Frederick (Max von Sydow), a dour and pompous artist; Holly (Dianne Wiest), once a drug addict, flits from one occupation or avocation to another, vastly unsure of herself. Only sensible Hannah (Mia Farrow), a retired actress, has the strength and peace of mind the others lack; she is the family's fulcrum. She is unaware, however, that her husband Elliot (Michael Caine), an investment adviser, is desperately and secretly in love with Lee. Also figuring in the story is Mickey Sachs (Woody Allen), Hannah's ex-husband, and a world-class hypochondriac who undergoes a life crisis when he believes he is dying of a brain tumor.

Clearly, *Hannah and Her Sisters* has a more intricate plot line than any of Allen's previous movies, and yet as writer-director, he manages to keep all aspects of the story in perfect balance. While there is no shortage of the usual Allen one-liners, the screenplay is much more concerned with revealing the subtle, bristling, and occasionally poignant relationships among these family members and their friends and acquaintances. Frequently, as characters expose their hopes and fears, laughter and tears exist side by side: Elliot's lust for Lee has its comic aspects (especially when he sprints after her through the streets like a gazelle in heat), but he is essentially a decent man, racked by guilt as well as desire, and he ultimately returns to Hannah. Holly's instability keeps her "career" spinning (from singer to caterer to playwright), but behind her hopeful smile, we can sense a deep hurt and resentment. And Mickey's despair over his imaginary fatal illness leads to some hilarious conclusions, particularly his attempted conversion to Catholicism (to demonstrate his sincerity, he takes home a loaf of white bread and a jar of mayonnaise). Allen, for a change playing only one of many characters rather than the central figure, makes Mickey a likable fool.

Allen brings a virtuosic style and rhythm to many of the film's key sequences. In the opening scene, a Thanksgiving dinner at Hannah's house reveals the family's multilayered relationships; without a wasted line of dialogue, or an intrusive camera movement, Allen tells us all we need to know about Elliot's passion for Lee ("I'm consumed by her!"), the sisters' contrasting personalities, and the important men in their lives, past and present. Even more potent (and perhaps the film's finest moment) is the scene in which the sisters have lunch together. As the camera circles them slowly, emotion rises to the surface, either in a distracted look or in words that sting. Here, the three actresses are especially fine, with

Dianne Wiest expressing every nuance of her troubled character. She won an Oscar as Best Supporting Actress for her performance, and Michael Caine won a Best Supporting Actor Oscar for his performance as Elliot. Woody Allen also received an Academy Award for his remarkably adroit screenplay.

With his next film, *Radio Days* (1987), Allen retained his love for New York City and reaffirmed his nostalgia for the recent past, but this time the nostalgia, rather than being tinged with melancholy, as in *The Purple Rose of Cairo*, is infused with affectionate parody. A freewheeling series of anecdotes and sketches, rather than a sustained narrative, the movie is set in the late thirties and early forties, when radio, at the peak of its popularity, was a dominant form of entertainment. Various story lines are threaded through the film, many of them involving top radio personalities of the time, but the main plot centers on a middle-class Jewish family, crowded together in a Queens apartment, and all faithfully devoted to the radio programs of their choice. Among them are Mother (Julie Kavner) and Father (Michael Tucker), constantly fighting over matters large and small (which ocean is larger—the Atlantic or the Pacific?); their young son, Joe (Seth Allen), a perennial mischief-maker who is the story's source of memories; Mother's ever-hopeful unmarried sister, Bea (Dianne Wiest); and another sister, Ceil (Renee Lippin) and her gullible, fish-loving husband, Abe (Josh Mostel).

These characters and other family members, recalled with warmth and humor rather than with condescension, make up the heart of *Radio Days*. The laughter is sympathetic for Mother's wistful regrets, Father's pipe dreams of get-rich-quick schemes, little Joe's obsession with his radio heroes, and Aunt Bea's indefatigable quest for a husband. Yet the movie frequently moves away from the family to deal with radio stars of the day, including the heroic Masked Avenger (Wallace Shawn), who fights "evildoers, wherever they may be," and the cheery morning talk-show hosts Roger (David Warrilow) and Irene (Julie Kurnitz), forever name-dropping and table-hopping. Most of the screenplay's attention, however, goes to a squeaky-voiced hatcheck girl named Sally White, played by Mia Farrow, who rises to radio stardom at the beginning of World War II.

Beautifully photographed by Carlo Di Palma, the vignettes for *Radio Days* are never less than amusing, and a number of them are inspired recollections of a long-vanished time, filtered through Allen's perceptive wit. Written and played with on-target accuracy, memories tumble forth one after the other: the anniversary of Joe's parents, when, for once, the bickering stops as Mother receives a fur stole; Joe's first awed visit to Radio City Music Hall with Aunt Bea and her latest suitor;

the family reduced to stunned silence as a nationwide broadcast reports the rescue of a girl trapped in a Pennsylvania mine shaft. This family portion of *Radio Days* is studded with lovely moments: Father, Uncle Abe, and Abe's daughter, Ruth, exuberantly singing along with Carmen Miranda's radio rendition of "South American Way," their thick bodies swaying to the rhythm; the family listening to ominous news about Hitler's invasion of Poland as Mother comments, "What a world. It would be so wonderful if it weren't for certain people."

Many of Allen's films in the late seventies and eighties included serious undertones, and some, such as *Interiors* (1978), *September* (1987), and *Another Woman* (1988), virtually eschewed comedy altogether. On the whole, these movies projected a worldview considerably grimmer and more pessimistic than the affirmative one he had offered in *Hannah and Her Sisters.* As the eighties waned, it was clear that he shared the opinion of a character in *September* that "the universe is haphazard, morally neutral and unimaginably violent." Nowhere was this more evident than in his brilliant 1989 film, *Crimes and Misdemeanors.* Once again, Allen focused on a diverse group of striving, largely upscale New Yorkers, but this time the comedy elements are overwhelmed by a cynical tale involving betrayal and murder. Martin Landau starred as a married, widely respected ophthalmologist who manages to have his burdensome mistress (Anjelica Huston) killed and then, after a bout of conscience, comes to accept his crime and returns to his old privileged life. Although the film contained scattered laughs, it depicted a bleak world in which the old moral imperatives no longer apply, where the guilty can overcome their anguish while the guiltless suffer pain.

Later in 1989, Allen returned to comedy with one segment of a three-part film entitled *New York Stories.* His screenplay for *Oedipus Wrecks* returned him to the familiar character of the neurotic, victimized New Yorker, here a fifty-year-old lawyer named Sheldon. The simple story revolves around a gimmick: burdened with the ultimate Jewish mother, a shrill, overbearing harridan played by Mae Questel, Sheldon is secretly relieved when she suddenly vanishes into thin air at a magic show. To his mortification, she materializes in the sky over New York, where she continues to berate him mercilessly. His efforts to be rid of this apparition lead him to a medium (Julie Kavner), whom he eventually marries. She turns out to be every bit as overbearing as his mother, who mysteriously returns to join his new wife in the "get Sheldon" game. *Oedipus Wrecks* is little more than a conceit, but a clever and amusing one. The other parts of *New York Stories* were Martin Scorsese's *Life Lessons* and Francis Coppola's *Life Without Zoe.*

Allen's 1990 film, *Alice*, kept him among the striving, angst-ridden New York-ers he always has favored, but this time he focused on the upper strata of society, the affluent people, and especially the women, whose pampered lives involve a nonstop round of parties, shopping, and personal improvement. His heroine (Mia Farrow), an Alice in Urban Wonderland, is a dutiful wife and mother with a gnawing sense of unease and dissatisfaction. Her life seems to have no purpose or meaning. By means of some mysterious herbs dispensed by an elderly Chinese acupuncturist (Keye Luke), Alice is rendered invisible, so that she can travel freely through time and space while learning some undeniable truths. By the end of the film, Alice has succumbed guiltily to an illicit affair, discovered her husband's recurring infidelity, and come to terms with her lifelong perceptions about her parents and sister. Above all, after all the years of self-recrimination, she has confronted the consequences of her lapsed Catholicism.

Although the film's substance may seem weighty and a mite pretentious, Allen succeeds in making *Alice* diverting entertainment. Some of the ingredients are familiar and welcome: the breathtaking photography of a New York City, which may exist only in dreams; the lush and lovely musical score. Again, Allen has turned to one of his revered film masters for inspiration: both in style and content, *Alice* strongly recalls Federico Fellini's *Juliet of the Spirits* (1965). Yet, as always, he has remained true to himself, investing the film with his own special perspective. Satirical thrusts at New York's striving well-to-do alternate with fantasy scenes that are both enchanting (Alice's disembodied flight over the city with a long-deceased boyfriend) and funny (her encounter with her muse, played by Bernadette Peters—Alice fancies herself as a frustrated writer).

During the eighties, the themes of Woody Allen's films had deepened at the same time that his skills as a filmmaker had increased. While his comedic sense never deserted him, he was no longer able to conceal fully the melancholy and painful aspects he perceived in life. At his best, however, he could balance the comic and the tragic, blending them into the virtually seamless entities of *Hannah and Her Sisters* and *Crimes and Misdemeanors*.

Happily, his movies will continue to explore the foolish, funny, and sometimes self-destructive ways in which we all tend to behave. As before, there will be moviegoers who find him too "special," too cerebral for their taste, or long for the gag-laden style of his earlier comedies. Many others, however, will be delighted to join him on his unique journey.

CODA

Today, in a world desperately in need of laughter, film comedy continues to fill that need. On the one hand, the jokes may be more salacious, the situations more sexually explicit than any burlesque or porno star ever may have fantasized. On the other, the best of today's comedy movies offer unvarnished home truths about the perils and pleasures of being a parent, a friend, or a lover. Like the comedies of every era, they make us laugh at our foibles, follies, and self-deceptions. They also feature performers who can comfortably, and also skillfully, embody these all-too-human traits.

If there is one thing missing from contemporary comedy films, it is the sort of nose-thumbing, larger-than-life humor provided by the enduring masters of early sound comedy. There are glimmers of this humor in a few of the genre parodies such as *Airplane!*—as well as in Mel Brooks's helter-skelter spoofs. Few of today's comic movies, for all their technical proficiency, can duplicate the sort of free-wheeling, irreverent entertainment that flourished in earlier decades, however. With a ripe sense of absurdity and an impudent wit, the icons of that era turned comedy merrily on its ear. It is true that they are linked inextricably with the past, but if they are, what a joy it is to know that their flickering images continue to cavort before our eyes, however small the screen.

Still, as in other times, there is no shortage of movie laughter to ease the burden of dull gray days, or to allay the terrors of the nightly news, if only for a few hours. On videotape or in multiplex theaters, the great comic artists offer their quips, gags, and wisecracks as a kind of perennial gift to all of us. It has been a pleasure to recall that gift in the pages of this book.

Photo Credits

MOVIE "LOBBY CARDS"

Going Bye Bye, 1934. For a film produced by Metro-Goldwyn-Mayer, Inc.

Animal Crackers, 1930. For a film produced by Paramount Pictures Corporation.

Duck Soup, 1933. For a film produced by Paramount Pictures Corporation.

Bombshell, © 1933. For a film produced by Metro-Goldwyn-Mayer, Inc.

After the Thin Man, © 1936. For a film produced by Metro-Goldwyn-Mayer, Inc.

Woman of the Year, © 1942. For a film produced by Metro-Goldwyn-Mayer, Inc.

COLUMBIA PICTURES

All Photos Courtesy of Columbia Pictures

Shampoo. Copyright © 1975 Columbia Pictures Industries, Inc. All Rights Reserved.

The Cheap Detective. Copyright © 1978 Rostar Films, Inc. All Rights Reserved.

Tootsie. Copyright © 1982 Columbia Pictures Industries, Inc. All Rights Reserved.

Roxanne. Copyright © 1987 Columbia Pictures Industries, Inc. All Rights Reserved.

The Big Chill. Copyright © 1983 Columbia Pictures Industries, Inc. All Rights Reserved.

Ghostbusters. Copyright © 1984 Columbia Pictures Industries, Inc. All Rights Reserved.

It Happened One Night. Copyright © 1934, Renewed 1962 Columbia Pictures Industries, Inc. All Rights Reserved.

Holiday. Copyright © 1938, Renewed 1966 Columbia Pictures Industries, Inc. All Rights Reserved.

The Awful Truth. Copyright © 1937, Renewed 1965 Columbia Pictures Industries, Inc. All Rights Reserved.

Twentieth Century. Copyright © 1934, Renewed 1962 Columbia Pictures Industries, Inc. All Rights Reserved.

His Girl Friday. Copyright © 1939 Columbia Pictures Industries, Inc. All Rights Reserved.

Mr. Deeds Goes to Town. Copyright © 1936, Renewed 1963 Columbia Pictures Industries, Inc. All Rights Reserved.

You Can't Take it with You. Copyright © 1938, Renewed 1966 Columbia Pictures Industries, Inc. All Rights Reserved.

Mr. Smith Goes to Washington. Copyright © 1939, Renewed 1967 Columbia Pictures Industries, Inc. All Rights Reserved.

The Fuller Brush Man. Copyright © 1948, Renewed 1975 Columbia Pictures Industries, Inc. All Rights Reserved.

The More the Merrier. Copyright © 1943, Renewed 1971 Columbia Pictures Industries, Inc. All Rights Reserved.

My Sister Eileen. Copyright © 1942, Renewed 1970 Columbia Pictures Industries, Inc. All Rights Reserved.

Born Yesterday. Copyright © 1951, Renewed 1979 Columbia Pictures Industries, Inc. All Rights Reserved.

The Marrying Kind. Copyright © 1952, Renewed 1979 Columbia Pictures Industries, Inc. All Rights Reserved.

It Should Happen to You. Copyright © 1954, Renewed 1980 Columbia Pictures Industries, Inc. All Rights Reserved.

Dr. Strangelove. Copyright © 1963 Columbia Pictures Industries, Inc. All Rights Reserved.

Divorce American Style. Copyright © 1967 Columbia Pictures Industries, Inc. All Rights Reserved.

Bob & Carol & Ted & Alice. Copyright © 1969 Columbia Pictures Industries, Inc. All Rights Reserved.

Loving. Copyright © 1969 Columbia Pictures Industries, Inc. All Rights Reserved.

California Suite. Copyright © 1984 Rastar Films, Inc. All Rights Reserved.

PARAMOUNT PICTURES

All Photos Courtesy of Paramount Pictures

Jumping Jacks. Copyright © 1952, 1991 by Paramount Pictures. All Rights Reserved.

Roman Holiday. Copyright © 1953, 1991 by Paramount Pictures. All Rights Reserved.

Sabrina. Copyright © 1954, 1991 by Paramount Pictures. All Rights Reserved.

Breakfast at Tiffany's. Copyright © 1961, 1991 by Paramount Pictures. All Rights Reserved.

The Odd Couple. Copyright © 1968, 1991 by Paramount Pictures. All Rights Reserved.

The Nutty Professor. Copyright © 1963, 1991 by Paramount Pictures. All Rights Reserved.

Harold and Maude. Copyright © 1971, 1991 by Paramount Pictures. All Rights Reserved.

Plaza Suite. Copyright © 1971, 1991 by Paramount Pictures. All Rights Reserved.

Trading Places. Copyright © 1983, 1991 by Paramount Pictures. All Rights Reserved.

Airplane! Copyright © 1980, 1991 by Paramount Pictures. All Rights Reserved.

WARNER BROS. INC.

Life with Father. © 1947 Katherine B. Day, Howard Lindsay and Russell Crouse. All Rights Reserved.

Auntie Mame. © 1958 Warner Bros. Pictures, Inc. Renewed 1986 Warner Bros. Inc. All Rights Reserved.

What's Up, Doc? © 1972 Warner Bros. Inc. All Rights Reserved.

The Goodbye Girl. © 1977 Metro-Goldwyn-Mayer, Inc. and Warner Bros. Inc. All Rights Reserved.

Blazing Saddles. © 1974 Warner Bros. Inc. All Rights Reserved.

Arthur. © 1981 Orion Pictures Company. All Rights Reserved.

Police Academy. © 1984 The Ladd Company. All Rights Reserved.

Crossing Delancey. © 1988 Warner Bros. Inc. All Rights Reserved.

Caddyshack. © 1980 Orion Pictures Company. All Rights Reserved.

TRI-STAR PICTURES, INC.

Look Who's Talking © 1989 Tri-Star Pictures, Inc.

Selected Bibliography

Adamson, Joe. *Groucho, Harpo, Chico and Sometimes Zeppo.* New York: Simon & Schuster, 1973.

Bavar, Michael. *Mae West.* New York: Pyramid Publications, 1975.

Benayoun, Robert. *The Films of Woody Allen.* Translated by Alexander Walker. New York: Harmony Books, 1987.

Blesh, Rudi. *Buster Keaton.* New York: Macmillan, 1977.

Brode, Douglas. *Woody Allen: His Films and Career.* Secaucus, New Jersey: Citadel Press, 1985.

Byron, Stuart, and Weis, Elisabeth, eds. *Movie Comedy.* New York: Grossman Publishers, 1977.

Capra, Frank. *The Name Above the Title: An Autobiography.* New York: Macmillan , 1971.

Daniel, Clifton, editorial director. *Chronicle of America.* Mount Kisco, New York: Chronicle Publications, 1989.

Dardis, Tom. *Keaton: The Man Who Wouldn't Lie Down.* New York: Limelight Editions, 1988.

Dickos, Andrew. *Intrepid Laughter: Preston Sturges and the Movies.* Metuchen, New Jersey, and London: Scarecrow Press, 1985.

Eells, George. *Mae West: A Biography.* New York: William Morrow and Company, Inc., 1982.

Everson, William K. *Claudette Colbert.* New York: Pyramid Publications, 1976.

Fields, Ronald J. *W. C. Fields: A Life on Film.* New York: St. Martin's Press, 1984.

Fields, W. C. *W. C. Fields by Himself.* Englewood Cliffs, New Jersey: Prentice-Hall, Inc., 1973.

Gehrig, Wes D. *The Marx Brothers: A Bio-Bibliography.* New York, Westport, Connecticut, and London: Greenwood Press, 1987.

—— *W. C. Fields: A Bio-Bibliography.* New York, Westport, Connecticut, and London: Greenwood Press, 1984.

Harvey, James. *Romantic Comedy in Hollywood from Lubitsch to Sturges.* New York: Alfred A. Knopf, 1987.

Hirsch, Foster. *Love, Sex, Death, and the Meaning of Life.* New York, McGraw-Hill, 1981.

Holtzman, Will. *Jack Lemmon.* New York: Pyramid Publications, 1977.

Kay, Karyn. *Myrna Loy.* New York: Pyramid Publications, 1977.

Kerr, Walter. *The Silent Clowns.* New York: Alfred A. Knopf, 1975.

McCabe, John. *Laurel & Hardy.* New York: Ballantine Books, 1975.

McGilligan, Patrick. *Ginger Rogers.* New York: Pyramid Publications, 1975.

Maland, Charles J. *Frank Capra.* Boston: Twayne Publishers, 1980.

Maltin, Leonard. *Carole Lombard.* New York: Pyramid Publications, 1976.

—— *Movie Comedy Teams.* New York: New American Library, 1970.

Mast, Gerald. *The Comic Mind: Comedy and the Movies.* 2nd ed. Chicago and London: University of Chicago Press, 1979.

Mordden, Ethan. *The Hollywood Studios: Home Style in the Golden Age of Movies.* New York: Alfred A. Knopf, 1988.

Moss, Robert F. *Charlie Chaplin.* New York: Pyramid Publications, 1975.

Ott, Frederick W. *The Films of Carole Lombard.* Secaucus, New Jersey: Citadel Press, 1972.

Sennett, Ted. *Lunatics and Lovers.* New Rochelle, New York: Arlington House, 1973.

Sinyard, Neil. *The Films of Mel Brooks.* New York: Exeter Books, 1987.

Selected Bibliography

Skretvedt, Randy. *Laurel and Hardy: The Magic Behind the Movies.* Beverly Hills, California: Moonstone Press, 1987.

Thomas, Bob. *Bud and Lou: The Abbott and Costello Story.* Philadelphia and New York: J. B. Lippincott Company, 1977.

Tozzi, Romano. *Spencer Tracy.* New York: Pyramid Publications, 1973.

Tuska, Jon. *The Films of Mae West.* Secaucus, New Jersey: Citadel Press, 1973.

Ursini, James. *Preston Sturges: An American Dreamer.* New York: Curtis Books, 1973.

Vermilye, Jerry. *Cary Grant.* New York: Pyramid Publications, 1973.

Weinberg, Herman G. *The Lubitsch Touch: A Critical Study.* New York: E. P. Dutton, Inc., 1968.

Widener, Don. *Lemmon.* New York: Macmillan, 1975.

Wolf, William. *The Marx Brothers.* New York: Pyramid Publications, 1976.

Wood, Tom. *The Bright Side of Billy Wilder, Primarily.* Garden City, New York: Doubleday and Company, Inc., 1970.

Yacowar, Maurice. *Loser Take All: The Comic Art of Woody Allen.* New York: Frederick Ungar Publishing Co., 1979.

Yanni, Nicholas. *Rosalind Russell.* New York: Pyramid Publications, 1975.

—— *W. C. Fields.* New York: Pyramid Publications, 1974.

Zimmerman, Paul D., and Goldblatt, Burt. *The Marx Brothers at the Movies.* New York: G. P. Putnam's Sons, 1968.

Zolotow, Maurice. *Billy Wilder in Hollywood.* New York: G. P. Putnam's Sons, 1977.

Index

Page numbers in italics denote photographs.